D1404509

On Our Own

Also by John DeFrain

Coping with Sudden Infant Death
(with Jacque Taylor and Linda Ernst)

Parents in Contemporary America
(with E. E. LeMasters)

Secrets of Strong Families
(with Nick Stinnett)

Stillborn: The Invisible Death
(with Leona Martens, Jan Stork, and Warren Stork)

On Our Own

A Single Parent's Survival Guide

by

JOHN DeFRAIN
JUDY FRICKE
JULIE ELMEN

Lexington Books

Lexington, Massachusetts • Toronto

Library of Congress Cataloging-in-Publication Data

DeFrain, John D.
On our own.

Bibliography: p.
1. Single parents—United States—Life skills guides.
2. Custody of children—United States.   I. Fricke,
Judy.   II. Elmen, Julie.   III. Title.
HQ759.915.D44   1987   306.8'56   86-27727
ISBN 0-669-15085-1 (alk. paper)
ISBN 0-669-15086-X (pbk. : alk. paper)

Published simultaneously in Canada
Printed in the United States of America
Casebound International Standard Book Number: 0-669-15085-1
Paperbound International Standard Book Number: 0-669-15086-X
Library of Congress Catalog Card Number: 86-27727

The paper used in this publication meets the minimum requirements of
American National Standard for Information Sciences—Permanence
of Paper for Printed Library Materials, ANSI Z39.48-1984.

ISBN 0-669-15085-1

87 88 89 90 8 7 6 5 4 3 2 1

Contents

Acknowledgments

M ORE than one thousand divorced mothers and fathers in single-parent families made this book possible. They volunteered time, energy, and emotion in hopes that their experience would help others who follow. We salute them!

Supportive professional colleagues have made life happier and enormously rich. A scholarly community, such as that of the University of Nebraska, creates a wonderful environment in which to grow. A thousand thanks to Hazel Anthony, Roy Arnold, Rod Eirick, Karen Eskey, Charlotte Jackson, Kathy Jordan, Larry Kagan, Kay King, Pat Knaub, Paul Lee, Martin Massengale, Lisa Morris, Irvin Omtvedt, Leon Rottman, George Rowe, Gale Smith, Nick Stinnett, Helen Sulek, Kendra Schwab Summers, Dale Vanderholm, Sally Van Zandt, Patricia Welker, Ginger Woodward, and John Woodward. Also thanks to Rebecca Braymen, Don Endacott, Jerry Fennell, Roger H. Johnson, Jeff and Sandra Keuss, Susan McClelland, and Richard Schmeling.

Much of the research for this book was supported by funds from the Agricultural Research Division of the Institute of Agriculture and Natural Resources, University of Nebraska, Lincoln. Dr. DeFrain holds a research appointment in the Research Division for studies of family strengths and families in crisis.

Once again, many, many thanks to Lexington Books. Our publisher's excellent staff has been a delight to work with over the years: Margaret Zusky, Marsha Finley, Margo Shearman, Mary Ann LaHive, Susan Cummings, Sylvia Todd, and Terrence Fehr.

And our families round out the circle of love that keeps us going when times are difficult: Nikki DeFrain, Amie, Alyssa, and Erica

DeFrain, Orville and Harriet DeFrain, Jim and Debbie DeFrain, John and Margaret Schulling, John Schulling, Jr., Rod and Sharon Schulling; Don Fricke, Julie, David, and Becky Fricke, Art and Dorothy Mortensen, and Dick and Joline Boettcher; Ken Gruys, Kjerstin and Hanna Elmen-Gruys, and Bob and Rita Elmen.

To all a sincere thank you.

A Note to the Reader

T HE stories in this book are true. Many names, dates, places, and other identifying details of very sensitive material have been changed or omitted to protect the anonymity of the people who told us these stories. Any resemblance to real people is, thus, purely coincidental.

1

Introduction

THE little boy and the psychologist walked along the shore of the lake. The autumn sun was shining low in the west, bathing trees and water and faces in a golden light that gave a dreamlike quality to the scene—or maybe only to the psychologist's memory of the scene.

The psychologist was on a painful mission. She had been retained by a judge in a divorce court to offer her opinion about what would happen to the little boy when his parents divorced. Should he live with his mother? Or his father? Who was to win custody?

The dilemma was a particularly difficult one. Father implied that the mother might be suicidal. Mother talked darkly, saying that the father could possibly be sexually abusive of the six-year-old child. Each parent was convinced that the other was crazy.

Substantiating charge and countercharge was enormously difficult. Understanding a family can be like stumbling into January fog on the Oregon coast. There are no landmarks to help you find your direction.

The psychologist decided that a good long walk around the lake would be soothing and conducive to a useful interview of the child. The pair skipped rocks off the water's surface, counted shorebirds, and soon the child was relaxed and the psychologist's blood pressure had begun to edge back toward normal.

It came time to tackle the toughest issue of all: "Now, *you* don't decide where you're going to live. That's not *your* job. The judge decides. The judge will decide whether you should live with Mommy or Daddy."

The boy nodded. He was listening closely. "But the judge is interested in what you think," the psychologist continued, haltingly.

God, she hated this job. "The judge is interested, even though she decides what will happen. Not you . . ."

The psychologist paused, hoping that she would not have to fumble on any longer. The boy was adept and took the cue to speak. "I think the judge should take a big knife and cut me down the middle, and give half to Mommy and half to Daddy," he said.

The psychologist did not know what to say. She smiled lightly, though her emotions were struggling between nervous laughter and tears. "Where did you get that idea?" she finally asked.

"I don't know," the little boy replied. "I think it's a good idea, don't you?"

"Maybe as good as any other," the psychologist conceded.

The Wisdom of Solomon

The little boy was probably referring to King Solomon's resolution of a dilemma. Two women had come to the king for judgment:

> "Oh my lord," one of them said, "this woman and I dwell in the same house, and I gave birth to a child there. On the third day after I was delivered, this woman also gave birth; and we two were alone in the house. This woman's son died in the night, because she lay on it; so she arose at midnight, and took my son from beside me while I slept, and laid it in her bosom, and laid her dead son in my bosom. When I rose in the morning to nurse my child, behold, it was dead; but when I looked at it closely, it was not the child that I had borne."
>
> "The living child is mine," said the other woman.
>
> "No, the dead child is yours," said the first.
>
> Then the king said, "Bring me a sword." So a sword was brought, and the king said, "Divide the living child in two, and give half to one woman and half to the other."
>
> Then the heart of the first woman yearned for her son. "Oh, my lord," she said, "give her the child, and by no means slay it."
>
> "It shall be neither mine nor yours," said the other. "Divide it."
>
> Then the king answered and said, "Give the living child to the first woman, and by no means slay it; she is its mother." All Israel heard of the judgment the king had rendered, and they stood in awe of him, because they perceived that the wisdom of God was in him (1 Kings 3:17-28).

The little boy may never have heard King Solomon's story told. He may have come up with the creative, though implausible solution himself.

We quoted the Biblical story at length for two reasons: (1) the average reader might enjoy having the details of the rich tale refreshed in his or her mind; and (2) it is a story of a judge's remarkable solution to the age-old problem of child custody. Who will rear the children?

There is no easy solution to this problem. This book is an earnest attempt to present the issues involved in divorce and custody as seen through the eyes of more than one thousand people who have been there. But we would be fools or zealots to offer only one approach to the problem, for there are probably as many valid approaches as there are people who adopt them. Divorce, like life itself, is an individual and family matter. We are all different, and we must decide for ourselves which road to take.

We urge parents to decide between themselves what is best for the children. We urge them to negotiate in good faith with each other. Even though they cannot live together, they can—if they choose—remain partners in the enterprise of childrearing.

We have seen too many families end up in court. We have been involved as professionals ourselves, counseling families about custody issues and acting as a court investigator in more than fifty cases. And we still get a bit sick at heart when people talk darkly about going to court "to fight for *my* child."

We are reminded, first, of Kahlil Gibran's wonderful poetry on children:

> And a woman who held a babe against her bosom said, Speak to us of Children.
> And he said:
> Your children are not your children.
> They are the sons and daughters of Life's longing for itself.
> They come through you but not from you,
> And though they are with you, yet they belong not to you.
> You may give them your love but not your thoughts,
> For they have their own thoughts.
> You may house their bodies but not their souls,
> For their souls dwell in the house of tomorrow, which you cannot visit, not even in your dreams.

You may strive to be like them, but seek not to make them like you,
For life goes not backward nor tarries with yesterday.
You are the bows from which your children as living arrows are sent forth.
The archer sees the mark upon the path of the infinite, and He bends you with His might that His arrows may go swift and far.
Let your bending in the archer's hand be for gladness;
For even as He loves the arrow that flies, so He loves also the bow that is stable.[1]

And we know that when a child custody dispute gets to court almost anything can happen. A parent may think that he or she has an airtight case, and a lawyer may agree (for a price), but the judge has to look at the situation from all angles and just may disagree. Two things are certain about a court battle: the hostility between parents will expand exponentially during the confusion and mayhem that is the legal process; and a lot of money will change hands, and most of it will not go to improve the lives of the children—the supposed benefactors of all this warfare. In the words of one attorney: "I can tell you that if my client's spouse didn't hate my client before I cross-examined him, you can rest assured that he did when I got through. Because my role was to destroy him. That doesn't make any sense to me."

In an earlier book written with Nick Stinnett called *Secrets of Strong Families* we explored the qualities that make up strong families. We wanted to know what made for positive marital and parent-child relationships. We interviewed and surveyed more than three thousand people. We were not surprised to find that happy families do not operate like a courtroom. An atmosphere of cooperation and trust fosters strong family relationships. A courtroom atmosphere—full of tension, hostility, mistrust, verbal combativeness, ultraformality, and communication in "legalese"—does not generally help mend the wounds of divorce. It is only a last resort in a chaotic situation. Many judges jokingly refer to their tour of duty in divorce court as doing time in Siberia. "Criminal court is easier and a lot more fun," one judge has said. In the words of Chief Justice Norman Krivosha of the Nebraska Supreme Court,

What we really need to do is we need to change it from an adversary proceeding to a mediating proceeding, with a court being involved. What you need to do is you need to say to both people who want a divorce, "We're going to put you in a room, with a referee." Not a lawyer. It might be a social worker, it might be a minister, it might be a prizefighter. I don't know what it's like with a policeman. "And you're going to sit here until you tell each other what you have to tell each other, and you agree on what the terms of the divorce are going to be. Now when that's through, you are submitted to the court." And sometimes in regard to child custody, people make agreements that aren't good for the children, so the court still has to play by its rules. But the people have to sit in a room and get their anger out. One time, and one time at least, he must listen to her. And that's the price he's going to have to pay to get his freedom. And they have to hear each other once and for all. And we would do it in a much more quiet way.[2]

Winning and losing may be the way people operate in courts and on the football field, but in the family such a mentality can easily lead to disaster.

The Current Study

The study reported in the following chapters builds on past research and bridges many of the research gaps of the past.

Two hundred and five interviews of fathers, mothers, and children involved in divorce custody battles in court were conducted and serve as valuable background.

In a statistical study we subsequently looked at 738 parents in forty-five states representing four distinct groups:

528 mothers with sole custody

114 fathers with sole custody

40 mothers and fathers with split custody

56 parents with joint legal and physical custody (152 parents had joint legal custody but a traditional sole physical custody arrangement)

As far as we know, this is the largest study in existence of joint custody, by far; it is the only study of split custody in existence to our knowledge; and it is the only study to compare statistically sole custody, split custody, and joint custody. These parents were not

selected from clinical populations, such as from a mental-health center or a court or a support group. Rather, they responded to newspaper stories asking for divorced people to participate in custody
research. They are of course volunteers, and volunteer populations
probably are biased toward the more educated, higher-income
classes. We believe, though, that this population is more representative of sole, split, and joint custody parents than would be a clinical
sample, which would be made up of people who are by the very
nature of the sampling procedure troubled.

Some of the people in our study were troubled. Some were not
troubled. All were challenged, certainly, by the difficulties of coping
with divorce and its aftermath.

Researchers operate on hunches a lot of the time, but research
jargon and fear of being considered unprofessional usually dictate
that hunches be hidden from the reader, being "unscientific."
Hunches do guide the direction almost all research takes, however,
and so it is important that the reader know why we took off in the
research direction we did.

We began seriously studying divorce and children in 1975. We
read many articles and books on the topic and in clinical work and
classroom seminars had the good fortune to talk with many, many
divorced people and their children. We developed a course called
"Coping with Divorce," and soon seventy to seventy-five people were
signing up for each eight-week sequence.[3]

One of the first things that impressed us was how wrong we
were about the divorce process. We had, in a very simplistic fashion,
assumed that all marriages ended with fireworks—conflict, violence,
alcoholism. Lots of heat and noise and emotion.

But talking with divorced people we found that in many cases
this was just not the case. These people described marriages that had
simply dried up and blown away on a dusty breeze. There was no
bang. Only, maybe, a whimper. An all-pervasive sadness, or perhaps
the absence of any feeling at all.

We began to call these "burned-out marriages" and were happy
to find that other researchers concurred with our findings. Dr. Maggie Hayes at the University of Oklahoma told us of her discovery
that so-called burnout was common in the divorced people she interviewed,[4] and Morton Hunt in New York likewise noted to us that
a large proportion of his survey respondents described a similar sce-

nario.[5] The so-called amicable divorce did have, then, a basis in fact. Maybe joint custody would work, we hypothesized, if people were not so angry after a divorce.

Another hunch we had came from our studies of fatherhood in two-parent families, which we began in 1973 at the University of Wisconsin, Madison. We found that fathers who shared child care and housework did a relatively good job, enjoyed it, and got along well with the children and their wives. A later study we did with Pamela Nelssen at the University of Nebraska, Lincoln, followed up the Madison research and found that fathers who shared child care were very common in Lincoln. The average father did fully 39 percent of the child care in Lincoln, while the average mother did 61 percent.[6]

Put the two ideas together: that divorce does not always end in hostilities and that the average father is very actively involved in child care. That makes for a pretty strong prediction that joint custody just might work in some families. Our research findings, you will see in the next chapters, bear this out. But joint custody is no panacea; there are many ways to arrange custody of children successfully. Each family is, indeed, unique, and no one can afford to be doctrinaire.

A Prospectus

What will happen to the reader in this book? In chapter 2 we will outline the issues and their importance. The results of past research on children, parents, and divorce by other researchers across the United States will be briefly reported and synthesized for the reader; we think as clinicians and researchers that it is important to lay down a strong foundation for the book, though previous studies are many and the issues complex.

Also in chapter 2 we will briefly explain to the inquiring reader how our own research was conducted, so that he or she will understand the process through which we came to the conclusions that we have. Finally in chapter 2 we will present brief, readable results of our statistical analyses comparing the four different basic groups of parents we studied and the varying ways they manage the many issues of divorce, custody, and single parenthood. The parent groups are:

Mothers with sole custody

Fathers with sole custody

Split custody (in which the father has traditional custody of one or more children and the mother has traditional custody of one or more children)

Joint custody (in which both the mother and the father share decision making and direct child care responsibilities in relatively equal segments of time)

Chapters 3 through 6 focus on each of the four different groups of parents individually. In these chapters we will present direct testimony from literally hundreds of parents from all walks of life in nearly every state of the nation. Their experiences will be related on a host of very practical matters:

1. Negotiating child custody arrangements: "Who gets the kids?"
2. Visitation
3. Courts, laws, and lawyers; mediation
4. Money: alimony and child support
5. Adjustment to divorce by the parents
6. Adjustment to divorce by the children
7. Where to go for help
8. Support systems
9. Stresses: money and work
10. Dating
11. Parenting skills: parent-child relationships
12. Relationships with the ex-spouse
13. Advice from the parents to other parents on custody (regarding the children and the adults)
14. Considerations that are unique to each particular custody arrangement
15. Sorrows
16. Joys

The heart and soul of the book will be found in chapters 3 through 6. The parents speaking in their own words will elicit many emotional reactions from the reader: shock, dismay, anger, disbelief, sadness, laughter, and tears, to name just a few. The stories the parents have told us are very real, very moving, and we feel honored that they have given us this mandate to pass on the love and wisdom they have gained experiencing the terrible crisis of divorce in a family.

In the final section, chapter 7, we will offer the reader our thoughts on how all these ideas can be applied to one's life. We also will encourage the reader to work through a semistructured thinking and writing process that we have developed from our interviews and surveys of divorcing parents.

In appendix B the reader will find a section on resources for families experiencing divorce and single parenthood. It contains a discussion of support groups, counselors, and social services for single-parent families. A section on suggested readings for both parents and children is also included. In this section we briefly describe many good books that we have carefully reviewed and recommended.

Divorce for many, many parents will be the most serious and disheartening crisis they will ever face in their lives. This book is, then, a gift from nearly one thousand people who have been down that painful road to others who may have the misfortune to follow. It is, ultimately, a hopeful book, a positive book. The parents who share their lives in these pages are wonderful sources of strength and wisdom; they are truly mentors for one of life's most challenging transitions.

Though the single-parent family in our society has been much maligned, our research and the research of many other professionals indicate that millions of children are successfully raised by parents going it alone.

2

Research Background, Design, and Results

Divorce and Children

The American family today assumes a variety of forms, each reflecting an adjustment to revolutionary social changes and to the stresses that inevitably arise from within the family. Although many families have successfully adapted, others have not.

The divorce rate has unquestionably been growing at a rapid pace in recent years. For nearly a decade now there have been 1 million or more divorces each year in the United States. Most of these divorces involve children; by the 1980s over 1 million children each year were involved in child custody decisions.[1] About 12 million children under age eighteen live with divorced parents.[2] One in every three white children and two out of three black children born in the late 1970s will see their parents divorce before the children are sixteen. Ninety percent of the children live with their mothers; most do not have a father in the home for at least five years. Most of the children acquire a stepfather because 60–70 percent of the younger divorced women remarry within five years.[3]

The average divorced mother has a difficult time of it financially. Her income has dropped dramatically from predivorce days, leading to a drastic change in life-style. The term the "feminization of poverty" was coined almost as a direct response to the epidemic divorce rate and the increase in the number of single mothers with low incomes in the past decade and a half.

A recent Census Bureau report says that more than half of all mothers and children ordered by courts to receive child support and/or alimony from fathers after divorce get less than what is due them; fully 28 percent get nothing. The so-called deadbeat daddy problem cuts across all socioeconomic, ethnic, and racial lines. The media are beginning to report rather dramatic responses to the problem: A Tallahassee, Florida, judge asks fathers who have defaulted on child support whether they drove to court, and if they have he seizes their cars; a Prince Georges County, Maryland, sheriff once rounded up eighty-one men and five women for delinquent payments in a predawn raid and jailed fourteen for contempt. There is a great hue and cry across the land.[4]

Divorced fathers without custody launch their countercharges. "We're broke," they lament, and tell plausible stories of the difficulty of trying to keep themselves afloat, to bankroll, say, a new spouse and stepfamily, and to care financially for their own children. These fathers tell us they are tired of being "sugar daddies" to their children. Many of them want more than occasional visits and friendly chitchat.

Barry Manilow sings about these "Sunday Fathers":

> *Sundays are theirs to explore alone*
> *By law one day to keep the two from turning to strangers*
> *Sunday father and son . . .*
> *Where are the words or the games*
> *A place to go*
> *Some way to let him know you want to be with him?*
> *Somehow it's always ending*
> *Just half begun*
> *Sunday father and son.*

The Sunday fathers often argue that the round-the-clock mothers jealously keep the children from seeing them. "She poisoned our friendship," they tell us. And many Sunday fathers plot darkly to even the score by not coming through on child support. "Why pay her for nothing?" they say at those times when they feel they can be totally honest.

"He wasn't interested in the children before the divorce," counter many mothers. "Why now?" they ask suspiciously. How could a man change so much? they imply.

The children are always caught in the middle, and "if we were living in a world governed by children's wishes, parents would rarely separate, no matter how badly they got along with each other."[5]

Child Custody Laws in Transition

Societal and legal presumptions about what constitutes "the best interests of the child" have evolved considerably through the ages. Between 500 B.C. and the late nineteenth century, children almost automatically went to their father upon dissolution of marriage. The child was seen as property and the father as the provider of services and income.[6]

In 1839 a tradition of noninterference in the father's common-law right to custody except in cases of paternal default was broken by the British court's Talfourds Act. This act established the doctrine of *parens patriae* under which the court assumed the power to decide custody for children under age seven.[7] This set the stage for the "tender years presumption."

In 1880 a precedent-setting ruling decreed that "The claim of a mother during the early years of an infant's life to the care of her child is to be preferred to that of the father."[8] Maternal custody was still seen, though, as a temporary exception to the age-old rule, and courts often returned children to the father after their early years.[9] By the end of the first quarter of the twentieth century, however, maternal custody was the norm.

Maternal preference recognized that the traditional role of the mother was to provide the primary care of the children in their early years. This tradition focused on parents' rights, specifically maternal rights.

Many fathers are currently challenging this standard, arguing that it may be the father who assumed the nurturant, "mothering" role in the family. Most states now have statutes that have replaced the maternal preference guidelines with the more neutral "best interests of the child" doctrine. And recently, an integration of all these different approaches has been proposed, an approach that purports to consider the needs of all parties concerned—fathers, mothers, and children. This is called, of course, joint custody.[10]

California was the first state to codify the presumption of the joint custody cases, and others have been quick to follow. Some argue that this is the fairest approach of all. Others argue that courts should presume nothing in a custody case and should endeavor to decide each case without any predisposed notions about what is best for the child or all involved.

The Movement Toward Mediation

The shift in the law from the "tender years doctrine" to "best interests of the child" was paralleled by a move toward no-fault divorce.

No-fault divorce was the legal system's response to the problem of people's lying. If one spouse did not want to live with the other anymore, a long list of excuses had to be conjured up to gain freedom. Chief Justice Krivosha is quite vivid in his explanation of how this response evolved:

> They wanted to get a divorce, and so somebody came to the court, lied about the adultery or lied about a beating or lied about a whole host of things. How we really got around it was that people said this was silly. If people don't want to live together, let them not live together. So we'll have no-fault. And what that did was it shifted the fight from divorce to property and custody.
>
> When fault existed a man came home and said, "I've found the woman I've been waiting for forever, and I want a divorce." And the wife said, "You'll die before I give you a divorce." So he said, "You can have everything, just give me my freedom." It would be wonderful, he thought. But two years later he was saying to the new one, "I've found the woman . . ." And in two years he hadn't gained much financially so he wasn't losing so much. The second time he wasn't nearly as wealthy.
>
> What happened was they shifted that. Now he comes home and he says, "I'm going to get a divorce." And she says, "I don't want you to," and he says, "Tough, I don't need your permission." So now what's left to fight about? The property and the children. We simply shifted. There are no fewer contested cases than there used to be, we just shifted.[11]

Now figuring out how to divide up property and money is relatively simple. Although the issue has recently been clouded by wives' claims for restitution for putting a husband through school and supporting him emotionally by building a stable home for him as his career took off, it still is easier, we believe, to divide up money than children. Put the money in a big pile, and slide half the pile in one direction and half in the other. The biggest problem is finding out how big the pile really is.

With children, though, we come right back to Solomon's dilemma and to that of the six-year-old boy and the psychologist by the lake.

Lawyers are not really trained in how to divide children, and many do not have the stomach for it. They studied the law to discover intricate, oftentimes beautiful ways of deciding difficult or ugly issues. The law can tell a lawyer ways to divide up property and money, but it is to the behavioral and social scientists that lawyers must turn when issues of child development and family relationships need resolution.

Judge Norman Fenton of Pima County Superior Court in Tucson notes that

> unfortunately courts are often parties to intensifying family conflicts by requiring that party members and family members take on adversarial roles. This is particularly true in contested custody proceedings or visitation fights. This adversarial position can destroy any future productive relationships between the parties, and have lasting psychological effects on the individuals involved. It can prolong the conflict and make future relationships impossible. Not only is it costly, but it interferes with the children's welfare and the relationship between the children and their parents, as well as the parents themselves.[12]

In his court, Judge Fenton has replaced the adversarial approach with mediation, a framework for negotiation and compromise. Rather than using lawyers trained for combat, he uses counselors—trained as educators, psychologists, or social workers.

Family mediation has increased greatly in the past fifteen years. Colleen Cordes, a journalist, offers a good working definition:

> In mediation, a neutral third party helps conflicting parties to negotiate their own settlement. Unlike arbitrators, mediators have no decision-making authority themselves. Unlike the criminal justice system, mediation assigns no guilt or innocence and emphasizes constructive cooperation between the parties at odds rather than casting them in adversarial roles. Moreover, in most instances, the parties involved in mediation participate voluntarily.[13]

Does family mediation work? A review of various studies came to these conclusions:

> People who work out their differences together through mediation are happier with the results than those who go through the traditional legal system.

People who succeed in reaching agreement through mediation generally see their agreements as fair and equitable and are more likely to comply with the agreements.

People save money having their disputes mediated rather than paying the legal system, though estimates vary. They also apparently save time.

Finally, a larger percentage of couples who go through mediation agree upon joint custody.[14]

What is not clear is the obvious question: What kinds of families can succeed in mediation and what kinds cannot?: Since people choose mediation voluntarily, they may be predisposed toward less hostile and more cooperative approaches to problem solving.

Kenneth Kressel, associate professor of psychology at Rutgers University, has been studying mediation for years and does some work as a mediator. He has identified four patterns among divorcing couples:

Psychologically enmeshed couples who use mediators and lawyers as tools to get at each other and keep the relationship alive by fighting.

Autistic couples who share a pathological history of non-communication.

Couples in open, direct conflict.

Disengaged couples who are burned out and have given up on the marriage.

Kressel says his research and that of others indicate that 20–30 percent of all divorcing couples do not do well in mediation. They are involved either in constant fighting or in complete lack of communication. These are the couples in the first two categories.

For the 70 or 80 percent in the final two categories—open, direct conflict and disengagement—there is a better chance that mediation will work.

"In my bones," Kressel said, "I know that five or ten years from now, after there's been more research, [what we'll find] is that [mediation] is very, very good for certain kinds of disputes and parties and not at all good for the other kinds of disputes and parties."[15]

The Child Adjusts to Divorce

"I'll be damned if I will let an eight-year-old tell me what to do," a New York City judge said when he heard the child's stated custodial preference.[16]

Children are the lost souls of a family in crisis. Parents are often so busy tending to their own hurts that the child is not consoled. An adult overwhelmed by crisis is in poor condition to satisfy the emotional needs of the young. And even when someone does listen to a youngster, the youngster's wishes are often ignored: "She is too young to know her mind," we adults are fond of saying, "too young to be privy to such an important decision." Or too inconsequential to get in the way of my fulminations, the judge in New York seemed to be implying.

Children in a divorce are just as likely to suffer negative consequences as anyone else, but they are less equipped intellectually or emotionally to deal with the crisis, and they lack power over the storms that buffet their lives.

In this section we will take a brief look at what the researchers and clinicians have to say about what conflict, marital separation, and divorce do to the young.

Many factors can influence the coping ability of families going through a divorce. Among them are the financial resources of the family, the ages of the children, and the coping skills of the individual family members. Factors relating to child custody arrangements must be considered as well. The role of the child in the decision-making process, the speed with which the custodial decision is reached, and the extent of parental involvement may all influence the postdivorce adjustment of both children and adults.[17] According to Mavis Hetherington, a psychologist, "The parents' response to divorce and the quality of the child's relationship with both parents immediately after divorce has a substantial effect on the child's coping and adjustment."[18]

It is clear that court decisions in which one parent is awarded custody and the other parent has limited or no access to the children involved may function to isolate children by inhibiting their chance for exposure to other adult role models and by severely limiting the network of enduring relationships available to them. This is not likely to produce an adaptive, emotionally mature adult.[19]

Joan Wallerstein, a clinician, studied thirty-four preschool chil-

dren at a counseling center who were interviewed shortly after their
parents separated. Some children coped with the marital separation
better than others and improved during subsequent months. Among
the factors that emerged as important in the environment of the improved children were: the ability of the divorcing parents to keep
anger and conflicts separate from their children; the availability of a
good school setting and teachers with time and sensitivity to give
individual support to the child; and the absence of overt rejection or
desertion by either parent. Children who were able to cope successfully with the stress of the parental separation were intelligent, per-
ceptive, and courageous. They also had the ability to make do with
less time and caretaking and to become increasingly independent, as
well as to develop supports outside of the immediate family. In order
to make the necessary adaptation it seemed important for the children to face the reality of the divorce and to be assured by trusted
parents of continued love and care.[20]

Mavis Hetherington has suggested that wide variability in the
quality and intensity of responses and the adaptation of children to
divorce exists. "Some children exhibit severe or sustained disrup-
tions in development, others seem to sail through a turbulent divorce
and stressful aftermath and emerge as competent, well-functioning
individuals."[21]

What are the long-term effects of divorce on a child? According
to one writer, "whether the children of divorce will dare to love, will
repeat the patterns of their parents, or will enter marriage better
prepared, are questions only time can answer."[22] We concur.

Some observers have noted the emergence of a preventive strat-
egy aimed at helping the increasing number of children facing family
crisis. Until recently, professional help for a child was thought of
only as a last resort—when the child became unmanageable or completely depressed. Counseling can help a child understand the feelings that often accompany a family crisis: "The idea is that if the
child can be taught to cope with the stressful situation while it is still
fresh, s/he may be able to head off emotional problems before they
get a chance to take root."[23]

Certainly not all children of divorce are in need of professional
help to adapt successfully to the reorganization of their families. According to Ivan Nye, a family sociologist, in most cases a new equi-
librium is established after a period of adjustment. Family members
will inevitably play new and less clearly defined roles but for the

most part will be free of the unbearable conflicts of the previously unhappy marriage.[24]

Several studies have been done that point to the emotional climate of the home as being the determining force affecting a child's adjustment. Many authors have expressed the view that it is not the divorce but the marital conflict that is destructive.

In order to gain insight into the effects of divorce, Deborah Luepnitz, a psychologist, examined a sample of college students whose parents had divorced before the young people were sixteen. The study attempted to explore the experiences of these students before, during, and after divorce. Which aspect of the divorce was the major stressor for each person? The results of the study indicate that 83 percent of the students reported feeling stress during at least one phase of the divorce—that is, predivorce, transition, or postdivorce. Half of the students revealed that it was the marital conflict that had produced most of their distress. Twenty-five percent were most stressed by postdivorce problems, 8 percent by transition problems, and 16 percent reported that the divorce was not a major stressor for them at all. The sample used in this study may have been unusually healthy because the investigation of a college population provides subjects who probably have managed to adjust adequately to the crisis.[25]

A study by Helen and Vernon Raschke gives support to belief in the negative effect of conflict rather than family structure on children's adjustment. Two hundred and eighty-nine third, sixth, and eighth graders were studied with respect to self-concept, family structure, and family conflict. Results of the study indicated no significant differences in the self-concept scores of children from intact, single-parent, reconstituted, or other types of families. Children who reported higher levels of family conflict had significantly lower self-concept scores. Another important finding was that for all children in the study, the greater the perceived happiness of the parents, the higher the children's self-concept score. The researchers suggest giving more attention to conflict and its effects on children in all family structures, and less attention to the "ills" of the single-parent family.[26]

Research findings seem consistent in showing that children whose parents have separated function more adequately than do children in conflict-ridden intact families.

Ivan Nye studied 780 high school students from "broken" and

unhappy "unbroken" homes. He found that although the groups did
not differ significantly with respect to delinquent companions and to
adjustment to school or church, adolescents in "broken homes" had
less psychosomatic illness, less delinquent behavior, and better adjustment to parents than did children in unhappy "unbroken" homes.
Nye also found that parental adjustment was greater in "broken
homes" than in unhappy "unbroken" homes.[27]

Judson Landis, a family social scientist, found that the emotional
environment of the home is most instrumental in personality development, rather than the actual structure of the family. He gave questionnaires to three thousand college students with the purpose of
comparing individuals with various family histories on factors of relationship to parents, dating, self-evaluation, and grade-point average. Few significant differences were found between students of divorced parents and those from unhappy intact homes. Landis found,
however, that students of happily married parents differed significantly on most variables from students of unhappily married parents
and divorced parents. Results were more positive for students of
happily married parents, except for grade-point averages, which
were lower than those of students from either other group. These
findings reinforce the idea that the unhappy marriage rather than the
divorce has a negative impact on the children of divorce.[28]

Initially, most children who have gone through the separation or
divorce of their parents experience a combination of responses.
Among these responses are fear, guilt, anger, and depression. It is
normally not until after the first year following divorce that tension
and anxiety are reduced and an increased sense of well-being begins
to surface. Mavis Hetherington suggests that "the point at which we
tap into the sequence of events and changing processes associated
with divorce will modify our view of the adjustment of the child and
the factors which influence that adjustment."[29]

The Parent and Divorce

Our research and that of many other researchers and clinicians
clearly indicate that a child's adjustment to divorce is closely related
to the parent's adjustment. If things are going relatively well for the
parent, it is likely—for a number of obvious reasons—that they will
be going well for the youngster too.

    In this section we will take a quick look at the research and clinical impressions of professionals who have studied mothers and fathers with sole custody, split custody, and joint custody.

Mothers with Sole Custody. LeMasters and DeFrain reviewed writings on divorced mothers with sole custody and identified six "generic features" of mothers without partners.[30] It is interesting how past research has tended to accentuate the negative:
    1. Poverty. Female-headed single-parent families have a median income that is less than half the median income for all American families. Financial stress is a major complaint, and in low-income families a financial crisis can hit on a regular basis. Some go without bus service or an automobile. Others do not have a television or a telephone.
    2. Role conflicts and overload. Being a single head of a household tends to be an 18-hour-a-day, 7-day-a-week, 365-day-a-year job. The woman must play both mother and father. When ill or working late, she cannot be relieved by the children's father. Most single mothers work outside the home, and work hours usually are in conflict with school hours for the children. The kids leave too late for school and get home too early, and have too many and too long vacations. And what about children's illnesses? Add to the work role and the parenthood role the girlfriend role, for most single mothers will remarry sooner or later, but it is difficult for most to begin dating again after being married for years.
    3. Role shifts. Since most single mothers do remarry, they will have to shift gears on parental roles twice: mother's role to mother-and-father roles back to mother's role. Try doing this with two different husbands with two different views of life and childrearing. No wonder stepparenting is the most difficult challenge of remarriage.
    4. Public attitudes. No matter how open-minded society becomes, divorced single mothers still seem to suffer from stereotypes and prejudice: that they somehow could not keep a marriage and are thus failures; that their children now, almost automatically, are suffering in a one-parent home; and that the women are probably loose—do not trust one around your husband. Now, certainly there are female single parents who fit these stereotypes, but there are many, many more who do not.
    5. The well of loneliness. When one is overloaded with work,

childrearing, and money problems, it is hard not to feel alienated and alone. Loneliness is a common problem for single mothers.

6. Historically, there has been a lack of institutional supports for single parents. In the 1970s and 1980s, as the number of single mothers skyrocketed, communities began to develop support groups for mothers, and the public schools set up after-school care for children of working parents. Counseling and classes for families were developed by human-service agencies. But unemployment and underemployment are still big problems for single mothers, and lower pay for female-dominated jobs plagues most women. Add to this that Aid to Dependent Children programs are notoriously stingy, and one is easily convinced that society is not ready to be very kind to mothers with sole custody.

Fathers with Sole Custody. The feminist movement of the past fifteen years probably influenced fathers as much as mothers. When one half of the parent team changes, so must the other. As fatherhood began to look more and more like motherhood, it was inevitable that upon divorce the issues would be clouded even further.

Fathers who had a big responsibility for child care before divorce were eager to continue after divorce. (As we shall see later, some fathers who did not do much with the children before the divorce also began to clamor for custody.)

In response to these changes in society, a number of researchers began looking more closely at divorced fathers with sole custody.

The U.S. Department of Commerce reported that in 1979, 17 percent of all families with children were maintained by the mother alone, and 2 percent by the father alone. Corresponding figures for 1970 were 10 and 1 percent. This indicates that though the numbers of male-headed families have increased, they have not increased dramatically and remain a tiny proportion of the total.[31]

After reading carefully the past research on fathers with sole custody, we believe that the following generalizations are valid:

1. Fathers with custody had difficulties, especially in juggling work and child care responsibilities, but these difficulties were surmountable.

2. Most fathers were successful at childrearing.

3. Most fathers did alter their life-styles in terms of their work habits, social lives, and recreational activities so that more time was available for their children. Loneliness and lack of adult companionship were problems for some fathers, because there simply was not time left in their hectic schedules for personal needs.

4. Most fathers reported that their parent-child relationships had improved since before the divorce.

5. Many fathers in their new role reported feelings of satisfaction, success, and personal growth.

6. Extended family, friends, and other community groups were needed for support and help.

It is interesting to note that studies of fathers tend to accentuate the positive more than do studies of single-parent mothers. We believe that society is biased on this issue: the fathers are somehow seen as a rarer, and thus more heroic breed. We think that this stereotype is basically nonsense, however. In chapters 3 and 4 this issue will be made more clear.

Comparing Mothers with Sole Custody and Fathers with Sole Custody. To our knowledge there is only one previously published study that statistically compares mothers with sole custody and fathers with sole custody. DeFrain and Eirick compared on a large number of measures mothers and fathers who volunteered for their study.[32] They found that fathers held a slight edge over the mothers in income, education, and the tendency not to move from their home and community after the divorce. But the researchers were startled when they statistically analyzed the thirty three fathers' and thirty eight mothers' responses to sixty three questions in the general areas of the history of the divorce process, feelings as a single parent, relations with the ex-spouse, and forming new social relationships. On sixty two of the sixty three questions, the fathers and mothers did not differ significantly.

In capsule form, the study found that:

1. The process of divorce was not essentially different for fathers and mothers. The causes of the divorce were not different, the children's role in the process was not different, nor did friends

or relatives behave differently toward the individuals depending upon whether they were males or females. Both groups saw the divorce as being a stressful event in their lives.

2. Both men and women were open about describing the stresses and strains of single parenthood, but agreed that if the situation were to arise again, they all would accept the responsibility. The marriage had become unbearable for them, and though a two-parent family was seen by most of these people as being potentially superior, a stable one-parent family in their particular circumstances was generally seen as better for the children.

3. The fathers and mothers described their childrearing philosophies and behaviors in essentially the same way. Fathers did not yell at or hit the children any more than did mothers. For a few fathers with teenaged girls, sex education was a minor problem, and the fathers usually had a sister or a friend talk about female concerns with their daughter.

4. The fathers and mothers described their children's behaviors after the marital separation in a strikingly similar manner. The vast majority of the children were doing well at home and in school; emotionally and physically most of the children were described as being healthy.

5. Custody arrangements with the ex-spouse were similar for both men and women. Most ex-spouses had the children for holidays, weekends, and summers. The one statistically significant difference between men and women did occur in the general area of relationships with the ex-spouse. Only one mother said that she encouraged the children to take sides in any continuing disagreements with the ex-spouse, while a third of the fathers encouraged this teaming up. The reason for this difference is highly speculative, but possibly fathers still believed to some extent the old stereotype that it is an even graver error for the mother to "abandon" the children than it is for the father to do so.

6. In regard to forming new social relationships, both men and women were equally interested in remarriage. The children of both generally encouraged them in their quest. We found that neither group fit the unkind picture of the care-free divorced person, hopping from bar to bar and bed to bed. To relax and socialize, most of the folks stayed home or went to friends' houses;

only ten of the seventy-one parents reported visiting a bar even on occasion.

Past research on fatherhood had led DeFrain and Eirick to predict that fathers would compare quite favorably to mothers in a study of single parents. They were surprised, however, to see how close the two fit together. On sixty-two out of sixty-three questions, to reiterate, there was no significant difference. The study by DeFrain and Eirick was a helpful pilot for the final study that this book is based upon.

Now, what does past research tell us about how fathers and mothers with sole custody stack up?

1. Fathers seem to be confident in their abilities as single parents, when compared with mothers. We cannot tell for sure whether this is false confidence or whether it is based on genuine skill in childrearing. We would guess, however, that it is a combination of both.

2. Fathers with sole custody have two distinct advantages over mothers with sole custody: they make more money, on the average, and society seems to look more favorably upon men (once they have been awarded custody). Sole fathers are seen, often, as heroic figures caring for their young after being "abandoned" by the mothers. They seem to get more offers of help: free dinners, child care offers, and so forth. Their position seems to be more "in" than does that of sole mothers, who vastly outnumber them.

3. Mothers have a major advantage over fathers. We have a distinct feeling, as do most people, that mothers still have a slight edge over fathers in a custody fight. Most people, including judges, have a gut feeling that mothers are better mothers than fathers are. And we concur that this is probably the case. Many fathers faced with sole custody often have a lot to learn about childrearing and housework; these are things that mothers usually already know.

4. All in all, though, fathers and mothers are very similar. They face loneliness, overload, and the vague fear that all is not as good as it could be for their children—the generic emotional challenges of the single parent, regardless of gender.

Split Custody. This, as the reader will recall, is a custody arrangement in which both the father and the mother have traditional custody of one or more of the children. A mother might have the two younger daughters, while the father has the teenaged son. To our knowledge there are no past studies of this variant family form in which siblings are split up after divorce. Whether to split siblings up is an issue that comes up in divorcing families and occasionally reaches a judge for a final determination. That is the logic behind our including split custody as one of the alternatives for divorcing parents. As it turned out in our research, split custody is a rather rarely used option.

Joint Custody. This option has gotten the most press recently, and people hold strong opinions about joint custody, both pro and con:

> If people had the ability to do a good job of joint custody, then they would never have been divorced in the first place.
> *—a professor of family studies at a major state university*

> Well, joint custody simply means that everybody gets an arm. Being pulled all the time is a hard way for a child to grow up. Now if both the parents operate in tandem, having joint custody isn't a problem. But they couldn't agree on their own life. How in the world are they going to agree on the child's? So we have one parent saying that staying up late isn't bad and one parent saying that going to bed early is better, and one parent saying that doing this is all right and one parent saying that doing that is better. Joint custody can be a very difficult problem.
> *—a chief justice of a state supreme court*

> Findings reveal joint custody to be a viable option for some divorced parents; in sharp contrast to the assumptions of Goldstein, Freud, and Solnit, these divorced spouses can continue to share parenting even though they have terminated a marital relationship.
> *—a professor of social work at a major state university*[33]

The difference between the professional reaction to shared custody and that of the people who are practicing some form of it is often amazing. During the last two years I have been researching and writing *The Child Custody Handbook* and have talked with numerous attorneys, psychologists, and judges on the subject. Not infrequently, I'd spend the day listening to learned arguments as to why such arrangements can't possibly work, and then have dinner with people who, not knowing that it was impossible, found it to be an eminently sensible way of doing things!

—an author-investigator of joint custody[34]

The Folly of Joint Custody:
Children Are Not Negotiable;
Bartering Them in Divorce Is Bad Law
and Even Worse Psychology

—title of an article by a psychotherapist and a human development professor[35]

Joint Custody of Infants:
Breakthrough or Fad?

—title of an article by a law school student at a Canadian university[36]

So, of all these presumably intelligent and well-qualified people, who is right and who is wrong? A review of the tiny amount of published previous research and of our own work reported later in this book leads us to conclude that there is an element of truth in what all the people cited above are saying.

In 1980 California adopted a law stating that the first-choice solution in divorce custody disputes is joint custody. On the basis of our reading of past research on joint custody and of our own investigation, this law does not make much sense to us. We would guess that the law *sounded good* to the legislators in a philosophical sense— it sounded fair to both fathers and mothers.

The trouble is, joint custody can be a disaster for a family and can enmesh the children in continuing conflict. We would rather see lawmakers make no presumptions whatsoever—not maternal presumptions, not paternal, not joint. Rather, on the basis of our data from more than one thousand parents in all fifty states, we would hope that judges first and foremost would be open-minded about all possibilities. We say this because many different approaches work. None is better than any other, across the board. In some families maternal or paternal custody works best; in others joint custody makes sense.

Let us review the tiny bit of research on joint custody before we are tempted to unleash much more rhetoric here.

Very little research has been done on joint custody, and figures are not available as to the prevalence of this alternative to traditional custody arrangements. But it seems apparent that the concept of shared parenting after divorce is becoming more and more common as our society calls for a more flexible definition of the postdivorce family. The concept of joint custody reinforces and facilitates several contemporary social trends. It is in accordance with the movement for sexual equality and its many corollaries.

Constance Ahrons interviewed forty-one divorced parents with court-awarded joint physical and/or legal custody.[37] She found that some divided parenting responsibilities fairly equally, but most did not. The majority (86 percent) reported satisfaction with their joint custody arrangements, though nonresidential parents reported more specific dissatisfactions than did residential parents.

In a second study Ahrons interviewed fifty-four pairs of divorced spouses one year following divorce.[38] She focused on the relationship between the ex-couple and found that the majority continued to interact with one another; those interacting most frequently were "the supportive and cooperative coparents."

Barbara Rothberg explored the satisfactions and dissatisfactions of thirty joint custody parents in New York.[39] Her conclusion:

> Joint custody can be a complicated arrangement for parents and children, but it does work. Despite many problems with this life-style, the parents interviewed in the study generally felt the arrangement was a positive one. Although the findings cannot be widely generalized because of the narrow sample used, they raise important questions and issues that need further exploration.

These three studies are the only major empirical ones we could find on joint custody. It is noteworthy that all conclude similarly, that joint custody *can* work under the right circumstances.

There are also those who are strongly opposed to the concept of joint custody. A referee of the Denver District Court, who hears noncontested dissolution actions, feels that couples who agree to joint custody are just delaying a final decision because they are not ready to dissolve their relationship with each other. He is against joint custody because he thinks it will call for further litigation when the court must modify to provide for sole custody. If the separation agreements involve shared custody arrangements, however, he will usually approve them.

One major argument made by opponents of joint custody is that a couple who could not get along well enough to stay married cannot agree on how to rear their children. Some people against the joint custody concept maintain that joint custody may be tough on parents since each parent must always consider the other parent's wishes. Still another argument is that children need the stability of one home and one parent making major decisions.[40]

According to Persia Woolley, psychologists are often skeptical of the concept that provides children of divorce with two separate but equal homes.[41] Just as some attorneys' arguments against sharing custody are largely based on assumptions of hostility and of the inability of divorcing parents to cooperate, the psychological arguments assume that parents are unable or unwilling to concentrate on the needs of their children in addition to their own.

Joseph Goldstein, Anna Freud, and Albert Solnit argued that in the event of a divorce, one parent should be granted sole custody of the children and should be given the authority to determine when and if visits from the noncustodial parent should occur. They reason that children who are shaken, disoriented, and confused by the breakup of their parents' marriage need an opportunity to settle down in the privacy of their reorganized family, with one person in authority upon whom they can rely for answers to their questions and for protection from external interference.[42]

Carol Stack counters that we are just beginning to recognize that the nuclear family is not the only workable family structure in our society. Yet, the old ideology of the nuclear family prevails, as those concerned with the pressures affecting families still regard alternatives to the intact nuclear family as pathological.

Stack is critical of the work of Goldstein, Freud, and Solnit, claiming that it reveals the influence of this very conservative attitude. She thinks that these researchers cling to the value of the intact family, labeling families lacking a typical married couple as malfunctional. They suggest that continuous relationships are essential for children, but argue that children freely love more than one adult only if the adults in question feel positively toward each other. In the absence of a two-parent nuclear family, Goldstein, Freud, and Solnit suggest a policy for what they consider to be a dysfunctional system: "The authors would prefer a child to be protected and isolated in what is left of the fragmented nuclear family."[43]

It seems apparent that no particular custody arrangement is equally suitable for all children and families, but it is important to

ask what factors should be considered in determining the best custody arrangement for each family on a case-by-case basis, according
to Robert Felner and Stephanie Farber: "Research should not focus
on seeking *the* best custody arrangement, but rather on the factors
that contribute to successful maternal custody, paternal custody, or
joint custody arrangements."[44]

Kenneth Kressel added to this discussion in a similar vein. According to Kressel, though the general public, the clergy, and the
helping professions express shock at the divorce rate and its effects
on families, the continuing bonds between ex-spouses are looked at
skeptically and are often seen as pathological or quasi-pathological.
Though people talk occasionally about amicable divorce, not many
actually believe that anyone really can be or can become amicable
after a breakup. Kressel and his colleagues surveyed lawyers, psychotherapists, and clergy and found that

> with a few notable exceptions, there was a general distrust of the
> ex-spouses' continuing involvement with each other as friends,
> business partners, or lovers, largely on the grounds that such at-
> tachments reflect separation distress rather than realistic caring,
> and they drain emotional and physical energies that would more
> productively be spent in forming new relationships.[45]

Our guess is that the professionals "in the trenches" will remain
skeptical of joint custody because they tend to see the more disastrous cases in which families come in crying for help. Clinical populations are made up of just that: troubled people. To base one's opinions of joint custody solely on experience with clinical populations,
however, would be like surveying the general health of the American
people in a cancer ward.

Research Design

We think that people should know how a study was designed and
conducted so that they can decide how much of the findings they
wish to believe and what they wish to remain unconvinced about.

In this section then, we will define terms; briefly outline the way
in which we found parents for our study; describe how we developed
interview and questionnaire techniques; explain how the statistical

material was analyzed; and then present the conclusions to which we have come based upon statistical tests.

In later chapters we will present information gleaned from reading nearly seven thousand pages of hand-written, qualitative testimony on the questionnaires.

Also, we will add the impressions we have gained from formal interviews of 225 people (fathers, mothers, children, grandparents, lovers, and others) involved in court custody battles; informal interviews of, perhaps, another 80–90 people going through a divorce; and questionnaires obtained from another 779 separated and divorced persons in previous studies with various colleagues.

Our Method and Procedure

The people involved in this study were divorced single parents in four groups: mothers with custody; fathers with custody; mothers and fathers with split custody; and mothers and fathers with joint custody.

Definitions
Joint Custody. An enormous amount of diversity exists in how parents and legal authorities define terms in regard to child custody. The two basic versions of joint custody are joint *legal* custody and joint *physical* custody. The former term refers exclusively to the shared major decision-making function. The latter term has the additional component of shared residence. In joint legal custody, only one parent has physical custody, that parent making the day-to-day decisions and being primarily responsible for the child's care. Under joint physical custody, the children live with each parent on an equal—or nearly equal—time basis, and minor as well as major decisions are made by both parents. There has been considerable confusion in regard to these two terms. An infinite number of ways can be found to work out the residential arrangements under joint custody. The time actually spent with each parent can range anywhere from a 50 percent/50 percent split (absolute joint physical custody) to 100 percent of the time's being spent with one parent (absolute joint legal custody).

For this research we defined *joint physical custody* as an arrangement in which neither parent has more than 60 percent of the total child care responsibilities (compared with the other parent's share), nor less than 40 percent. Other behavioral science researchers have defined it slightly differently (a ratio of 67 percent to 33 percent or closer). The important point is not percentage hairsplitting but whether both parents have a major share of the child care responsibilities or not. A detailed procedure for calculating joint physical custody is included in chapter 6, "Joint Custody."

The essence of joint custody is that responsibility and authority with respect to the children are shared by both parents. This requires parental consultation and agreement on all major decisions affecting the children. Matters having a significant impact on the children's lives, such as education, religion, and financial support are dealt with jointly by the parents. Medical or psychological help, if needed, vacations, summer camp, and extracurricular activities are usually also included in the joint decision-making process. These decisions and the specifics involved are normally left to the parents in a joint custody arrangement; the parents are on an absolutely equal footing in the eyes of the law.[46]

As behavioral scientists we are somewhat interested in joint legal custody, but we are more interested in joint physical custody because we believe that it offers a viable alternative to traditional custody for *some* families.

Sole Custody. This term refers to an arrangement in which one parent assumes considerably more responsibility for the child after divorce, spending more than 60 percent of the total time with the child.

Split Custody. Split custody refers to an arrangement in which one or more of the children lives primarily with their mother after divorce (more than 60 percent of the time) and one or more of the children lives primarily with their father after divorce (more than 60 percent of the time). It is simply "the traditional sole custody arrangement with brothers and sisters divided: each parent is given complete, full-time custody of at least one child."[47]

Sampling Procedures. We used the *Ayers Directory of Publications* to obtain a list of daily newspapers in the United States. Using every other listing in the directory, seven hundred letters were mailed to editors of daily newspapers in every state. The editors were asked to run a brief story about the research project and about the need for divorced parents to participate. An unknown, but obviously substantial number of newspapers obliged by running the story. Within eight weeks of the time the letters were sent to the newspapers, the researchers had received 1,050 letters and cards from the divorced parents indicating interest in participating in the study. Of the 1,050 questionnaires sent out by mail, 738 (70 percent) were returned and used for statistical analysis.

Any sampling procedure has certain inherent difficulties and theoretical problems. Our approach was no exception to this rule. The parents who participated are obviously volunteers and may be quite different from people who choose not to participate in research. But every study is really a study of volunteers.

We also wanted to find a large population of parents that would represent all four groups of parents (mothers with custody, fathers with custody, split custody, and joint custody). Divorced single mothers with custody are quite easy to find, but single fathers, split custody parents, and joint custody parents are much less common, and we knew from past experience that we would have to cover the entire United States if we were to obtain a large sample.

Finally, the parents in our study are not a random sample, but we did not really set out to see what "average" looks like in regard to child custody. Rather, we wanted to compare large groups of families in all four situations. We wanted to know, statistically, whether for example fathers are doing as well as mothers or whether joint custody parents are doing better than sole custody parents.

What we have, then, are 738 parents who each volunteered several hours of their time to tell us how they were doing. They may not be random or "average," but they were surely helpful, and we are confident that our results are a valid statistical comparison of single mothers and fathers with custody, split custody parents, and joint custody parents.

The Questionnaire. Our questionnaire focused on parental adjustment to divorce, child adjustment, the ex-spouse relationship, the parent-child relationship, and general information about the divorce.

Between 1975 and 1980, one of us, John DeFrain, participated in several studies of divorce that aided in the construction of this questionnaire. Previous studies included studies of parents' perceptions of children's adjustment to separation and divorce[48]; a study of children's adjustment to separation and divorce done by interviewing the youngsters[49]; a study of religion and how it affects people's ability to cope with divorce[50]; a study of how churches help (or hinder) divorcing people[51]; a study of how parents feel when their adult children divorce[52]; and a study of how single fathers with custody adjust to divorce as compared with single mothers with custody.[53] A total of 779 parents and children in almost every state participated in these earlier studies.

The questionnaire for the current study of 738 parents was pre-tested with many people, validated by half a dozen professionals in the field of family studies, and put through four drafts before we were convinced that it was ready to be used.

The questionnaire was prepared to be administered to the parents, but it was designed to obtain information about the children involved as well. The researchers recognize the disadvantages of this method, but because of the size of the sample and the scope of the study, use of this method was imperative. Even so, when answering questions about the adjustment of the children involved, the parents may have given biased or inaccurate responses.

A valid question the reader may ask is, why send a questionnaire instead of interviewing people? Interviews in many ways are obviously superior. But we needed to find many fathers with custody, split custody, and joint custody families. And to find as many as we did, we would have had to spend enormous amounts of money and send interviewers to every corner of the United States. Besides, John DeFrain at the time the questionnaire study was being conducted was also interviewing 225 people in forty-six families as a court investigator/expert witness and mediator in custody disputes. Furthermore, the questionnaire is a mix of quantitative-type questions ("How long?", "How much?" "When?" and so forth) and open-ended, qualitative questions ("What are the joys and sorrows of your particular custody arrangement?" and so forth). The open-ended questions generated many long, hand-written responses from the parents. They wanted to tell us their stories, as the reader will see in chapters 3 through 6. The questionnaire served its purpose extremely well: it provided us with a large amount of data (74,538 pieces of information, to be precise) for a relatively modest amount of money. If we had it all to do over again, the changes we would make in our method and procedure would be minuscule, indeed.

Analyzing the Data and the Results

We need to describe the parents who participated in our study statistically here, so that the reader can better interpret the findings presented later. Bear with us on this—it will be very brief.

The People in Our Study. Of the 738 divorced parents completing the questionnaire, 80 percent (590) were women and 20 percent (148) men. The average age of the women was 36.6 years, while the average age of the men was 35.5. Ninety-eight percent of the total sample of parents were white, 0.7 percent were black, 0.1 percent were American Indian, and 1 percent were Hispanic Americans.

Seventy-three percent (534) of the parents described their *legal* custody arrangement as sole custody; 21 percent (152) of the parents described their *legal* custody arrangement as joint custody; and 6 percent (40) described their *legal* custody arrangement as split custody.

We then asked the parents to calculate the time in an average week the mother and the father spent actually caring for the children. This way we knew how the courts and lawyers defined the situation, on the one hand, and how it actually worked out in reality. In regard to their actual *physical* custody arrangement, 86 percent (642) of the parents indicated that theirs was a sole custody arrangement; 8 percent (56) indicated that theirs was a joint custody arrangement; and 6 percent (40) indicated a split custody arrangement. (Tables 1, 2, and 3 in appendix A summarize this information.)

Genuine joint physical custody, in which both parents actually care for the children on a day-to-day basis, is apparently rather uncommon, as is split custody.

The average age of the children whose parents were participants in the study was six years. Fifty-eight months was the average length of separation from the ex-spouse. Eighty percent (591) of the parents had been married once, 17 percent (122) had been married twice, 2 percent (18) had been married three times, and three of the parents had been married four times.

In regard to the type of residence, 60 percent described themselves as homeowners; 39 percent described themselves as renters; and 1 percent of the parents indicated that their housing was provided by an employer. Thirty-seven percent of the parents had not moved since the marital separation; 32 percent had moved within the community; 12 percent had moved up to one hundred miles away; 6 percent had moved one hundred to five hundred miles away; and 13 percent had moved more then five hundred miles away. Participants had lived in their present communities an average of 9.6 years.

Two percent of the parents in the sample lived on farms; 5 percent lived in rural but nonfarm areas; 2 percent lived in towns with populations below 500; 7 percent lived in towns with populations between 500 and 5,000; 26 percent lived in towns with populations between 5,000 and 20,000; 18 percent lived in towns with populations between 20,000 and 50,000; 25 percent lived in cities with populations between 50,000 and 200,000; 7 percent lived in cities with populations between 200,000 and 500,000; and 8 percent lived in cities with populations of more than 1 million.

Of the 738 divorced parents who participated in the study, 51 percent (369) were Protestant; 25 percent (182) were Catholic; 5 percent (33) were Jewish; 11 percent (77) indicated no religious preference; and 9 percent (67) had a religious preference other than the choices listed.

We broke down the data by sex to look at differences between all the mothers and all the fathers. The mothers averaged 14.3 years of formal education; the fathers averaged 15.2.

The predominant occupation of the fathers was professional, and those of the mothers were professional and clerical worker. (Table 4 indicates the occupational distribution.)

The average income level was higher for the single-parent fathers than for the single-parent mothers. The fathers' mean income was $26,304, and the mothers' was $14,140. The fathers' average number of hours employed per week outside the home was 40.1 and the mothers' was 35.7.

Sixty-one percent of the mothers and 57 percent of the fathers lived in their own homes. Thirty-eight percent of the mothers and 40 percent of the fathers were renters. Finally, 1 percent of the mothers and 3 percent of the fathers had their housing provided by their employer.

When asked if they had moved since becoming a single parent, the majority of the mothers (64 percent) and fathers (59 percent) answered that they had moved. The average number of times the mothers had moved since their separation was 2.6, and the fathers' average was 2.5. The average length of time that the single parents had lived in their community was 9.3 years for the mothers and 11.2 years for the fathers.

In indicating their living arrangements, the largest percentage were living alone with their children. Eighty-five percent of the mothers and 67 percent of the fathers were living alone with their children. Three percent of the mothers and 18 percent of the fathers were living with a female friend and her children; 8 percent of the mothers and 4 percent of the fathers were living with a male friend and his children; and 4 percent of the mothers and 11 percent of the fathers were living with relatives and their children.

Comparing Sole Custody Parents with Joint Custody Parents. A major goal of our research was to compare statistically a large number of joint custody and sole custody parents on numerous dimensions.[54] We will simply summarize the results of our statistical tests, which we find fascinating:

1. A very positive correlation exists between the parents' adjustment to the custody arrangement and the children's adjustment to the custody arrangement. If the parent is doing well, the children very often are reported to be doing well also.

2. Feelings of being overburdened by the children are significantly less prevalent among parents with joint custody than among parents with sole custody.

3. Parents with sole custody claimed to be experiencing a significantly greater level of stress than were parents with joint custody.

4. Parents with sole custody had acquired significantly more nervous habits than had parents with joint custody, since assuming their custody responsibilities (nail biting, smoking, overeating, and so forth).

5. No significant differences in adjustment were found between children in sole and joint custody arrangements. Children in both types of families, on the average, were doing relatively well, according to the parents.

6. Parents with joint custody reported living significantly closer to their ex-spouses than did parents with sole custody.

7. A significantly higher percentage of joint custody parents than sole custody parents reported feeling positive toward the ex-spouse at the time custody was set up.

8. A significantly higher percentage of joint custody parents than sole custody parents indicated that their custody arrangement was a mutual, friendly agreement between parents.

9. A significantly higher percentage of joint custody parents than sole custody parents felt that the ex-spouse spent about the right

amount of time with the children. (Sole custody parents with custody often felt that the noncustodial parent was out of touch with the children.)

10. A significantly higher percentage of joint custody parents than sole custody parents claimed currently to have positive feelings about their ex-spouse.

11. Parents with joint custody had discussed child custody options with their children significantly more often before the divorce than had sole custody parents.

12. Children in joint custody situations were found to have significantly more positive relationships with the other parent than were children in sole custody situations.

13. Parents with joint custody felt significantly more strongly than did parents with sole custody about the importance of children's having close relationships with both parents.

14. Parents with sole custody arrangements reported significantly lower gross yearly incomes than did parents with joint custody arrangements.

15. Parents with joint custody arrangements reported significantly more positive changes in their social lives since assuming custody than did parents with sole custody.

Comparing Mothers with Sole Custody to Fathers with Sole Custody. Joint custody sparks a good deal of controversy when people discuss the issue. And the subject of maternal versus paternal custody is also certain to raise the hair on the back of debaters' necks, for the issue has its foundation in the centuries-old, silly argument over which sex is "superior."

We looked, statistically, at the mothers with sole custody in our study (number = 529) compared with the fathers with sole custody (number = 114). This is what we found:

1. The mothers were, on the average, more likely to have initiated the divorce proceedings than were the fathers.

2. The mothers were, on the average, more likely to have sought professional counseling than were the fathers.

3. More fathers had cohabitated with a lover than had the mothers after the divorce.

4. The fathers were more sexually involved than were the mothers.

5. More mothers than fathers reported that their children wanted them to remarry.

6. More mothers than fathers talked to their children about their sexual involvements.

7. The mothers reported that their children preferred to live with them more than the fathers reported that their children preferred to live with them. (Children of fathers were more likely to want to live with both parents.)

8. The fathers discussed the custody options with their children more than did the mothers.

9. The mothers felt more overburdened by the children than did the fathers.

10. The mothers reported a more positive effect on their personal lives from the arrangement than the fathers.

11. The fathers were more liberal in their sexual views than were the mothers.

12. The fathers were more positive toward their ex-spouse than the mothers were.

13. The fathers were more positive about what they say to their children about their ex-spouse than the mothers were.

14. The mothers encouraged their children to take sides more than the fathers did in continuing divorce controversies.

Our statisticians ran ninety-five statistical tests to explore the differences between mothers with sole custody as a group and fathers with sole custody as a group. We constructed several questions in each of the five basic categories: parental adjustment; child adjustment; the ex-spouse relationship; the parent-child relationship; and general information about the divorce.

In sum, only fourteen out of ninety-five statistical tests revealed any measurable quantitative differences between sole mothers and sole fathers. In eighty-one out of ninety-five tests there was no significant difference between the groups. This indicates to us that when using questionnaire survey techniques alone, we as researchers cannot find much difference between mothers with sole custody as a group and fathers with sole custody as a group.

In chapter 3, "Mothers with Sole Custody," and chapter 4, "Fathers with Sole Custody," we will look more closely at case study material to see whether any qualitative differences can be detected. The examination of the issues in chapters 3 and 4 will be more philosophical in nature, and not statistical.

Comparing Joint Custody Mothers and Fathers. When we compared these two groups of parents statistically, we found very few differences. Out of ninety-five statistical tests only four revealed differences between joint custody mothers and fathers:

1. The mothers said that they discussed custody options with their children before the divorce more than fathers did.
2. More mothers than fathers were sexually involved with someone.
3. More mothers than fathers reported that the children were aware of their sexual involvements.
4. The mothers were more positive toward their ex-spouse than the fathers were.

Comparing Split Custody Mothers with Split Custody Fathers. Statistical differences between split custody parents were also few and far between. Though our statisticians performed ninety-five tests on the data to compare responses of mothers (number = 25) and fathers (15), only four tests showed any statistical differences between the two groups:

1. The mothers perceived that they received less support from their friends and relatives than did the fathers.
2. The mothers felt more guilt about the care that they were giving the children than did the fathers.
3. The fathers were more liberal in their sexual views than were the mothers.
4. More mothers than fathers encouraged their children to take sides in continuing divorce disputes.

Split custody mothers and fathers were as a group extraordinarily similar.

In Conclusion

Four major findings emerge from the data used to compare mothers and fathers with sole custody, split custody, and joint custody:

1. Both mothers and fathers feel that they are coping well with their custody arrangement.

2. Although both mothers and fathers are adjusting well to their custody arrangement, the fathers appear to be more confident in their parenting skills and more satisfied with their relationship with their children than do the mothers.

3. The mothers admit to being slightly more frustrated than do the fathers with some aspects of their custody arrangement. The mothers are more likely to seek professional counseling and other support than are the fathers. And the mothers admit to having developed more nervous habits than do the fathers. Financial worries could be a factor here, because the mothers' average income ($14,000 per year) is only slightly more than half of the fathers' annual income ($26,500).

4. The adjustment of the children to the custody arrangement is positive as perceived by the parents. However, the mothers feel significantly better than the fathers do about the level of their children's self-esteem.

The age-old argument over who is better, men or women, is being waged on the new battleground of parenthood. As far as we as researchers can tell, the result of the battle is a draw. Custody battles cannot be waged with statistical studies. Each case will have to be decided on the merits of the individuals involved. Asking "experts" to produce generalized research findings in an effort to resolve Solomon's dilemma easily is pure foolishness.

In this book we seek to increase the reader's understanding of divorce and child custody issues by focusing on the essence of the problem: the emotional upheaval that occurs when families are faced with the terrible dilemma of deciding what is best for the children after a breakup. The remainder of the book will be devoted to a large amount of case material gleaned from our research data and clinical experiences. The case material will breathe life into the statistics from this chapter.

3

Mothers with Sole Custody

One Mother's Story

Authors' Note. A Massachusetts mother describes the long and painful court battle she waged with her ex-husband over their young son. Though every family is unique in the world, this woman's story has a power and dynamics that many people will immediately recognize from their own experiences. Many details in the story have been changed to protect the anonymity of the people involved.

I worked out most of the property settlement directly with my ex-husband. My lawyer helped some. It took over a year to come to an agreement. Fred would not read the settlement for a month or so, and then he would read it and say, "Make these changes." I'd make the changes, and then he wouldn't read them for some time. And he'd ask for more changes, and I'd make them. This process was repeated five or six times.

The custody issue was addressed, and he felt Jimmy should choose. Jimmy was only six years old. I told him that I would not agree. Jimmy wasn't capable of living with the decision and the possible guilt. Finally Fred signed the agreement with me having custody, and he had the right to see Jimmy almost any time he desired.

I told my ex-spouse I would probably be moving to New Hampshire. The court had really not set up visitation in any formal way when we divorced. I told Fred he could see Jimmy every other weekend, every third or whatever, but that he had to commit to some regular schedule for planning purposes. I also said that if he did not want to commit to a plan then he would simply have to ask me on each occasion, and I would do my best. But I would not simply wait for him before making my own plans with Jimmy. He did not like this, but he accepted. He usually makes his requests through Jimmy and not to me directly.

I had a discussion with Fred and explained I would definitely be moving. At that time I asked that he keep Jimmy until school was out and then he would move with me. Not long after that I was served with a notice to appear in court to prove why my ex-husband should not have custody. He had remarried and felt he could offer a better "family environment."

I have reason to believe that while he may love his wife he may have remarried primarily to try for custody. I say this because he had been living with her for over a year and he moved out because he found her children "unbearable." She has two boys, nine and twelve. It was during this period that I told him I would probably move to New Hampshire. Two weeks later he announced his plans to marry.

From the date I was served notice to appear in court I changed my plans. I rushed the buying of a home, got the headmaster off vacation to interview Jimmy for school, made sitter arrangements, got a lawyer, etc. I went into court with everything well planned! I received very little guidance from my lawyer. I had taken Jimmy to a child psychologist, who was my primary witness.

Fred had twelve witnesses, and they primarily portrayed him as a loving, devoted father. This is true, but I often feel he is more of a playmate than a father.

Nothing really bad was said against me. In some ways I was portrayed as a little too ambitious and career oriented, and maybe not as carefree or loving as he is.

The psychologist stated that Jimmy should live with me and gave his reasons. I feel that the psychologist was the primary reason I retained custody.

The judge asked Fred, "If your son tells me the same thing as he told the psychologist, will you drop this suit?" After a long pause, Fred said, "Yes."

Fred felt I had brainwashed Jimmy. During the time I was preparing for court I kept Fred and Jimmy apart. Fred was supposed to see him a few days before court. But on the appointed morning I called Fred and left a message that Jimmy would see him in court instead. This was primarily done because of my lawyer's advice, but I was also scared to death Fred would do a number on Jimmy.

Jimmy was told of the pending suit a week or so before. At that time Jimmy cried and wanted to know why Fred would do this. I explained that it was because he loved him and knew I would not agree to let him live with Fred. Jimmy said he wanted to stay with me, and one of the main reasons was "because I know what it is like to live with you. That's where I have always been."

A week before court Jimmy was interviewed by my lawyer, and he took him on a tour of the courthouse. That afternoon his father called and asked where he had been and Jimmy explained. He also told him he wanted to stay with me and visit his father. When I asked him why he did that, he said, "Can't I?" And I said, "You can say anything you want to say." He broke down and said, "I feel so out of control, I don't think I know all that is going on and I have no say in the matter." I explained that he had been told most everything, and that he would have a say because the judge would listen to him.

I told Fred he should drop the suit. He had heard what Jimmy wanted and this was very difficult for Jimmy. Fred refused.

A few days before court, Jimmy was evaluated by the psychologist, and then we left town for the weekend. I let Jimmy call his dad so Fred would know he was all right.

In court late in the evening, Jimmy saw the judge. He initially stated that he wished we would get back together, but failing that he wished to live with his "mommy." The judge then talked to Fred and me asking us to resolve, and evidently expecting Fred to back off. Fred would not. The judge stated that he could hear the rest of our witnesses but didn't feel it would change anything. We agreed not to put forth the other witnesses, and I received or retained custody. Fred broke down and sobbed. Jimmy saw this. On our way home his cries would have broken even the coldest of hearts. He has had a great deal of difficulty in living with his decision. He said, "I got what I wanted, but I didn't know it would be this hard." The year following the court decision was very painful for us all. Jimmy and I talked a lot, and he got much better. He explained the problem this way: "Daddy's grumpy because I moved. I'm grumpy because he's grumpy, and you're grumpy because I'm grumpy."

I asked him if he would be happier living with Fred and although I would prefer him to stay that he could move if that's what he wanted. He decided to stay.

Reflecting back on the year following my custody suit, I would have to say it was the most difficult year I've had.

There were a couple of months where I visited a psychologist. I wanted Jimmy to go, but he was opposed. The psychologist helped me learn how to talk to Jimmy by role-playing. Jimmy did go for one visit. After the visit the psychologist reviewed with me (in Jimmy's presence) what had been discussed. She felt Jimmy was very angry at the whole situation and at me for moving him away from his dad.

At a later meeting the psychologist stated that she knew what my problem was. I asked, and she replied: "You expect too much. Jimmy is very angry, and he is going to make life miserable for awhile." The psychologist felt it was better than Jimmy keeping it all inside and possibly becoming very depressed.

In some ways that seems such a long time ago and in other ways I still shudder.

I made a decision not to move because of Jimmy. But as time goes by I get more pressure to consider a relocation. Jimmy is against being farther away from his dad.

A few summers ago I seriously considered a position in Claremont, California. Jimmy was going away to camp and would be gone during the period I felt I would be making a decision. I called him (at his dad's) and told him I wanted him to go with me on the following day to Claremont. I explained that the trip was for a job interview. He appeared uninterested in going. I explained that this might be his only opportunity for input into the decision, and I felt he should go. He did. We had a delightful three days house hunting and visiting the city.

After camp, in a phone conversation, I explained to Jimmy that the position in Claremont was not going to happen. His reaction was, "Why not? I'm disappointed." I asked why (having felt he would be relieved). He said, "I've spent the last two weeks thinking only of the positives."

Since the move to New Hampshire, Jimmy has had some problems in school. They were mostly peer problems. He had a lack of self-confidence and was very vulnerable. He has always been more confident around adults. He spends a reasonably large amount of time around my adult friends. During the period of peer problems his grades suffered somewhat.

Jimmy has since improved peer relationships. He seems much happier. He considers himself "somewhat popular."

Jimmy is currently in seventh grade at a junior high school near our house. His grades are good. He was an honor student last year. He is in an advanced English program. He is tall, thin, and very handsome. He is developing physically but is late compared to his classmates.

Overall I would say he is a positive boy, and I enjoy him immensely. We seem to communicate fairly well.

I date a man, and that causes some jealousy for Jimmy.

Jimmy went to spend the summer with his dad and was somewhat reluctant to set a date for it to begin. He used my sister's illness as an excuse: "Well, if Betty gets better or worse, we'll be going to see her so I can't set a date."

One of the biggest problems appeared to be that Jimmy was going to have to start sharing a bedroom with his oldest stepbrother. His father was going to redecorate what had been Jimmy's room and let Jimmy and Tim share. This was a result of the new baby moving into another bedroom.

Jimmy has very little positive to say about his stepbrothers. He feels they are snobbish, mean, or rude to his dad. Jimmy also has recently had a great deal of difficulty with his stepmother.

Jimmy says this about Ann, his stepmother: "She always makes me be the one to pick up, not the other boys. I never do anything right for her. If I say anything she tells my dad."

I tried to discuss with Jimmy that he has to try. And maybe he is very difficult or rude to Ann. I used an analogy of the daughter of the man I date and how I feel when she is rude to me or unfair. Jimmy has come back with "I'm really trying," etc.

I strongly feel that Jimmy is not all "innocent" in this problem. He resents sharing "his dad" with these other people. He also whines or feels sorry for himself and probably has generated a lot of hostility toward himself. He appears to be maturing and may genuinely be trying harder but may have a lot of sins to pay for.

I have thought of discussing the issue with his dad but feel that would only cause Jimmy more problems. Fred still appears to be very competitive with me and interprets my comments in that manner. About a month ago he did briefly mention want-

ing to discuss Jimmy's behavior with me at a later time but has
not followed up on it. Fred pays child support (minimal) and is
usually three months behind. He views me as not needing the
money, so he pays when it is convenient. I occasionally nudge
him, or he probably would let it go.

Challenges and Accomplishments of Mothers with Sole Custody. Fatherhood
has gotten a tremendous shot in the arm in the past decade or so.
The women's movement has helped make it a bit easier for mothers
to enter what some people glibly call "the working world." As mothers poured into the marketplace in the 1970s, fathers were pressured
and encouraged to become more active in the home.

Many fathers have responded to a large degree to the need to be
more helpful around the house and more active with the children. In
a growing number of what we call "androgynous families," the roles
of mothers and fathers are almost indistinguishable from each other:
Moms work outside the home and care for the kids and the house,
and dads do likewise. Many fathers are active with the children not
only because the mother's outside work makes it essential, but simply because the fathers enjoy their youngsters. The company of children can be very pleasing to most parents, if kept in manageable
doses.

But in spite of all the interest and encouragement fathers have
gotten over the past few years, in divorce situations tradition usually
wins out. Solid national statistics are difficult to obtain, but in our
study giving one parent sole custody was still by far the most common approach in a divorce situation. Fully 87 percent of the 738
parents who responded to our questionnaires were parents with sole
custody. And 82 percent of the 642 parents with sole custody in our
study were women. We have good reason to believe that the 18 percent figure for fathers with custody may be rather high. One estimate, for example, is that 80 percent of the children in divorced
families live with their mothers, 6 percent with their fathers, and 14
percent live with other relatives.[1] Fathers may have been more anxious to respond to our call for volunteers because they may feel "special" in some way. Also, mothers with custody tend to have far less
money than fathers, and may have less time to spend filling out questionnaires for researchers when they could be spending time figuring
out ways to pay the bills!

Our discussion in this chapter of the unique challenges and accomplishments of mothers with sole custody, then, is based on questionnaire data from 528 mothers. These mothers spent countless hours laboriously filling out the nine-page questionnaires. Many of them included page after page of additional information as they wrote their stories for us. We found the stories extremely moving as we pored over the more than five thousand pages of material that these good people gave us.

Computers gave us a solid statistical composite picture of these mothers with sole custody. But to get to the heart of the matter, to the emotions and struggles these women are going through, we had to read and read and read. Our reading was filtered through our experiences over the years as counselors, teachers, and researchers. In addition to having the research data from these 528 mothers, we have had the good fortune of formally and informally interviewing approximately another 300 single mothers.

When we make statements based upon our empirical research findings in this study we will tell you, the reader. When we speak to you on the basis of our "gut-level feelings" as clinicians with a lot of experience with divorced people, we will point this out, too.

Our discussion in this chapter will focus on the following important issues that the mothers made very clear to us: Custody arrangements: when does Dad get the kids?; how was custody negotiated?; courts, laws, and lawyers; money: alimony and child support; how mothers adjust to divorce; how children adjust to divorce; support systems: where to go for help; dating and sex; personal advice for mothers from mothers; advice for mothers about children; sorrows; and joys.

Custody Arrangements: When Does Dad Get the Kids?

There seems to be an almost infinite number of ways mothers with custody schedule dads' visits with the kids, and few rules of thumb to go by exist on this very individualized issue. We found basically three groups of families by studying the data from the mothers: (1) families who have worked out unlimited, open-ended visitation, (2) families on fixed schedules, and (3) a large group of families with unusual schedules that defy categorization. It is quite clear from our reading of the data that some mothers in each group feel successful, and some mothers in each group feel that the arrangement is a failure to some degree.

Unlimited, Open-ended Visitation. This is the most flexible option for most single-parent families. Some mothers give it high ratings; others are not as enthusiastic.

A very positive mother notes that her ex-husband lives with his mother across the street from her house: "The kids see him as often as they wish. We had no set times set up in our divorce papers. I never have refused him seeing them, as I know he loves them as much as I do. We have never had a problem with this in nine years."

Another mother offered flexible visitation to her ex-husband and noted that the man had not even seen the children in the past year. A similar situation caused one mother some grief. She told us that the father might not visit his son for six or eight weeks and then would call twice a week for a period of time. "My son sometimes questions his father's absence with disappointment, and that upsets me."

Reading between the lines, we would guess that one father was caught in a bind between "old" family and "new" girlfriend. The mother wrote that even though the father has an office a mile from her house, he sees the children about once every three or four weeks for only twenty-four hours. "I need some time alone," she said, voicing the all too common complaint of single parents. "And the children would like to see him more often." But the children's only option is to spend the twenty-four hours with their father and his girlfriend, with whom he lives. "They resent never getting to see him alone and have asked, but their father refuses. My son feels especially rejected."

Fixed Schedules. There are many different types of fixed visitation schedules that divorced parents adopt. A common one is for fathers to have responsibility for the children every other weekend, alternate holidays, and two weeks in the summer. One mother noted that the attorneys negotiated this arrangement during a period of great emotional upheaval on all sides: "Luckily it has worked out well." Though this is a common visitation plan, it guarantees only minimal time for the father with his children. Some fathers complain of this, while others do not even take advantage of the little bit of time they do have: "My ex-husband only sees the children about half of his scheduled time," a mother noted. Another mother said that her ex had not seen his son for two years and only lives five miles away. Two years earlier this same father had taken his ex-wife to court to plead for more visitation and lost. Fading away of fathers after court battles is a rather common occurrence. Mothers often charge that the fathers were insincere in their apparent love for the children; fathers often countercharge that the mothers have poisoned the relationship with the children and that the situation is hopeless. "It's easier to crawl away than to go on fighting," one whipped dad explained.

Another common fixed visitation schedule is for fathers to have the children every weekend. One ex-couple lives three hours apart. Each parent drives halfway every Friday and Sunday. They also alternate holidays. Another father with the same type of visitation schedule rarely takes advantage of it. "When he does, he takes them to bars, so they don't enjoy it much. When sober, he's devoted and loving as a father. When drinking, he is not." Another mother charges her ex-husband with workaholism. Although he could have them every weekend, which figures out to be a relatively large amount of time, he ends up "calling a few times a year and visiting them at Christmas."

One father spends one evening a week with his children and some weekends and holidays. This is mutually agreed upon by the father, mother, and children. "It works well, though it takes lots and lots of communicating among us." One father watches the children two hours once a week while his ex takes a class.

Distance for these parents can be a difficult problem to overcome. The court agreement originally read that one father was to have his son two months in the summer and one week every other Christmas. The mother moved, taking the boy 1,200 miles away. The father was angered by this move. On one occasion the mother had to fly to the father's town and enlist the help of the courts to get her son back after the father threatened not to return him.

Father's burnout is a common theme in these situations. An almost classic example was given by one mother, who told us of very specific visitation rights:

My children may spend alternate national legal holidays with their father, up to two consecutive days in each calendar week, and up to thirty consecutive days during the summer vacation.

He lived here in town for the first few months after the divorce, so he had the children fairly often, except when his shift work at a federal facility preempted his time with them.

Then he moved several hundred miles away and married someone with three children. That was two years ago. The children spent Thanksgiving of that year with him, and that was the last time they spent with him. He wanted them last summer right after he quit his job for health reasons.

I thought, however, that it was stupid to send two small children several hundred miles away to live with someone who was too sick to work and who had quit paying alimony, child support, the children's health insurance premiums, and half of the youngest's preschool fees as stipulated in the divorce.

Now he's moved again. Even farther away. He does not see the children and rarely calls.

I was afraid he would steal the children last summer. I'm glad he's gone. The kids miss him. But he's so depressed. And he can't get his finances in order. He's compulsive about abusing credit cards.

From our experience interviewing people in divorce wars, we know that this man would have a very different story to tell in return. The main point, though, is that in many situations of "holy deadlock," the father drifts away. "Sometimes it's just easier to bury the old life and start a new one," as one father told us.

Unusual Schedules. A number of families have unusual schedules for visitation that defy categorization.

"My ex has not seen his children in over ten years," one mother told us. "It is his choice. He says he feels too bad after seeing them." This is a common occurrence. Some fathers simply lose interest, as many mothers allege; other fathers find the combination of pain and impotence in the situation too difficult to handle.

"My ex-husband is only allowed to see my son as long as another family member is present," another mother wrote. "He sees him once or twice a month. This arrangement was made after he was institutionalized due to his drinking and drug dependencies." The mother said that this arrangement worked well for her, and the boy seemed relatively content: "He considers his father like an uncle and not a traditional father figure. His grandfather is his father figure." In our experience in the courts, we have seen many cases like this. Judges often agree that it is too risky to leave father and child alone, especially if drugs, including alcohol, are implicated.

One family told of how they had to work the father's visitation around his schedule as a police officer. Another ex-husband could visit the child "on reasonable notice," because he lived a long distance away. The mother's description of the situation is instructive:

> Because of the distance involved, it usually takes a week's notice to make airplane reservations. Visits are limited by school, so they have resulted in long weekends and ten days over Christmas. So far these visits have been less frequent than I would prefer, but my ex-husband is responsible for the cost of the airfare so the visits are at his timing. The arrangement is acceptable to me, although I would like to know when my son will be visiting farther in advance. His father is bitter over my having moved so far away, but the flexibility and my willingness for my son to visit have made it easier. I am in control totally, and I prefer it this way for the moment. This may change. My son accepts the situation but would like to see his father more often.

This story is quite representative of a number of situations, so we would like to continue discussion of it at some length. Before the mother moved away the father saw the boy on twenty-four hour notice almost every other day. The mother explained that she had wanted the divorce and cited money problems as a major reason. The boy has visited his father several times since the move, but the mother is uneasy about these long weekends because she does not know much about her ex-husband's living situation.

The mother stated that she felt the father-son relationship was important, and she did not want "to stand between them." But she did know at the time of the divorce that she would be moving and did not tell the spouse of the plan she had. "He must have known of the possibility, though, since I had no relatives in the area. All my relatives are in the general area of where I live now."

From our experience we would guess that this family would have a very difficult time resolving all of the problems inherent in their situation. The mistrust and game playing over the years have built a wall of anger too high to scale.

Another mother wrote, "My husband took the children to a friend's house one day when I was at a convention, and he didn't return with them for two years." Stories like hers of alleged "kidnapping" abound in divorce situations. When the children are seen by both parents as a "prize" to be held on to at all cost, it is difficult for an outsider to make a judgment as to who should be the "winner" and who the "loser."

The complexities of yet another arrangement are worth outlining:

> My ex-husband is in the Navy, and he is stationed in California. He sees the children with *my permission* when he is in town. This visitation takes place at his mother's house.
>
> This arrangement is good because the grandparents get a chance to visit with the children, and I get a free night out. Best of all, the children are around people who love them—not only their mother.

This apparently happy arrangement was not worked out without considerable struggle, however. It seems that the mother-in-law initially tried to get custody of the children, preschoolers at the time of the battle. The young mother was investigated by social service agencies. Interviews took place in her home and in the agency offices. Friends, family, and the woman's boss were also interviewed. "My mother-in-law finally dropped the proceedings. I got the kids. We went through all these hassles for nothing."

It is amazing to us how many stories end up this way: with no clear-cut victors, but plenty of storm and stress.

Finally, a mother told us the curious story of her ex-husband, who rarely saw the children for two and a half years but currently takes them every other weekend because "I pleaded with him." She explained that the man does it only "so he can claim one of the children as an exemption on his income taxes."

This story sounds rather strange and needs elaborating. Remember, once again, that it is told only from the mother's perspective:

> At first he tried to get the children six months of each year. I said no. I felt he was an undesirable influence. He felt his rights

as a father were being denied, so he refused to be involved with the children at all.

The children were terribly upset by this denial. One daughter felt he hated her and blamed herself. When I realized what was happening I began trying to get him to change the situation. It was a long, difficult struggle. Now he maintains he takes them only as a bitter favor to me. And as a tax break.

Life is, indeed, full of interesting twists and turns.

How Was Custody Negotiated?

Tradition. For some families negotiating custody is not a particularly traumatic process. In these cases both parents explicitly or implicitly buy into the traditional notion that moms raise kids and dads pay child support:

My divorce occurred in 1965 when there was generally little contention over custody. I filed for divorce, and child custody just "naturally" was assumed for the mother. My ex-husband could possibly have sought custody but did not. Our child was still a baby, and it was standard then for women to be responsible for the care of small children.

The "tender years" doctrine was in full bloom. In this case, the mother simply left the details to the lawyers. Her story is very common.

Communication. For many other parents the negotiating process is more difficult. A great deal of communication between divorcing parents is necessary in these cases, and people are subjected to a ride on an emotional roller coaster: "I had a multitude of mixed feelings. Depression. Rage. Resentment. Heartache. Rejection. Hate."

Some parents, fortunately, are models of reasonableness:

We worked it out ourselves, the most important factor being that the kids come first. We agreed that financially he was more capable of supporting the children, but emotionally I was more capable of handling them. We decided that because of their ages they should live with me. His job causes him to be away from home overnight quite often, sometimes up to a month. This was another logical reason for my having custody.

> There really wasn't any way to have joint or split custody. I
> agreed that he can see the kids at any time. No matter what
> our differences are, he is their father and has every right to see
> them and share their growth and development.

Another mother voiced a number of very important considerations:

> I felt very strongly that I should have custody of the children. I
> had been a full-time homemaker since the birth of the oldest
> child, and being a mother was my self-identity. . . . We talked
> with the oldest child about what he wanted, and he seems to
> be happy in the present arrangement living with me, but seeing
> and talking on the phone with his father often. . . . We have
> remained with the original decision until now, but negotiations
> will probably continue for many years. As the boys get older,
> they may prefer to live with their father, and depending on his
> circumstances at that point, I may agree that that arrangement
> is best.

This mother feels that motherhood is her primary identity but is
willing to be flexible because she realizes that she may change in the
future and that her children's needs may change. The need for communication between ex-spouses goes on forever, it seems. A marriage may end in divorce, but it is often impossible to break off the
coparent relationship cleanly and honestly.

Besides a lot of talking, some arrangements take lots of hard
work. In a case we mentioned earlier, one mother explained that her
daughter lives with her during the week and spends weekends and
holidays with the father. The hitch is that the parents live three
hours driving distance from each other. "I drive up halfway on Friday and Sunday nights, and he drives down halfway." Why such an
effort to meet in the middle? "Our daughter wanted to stay in the
city I live in and go to her school. But she still wanted to see as much
of her dad as possible." The "flavor" of the negotiations that led to
this arrangement was "studiously amicable." "We did not want to
upset her further by making arrangements for our own convenience
and not for her best interests." The parents felt that if they could not
provide their daughter with a model of a healthy marriage anymore,
they could at least provide two willing and able parents.

The Father Loses Interest. A very common story the mothers tell is of the father who fights in court, loses, and breaks off contact. We cannot know the motivation of these fathers, but the mothers' stories are interesting:

> He had the kids as much as he wanted, whenever he wanted, until five years ago. Then he filed a custody suit against me, and he lost. (He only wanted custody of my two oldest children, who are boys.) He has not had any contact whatsoever with them since then. No phone calls, no visits, no letters. He and I have also had no contact.

The Father Who Is Not Interested in Custody. "There was never any discussion about who would have the children," one woman wrote. "It just appeared in the divorce agreement from his lawyer that the children would live with me." Another told of how her ex-husband could not cope with two deaf sons and therefore was not interested in custody:

> I think that was a large part of our problem. With five kids, two of them handicapped, and a full-time job, there was not enough of me left over to be a wife. On the other hand, he demanded as much attention as a child, and was no help around the house or with the kids. I am very happy now. I really don't care if I ever get married.

A number of mothers expressed the belief that deep down their ex-husbands really loved the children but did not know how to express their love: "I feel he misses the children very much but cannot express that feeling to them because he has kept it hidden for so long." Career concerns often took precedence over the children, even though

> he does, I believe, love them as much as he loves anyone at all, but he finds it difficult to acknowledge this and express it. Therefore, he does not really know them well, nor do they know him well. Sometimes, in oblique ways, he expresses this and seems to feel some regret. But so far he has not taken any steps to dramatically change the situation.

The tragedy of the inexpressive male is played out on yet another stage.

The Girlfriend. Negotiations over custody are complicated when female friends are added into the equation: "I requested total custody because the father was living with his girlfriend. I may have to give him up to her, but I won't give up my children. I'll see him in hell first!"

Another mother told of how her former husband came home from work one evening and announced that he was "screwing around with another woman" and no longer wanted the responsibility of three teenagers. The mother had been considering divorce because of the husband's alcohol problems, and he finally moved out several months later when the mother objected to his spending four to five nights a week with his girlfriend "and arriving home just as the children were getting on the bus for school." Three months later the oldest daughter's drug-abuse problem came to the surface. The mother's ultimatum: stop using drugs, enter a treatment program, or live with the father and his girlfriend.

The daughter chose the third option but moved out five months later after the second beating she had received from her father for smoking pot. Both parents at that point gave up on her for the time being, and at age seventeen she became an "emancipated minor," sharing an apartment with a female friend.

Electricity does not always surge in situations involving the husband's girlfriends, however. One mother expressed surprise when her husband told her he was leaving her for another woman. He had thought about custody arrangements before leaving and rejected the notion of joint custody that the mother suggested. "I figured that if he didn't want the children, it wouldn't work out very well, anyway." She noted that "all negotiations were amicable." The couple came to their decisions regarding financial support, living arrangements, and division of property without consulting friends, relatives, or professionals. A lawyer wrapped up the details.

Mother Moves. Mothers often pack their bags and move away with the children at the end of a marriage. They state that such a move was made to reduce friction, to make for a quick, clean break, or, sometimes, to save their lives. One young mother escaped from her abusive husband in the dark of night, taking only the children, a beat-up old car, a few clothes, and her stereo from high school. This approach works in many cases. The tension in the family is dissipated, and peace is quickly restored. In other cases the father responds by tracking the mother down, sometimes "rekidnapping" the kids. "He drove 1,500 miles to our hometown, walked into the elementary school, told the teacher Krissy was to go home with him, and drove 1,500 miles back to Spokane. I about lost my mind."

The Children Are Caught in the Cross Fire. In many cases it is very difficult to keep the children out of the battle. Children of course need to know what is going on in a divorce, but they do not need to be bombarded by gory details on a regular basis. Sometimes, however, the bombardment comes no matter how conscientious a parent may be about protecting the children:

> The process was filled with hostility. Right from the beginning he scared the girls by saying they were going to be with him even if he had to go to court to make it happen. He was out to prove me a bad mom, even though he was having an affair. I never trusted his words in this, as he had completely changed his life-style and knew the girls were not going to fit into the picture easily.
>
> At one point I considered joint custody, thinking it would be best if the girls could remain close to their father, but I also knew I couldn't communicate with him on every issue with respect to the girls. So, I decided to hold my ground and fight to keep them with me.
>
> I also felt (and still do) that every time I would want the girls to do something (camp for summer, etc.) we would have to agree. If he had had that power to block me all the time with his veto, the girls would have been subject to the fighting and disagreement between us continually.
>
> Furthermore, I didn't want my girls (and still don't) to take on his value system, which went out the window when he decided to "find himself." Although I'd like my girls to be closer to him and spend more quality time with him as I think that is the healthiest in the long run, I don't want them getting lost while he looks for himself.
>
> He had the court send a probationary officer to our home after he moved out, and when it became apparent that he didn't have a chance to win, he negotiated our kids. The constant threat of court was used to scare them and to try to scare me, even though he's the one who would have looked bad. I

negotiated to keep out of court (for myself and my children) and will never forgive him for the trauma he caused in the negotiation process.

I made the correct choice taking sole custody, even though sometimes it's difficult to parent alone. The lawyers were not helpful; the judicial system took too long and is not set up to help people, as my ex was not willing to go to counseling, so we were left to push and pull alone. Overall, the process took about one year. It was a hellish time.

Persistent Fathers and Patient Mothers. One mother told of how both she and her husband wanted sole custody. She alleged that he even got passports and was ready to run away to Europe with the children, but his lawyer talked him out of that idea. The father had always agreed that the mother was very capable, so in the end they decided that she should have sole custody and that he could visit the children two nights a week and have access to the house. But "having him in the house did not work out. I would leave, and then he'd let the children jump on the couches, etc., and he would go through my personal stuff. They'd play a game called 'jump on the couches.'" The mother also alleged that the father came to the house late, sometimes drunk. After six "horrid" months of this, the father moved out of his mother's house and got an apartment. He stopped coming around to the ex-wife's house, and things got much better. Ultimately, she decided that the problem centered on the difficult issue of access to the home, and it was exacerbated because the father felt a legitimate claim to the property.

Another father was particularly fretful because he was afraid that the mother would move away, taking the children. The mother's lawyer calmed him down, noting that in their particular state the parent with custody could not move away without the "permission" of the father. The mother claimed that he was at times bitter and depressed, and threatened to fight for custody. But after the smoke cleared things worked out pretty well: "He spends more time with them now than when we were married. He is a better father now."

The Father Returns After a Long Absence. As social and behavioral scientists we would like to make an effort to classify and catalog divorce situations in some meaningful way, so that the human mind can better understand all the complexities. But as family counselors we are more convinced that every divorce is unique and that most situations defy categorization. The story of how one father returned after a fourteen-year absence is just such a case:

"At the time of our separation I was unable to care for the children, and they were placed in foster homes under the custody of the Department of Social Services," one mother began. It was a poor setup. The mother was unhappy, and the children—all in separate homes—were unhappy. At that time she said that the law provided for no financial assistance to the mother and children until after the divorce was finalized. Since the father provided no money, the mother had to find a job, and it was very difficult for her. And after she started work, she was forced to pay in part for the children's care in the foster homes, though she would have preferred that they be with her.

After a year and a half she regained custody of the children, quit work, and made a home for the children while living on meager welfare payments. "Custody was returned to me, and the father did not appear in court at the time of the hearing. Any news about the father was rumor. He did not visit, and he did not provide any money."

The young mother finally went back to school at a technical college and has now been employed for ten years. Eight of those ten years she was aided by Social Services.

Just a few months before she wrote to us, the father finally surfaced after fourteen years. She says he now provides minimal support and sporadically visits the children. The children are now old enough "to decide for themselves if they want to stick around during the few hours he gives. Oftentimes they leave after saying hello."

The father's side of the story would have been fascinating to hear, but it was impossible to obtain.

"Not with a Bang but a Whimper." In a number of families there is little argument over where the children will go. For example, one mother stated that "negotiations were no problem because my ex-husband is gay. He knew if it came out in court he wouldn't have a chance." In our own experience working with the courts we have seen that homosexuality is not a cut-and-dried issue; a person's sexual orientation often has little to do with how well he or she cares for children, and many judges apparently realize this. But the father in this particular case was "a transient type, moving around a lot from Chicago to San Francisco to Canada" and "didn't really want to have the child."

A few mothers noted that Vietnam changed their husbands. "Child custody was just understood. Never discussed. He left without saying anything, without any reason," one woman wrote us. The father sent child support and 40 percent of his military retirement check "very punctually." "He was in Vietnam, and I do believe that it caused him to change so drastically. We are adjusting, and I feel we have done good. As a family we do seem closer. I would not take him back," she added. The woman was fifty-seven years old at the time of writing and had children aged twenty-seven, twenty-four, eighteen, and seventeen.

Other mothers wrote of workaholic husbands. "He worked seven days a week from 6:00 A.M. to 2:00 A.M. and rarely had contact with the children" one woman told us. The father insisted, however, that he had a good relationship with them: "Every night before I go to bed I go into both their rooms and kiss them while they are sleeping," he told her. When the divorce occurred, his lawyer told him that he had little chance of gaining custody, and he rarely sees the children now.

Health problems sometimes are so devastating that there is little question or discussion about the fact that one parent will have responsibility for the children after a divorce. One forty-eight-year-old mother wrote that her ex-husband had a rare, progressive, and incurable neuromuscular disease. "I had full responsibility for the children a good ten years before the divorce, so there was little question on this issue." The woman stated that she tried to encourage the children to call their father and visit him, but the illness limited contact. "We invite him for all family celebrations, but he usually doesn't come. . . . He accused me of turning the children against him, when in fact I was trying very hard to get them to call and see him."

The family tried counseling at several different agencies, but "we were made to feel that because he was sick we should be forever forgiving." The father had one brain operation at a veterans' hospital and went to Houston three times to a famous neurosurgeon, "who I really felt understood what we as a family were being subjected to." The father was on several different drugs, sometimes slept two days at a time, and went two weeks without a bath or a change of clothes. "The frustration I felt at trying to take care of a stubborn, sick man and deal with the many psychological problems was too much. The children and I feel so much better since the divorce." But, she added, "we still deal with the negative connotations of divorce from society. Nobody could believe what torment we've been through." She had six children, aged twenty-nine, twenty-eight, twenty-two, twenty, fifteen, and thirteen.

Courts, Laws, and Lawyers

"There was little discussion as to who would have custody," one woman wrote. "As the mother I wanted custody, and my ex-husband's lawyer, as well as mine, reaffirmed our beliefs that a court would uphold my wish for custody. My ex-husband then ceased trying for custody."

This mother apparently believed that there is an almost mystical power in motherhood and that a mother's wishes could not possibly be denied. As far as we can tell, the court also accepted this line of reasoning. How this particular family worked out the details, after the initial assumptions were set down, is instructive:

My baby was only six months old when I filed for divorce. Because of her age and the fact that we would be living 1,200 miles from her father, I was very concerned about visitation.

We could not work things out, so I set a court date to have a judge decide these things. When we appeared at court there was an overloaded docket and few available judges. The lawyers were advised to try to negotiate settlements if possible and to return only if agreement was impossible.

My lawyer, myself, my father, my husband, and his lawyer went into a room and began negotiating. We spent nine hours in this room going over every date, holiday, weekend, etc. My decree because of this is very specific as to visiting dates, hours, times, places, etc. These are spelled out until she is of school age when they revert to two weekends a month, two weeks in summer, one week at Christmas, alternating holidays.

The atmosphere in that room was very strained, very deliberate, and neutral as far as hate/love. The lawyers did most of the talking between all parties. We were able to work out everything but money. At the last possible moment we found a judge to make a decision.

Because it was after hours and we had no court reporter it

was not legal. But we accepted it, and the woman judge pro-
nounced us divorced!

The child's father never exercises the time with her he
fought so hard for. He sees her about twice a year for a couple
of nights each. I never argue when he wants her except for
Christmas Eve day. Although she doesn't see him often, she
loves him very much and looks forward to his visits.

Another mother explained that she and her husband had wanted
joint custody of their children, but a lawyer convinced her that there
were "a few legal problems with that setup." The parents settled on
the mother's having legal custody, but the father's having joint custody in terms of liberal visitation.

At first, we set up exact times for pickup and return. Then I was
advised by my lawyer that it would look more favorable if we
wrote into the agreement "unlimited visitation privileges." I
was told that it usually happens that over a long period of time
the father or absent spouse has a tendency to make visitation
less frequently. . . . It is now just a mutual understanding between the two of us that he will have them every other
weekend.

This mother was very concerned about her husband's rights. She
had three young children, all under the age of ten. "I felt they needed
their dad. Although I was very bitter, I realized I might need his
help down the road." She was also concerned that the children
should be consulted in divorce custody cases. "At what age do they
take into account what the child actually wants? Too often the
mother receives custody, even though she is not always the best parent." She argues that a panel of three people should decide custody
cases, adding that "from what I've seen, many judges think they can
walk on water and closed their minds years ago to any new ideas."

We would concur: though the legal system must be involved in
divorce because divorce is a legal matter, we believe that many other
people should also be involved. Divorce is a family matter, first and
foremost, and all members of the family should be consulted:
mother, father, all the children, almost regardless of age, grandparents and other important relatives, and old friends. Furthermore,
lawyers and judges are trained in the law and learn about families

only as a secondary matter; lawyers and judges thus are not in a position to make decisions or to give advice about vital matters concerning continuing family relationships. Specialists who focus on family issues are generally going to be more knowledgeable when it comes to child development and interaction patterns between ex-spouses. When your car breaks down you certainly do not call a plumber.

Money: Alimony and Child Support

Money is a tremendously controversial issue in a divorce, and the debate over it is being carried on at all levels: divorcing families argue about it; local, state, and federal agencies argue about it; and presidents and presidential candidates offer their own ideas.

The wheels of government grind slowly, and we would never counsel anyone to wait for government to fix things up. Until that great day dawns, divorcing families will have to work out the money issues pretty much for themselves.

If it is at all possible, it is in the parents' best interests to bargain straightforwardly and in good faith. Many, many fathers do not pay alimony or child support or are behind in their payments, as a spate of studies has indicated. For example, a nationwide study issued by the House Select Committee on Children, Youth, and Families found that 79 percent of divorced fathers do not support their children. The reasons for this are of course varied. Many fathers claim, honestly, that they are simply broke; because of low pay or unemployment they cannot come through with much money for their ex-spouse and children. The most common dynamic we see operating, though, is the situation in which the children become pawns in the war: Dad thinks Mom poisoned his relationship with the children and fights back by dragging his feet on support payments; Mom thinks Dad has no right to see the kids if he will not help feed them and stonewalls his honest and sincere efforts to build a relationship with them. Each side accuses the other of being dishonest and manipulative, and both sides are correct in this allegation. Each also fails to see that the other person is sincere—sincerely in love with the kids, and sincerely in need of money.

When each ex-spouse is unable to see the good side of the other (which is there in 95 percent of all the cases in which we have been involved), the solutions to the problems come few and far between. What you are left with is a pathetic story. A sad story, such as the following:

> The hang-ups began when he quit paying alimony and child support and then left town so I couldn't even depend on him to take the children occasionally to give me a break from all the responsibilities in terms of time, money, and energy. And the kids thought he didn't love them anymore.

or

> My ex-husband offered to pay child support of $275 per month. The lawyer wrote $50 per child per week. And my ex-husband now pays $200 per month per child, which he has paid regularly even before the divorce was final. I work full-time, but we just hardly scrape by. He included extra money one month when the children were both sick with pneumonia.

or

> Our divorce was final in April 1981, and he stopped paying child support in December 1981. The next spring I took him to court for payment of back child support, and he skipped the state, and we haven't seen him since.

We found one mother's struggles over money especially instructive and pass them on to the reader almost verbatim:

> I am including this additional volunteering of information as I feel it is very important and yet is so overlooked in books written, in articles on divorce, and the like.
>
> At the time of the divorce, I was employed full-time (and still am). The decree stipulates that I am to receive $200 per month in child support. There is no alimony or maintenance.
>
> The laws governing child support are absolutely archaic. I will cite my own situation, which is obviously important to me. This situation, above anything else, has been nothing but a continuous hassle and has been the one thing that, since the time of the divorce (over five years ago), has caused me mental anguish and anxiety.

Our divorce took place in Missouri. At the present time I live in Minnesota, and my former husband lives in Kentucky. He is to pay $200 per month to me for child support; however, it is on the honor system. At this point in time, he is in arrears to the tune of $3,000. This may not seem like a large amount of money; however, it would certainly take the worry out of my month-to-month budget to have it on a regular basis.

The usual statement made to me is, "get yourself a lawyer and go to court." It is not that simple. To go to court means that I must hire an attorney in the county where the divorce decree was issued (which in this case is 615 miles away). Then there is the attorney retainer fee ($200–$500). I do not have a savings account; therefore, there is no money for a retainer fee. Once the attorney has been retained, then a court date is set up. Then there is the expense of taking off time from work, traveling to the county in question, court costs, and going to court. If I were to go to court at this particular time, I would be "lucky" to come home with $1,500 out of the $3000 in question.

The reciprocity laws between states pertaining to child support are very bad. If one is on welfare or ADC [Aid to Dependent Children] there are avenues to pursue through the local county agencies. However, I am not on welfare, and I do not receive ADC (or any other type of assistance), therefore I do not qualify for any type of legal assistance in obtaining the child support. This past year my salary was $15,500 before taxes. It is very difficult to maintain our residence with costs at their present level.

The struggle in my mind is ever present. This month should I initiate the court action and pursue obtaining the money that is legally due me? Do I want to go through the entire hassle again like I did three and a half years ago when I took him to court for child support arrears? Mentally, it has got to be one of the most anxiety ridden, degrading situations I have ever been exposed to. There have been times when I have felt like throwing in the towel, so to speak, and just saying to hell with it all and allowing myself to go on welfare. I would never do this—I am merely expressing inner feelings. The financial situation has got to be the most depressing aspect of the entire experience.

Examples: Since the divorce, I have not had a vacation (vacation in the sense where one travels, stays in motels, etc.). I have had weekend vacations visiting friends in other cities, or a day or two with my son visiting friends, but an actual vacation per se has been nil. This is very disconcerting.

One cannot discuss the financial situation with my ex-husband because he does not care. He feels that he (our son) is living with me; therefore, he is my responsibility. If I call him in an attempt to extract money, he will hang up on me if he so desires.

I wrote the judge that presided over the divorce proceedings asking for his assistance, thinking perhaps there was an agency I could turn to for help. He replied and advised me to retain an attorney.

You asked about my feelings toward the ex-spouse. If for no other reason than money, an animosity is there. One resents his taking vacations to Arizona, a winter vacation in Mexico, a jaunt to Reno. Advice from family and friends is, "don't think about it." This is rather hard to do when raising a twelve-year-old son when the expenditures run high.

At the time of the divorce I sought the assistance of a qualified psychologist. Why? Because I felt I was coming apart—I didn't really have anyone to talk to. At this point in time, in retrospect, I feel there is a definite need for counseling—not counseling from a psychologist or psychiatrist, but someone an individual can talk to. I am not saying the aforementioned are not good. What I am saying is that one doesn't really need the services of a psychologist or psychiatrist. One needs to talk with someone one can identify with.

At the time, I felt like I was the only individual in the world who was going through the trauma, that I was the only person who was experiencing what I was experiencing—feelings, thoughts, loneliness, being afraid. I was afraid of living alone, afraid of being single, afraid to raise my child as a single parent.

One doesn't need the services of a $50–$60 per hour psychologist/psychiatrist to discover that all of these types of feelings are very normal. Again, one cannot talk to family and friends because they are biased and make statements like "forget him, he's not worth it" or "it's all in the past—put it behind you," or "things will be better tomorrow." It doesn't take a Ph.D. to find that no one really wants to discuss these types of things with you—thus, you really have no one to talk to. Groups like Parents without Partners, Single Club, and the like are more socially oriented. In addition, one doesn't feel comfortable walking into a group of total strangers and discussing very personal, intimate things. The adjustment to going from a married existence (good or bad) to a single existence, raising children, in your thirties or forties is very hard. I have a phrase that I use when I think back on that first year—un-from-gether.

Perhaps after reading the above you are wondering what type of an individual I am now. I am very self-reliant and self-sufficient. My son and I live in a two-bedroom duplex, with a living room, kitchen, dining area, 1½ baths, and a recreation room. We take care of our own lawn mowing, trimming, etc., as well as snow shoveling. The car is maintained well at all times. Our home is the hub of activity, with my son's friends coming over all the time. I will not allow myself to become depressed, though at times I miss the intimate relationship of being married and having a spouse. However, I will not marry for the sake of being married; thus, five years plus have passed.

How Mothers Adjust to Divorce

The first year or so after the divorce is critical. Shock, fear, panic, anger, sadness, depression, the fear of being alone, and loneliness itself are common feelings the mothers share. "With great effort after those two years I learned to like my life," one noted.

Many of the mothers counseled patience and emotional preparedness for the long haul:

Be aware of the hills and valleys. When you're in a valley, know you can climb up tomorrow.

Give yourself time to get over the worst part. I'd say don't expect too much of yourself. It takes at least a year to develop a positive attitude and to get over the worst of the hurt.

Recognize that there will be a good many "down" days as well as panic and anxiety. Try very hard not to make any major decisions, apart from the divorce and settlement procedures. The adjustment does not happen overnight, especially if you were the divorced party. Give yourself time.

In a number of studies over the past several years, we have found that the majority of divorced people are happier after the breakup than before. It seems that for most, the pain of a dead or hostile marriage is worse than the challenge of going it alone with the children. Our colleague Kendra Schwab Summers found, for example, that within three months of the marital separation (this is even before the actual legal divorce), the average mother feels that she and her children are doing better than they were before the father left.[2]

In counseling we see this demonstrated time and again. One young mother had been dragging through life for two years, plagued by arthritis-like pains that almost completely incapacitated her. She missed many days of work, and her doctors could not figure out what was going on. It seems that her husband had been having an affair, and she repressed her feelings about this as best she could, but the tension was expressed in her body. We saw her just the other day, and she was walking on a cloud: smiling, relaxed, and calm in her conversation. What happened? "I kicked him out," she said in triumph.

A mother in the current study noted that though life looks better now that she is separated, it is by no means easy:

> I indicated that our present, postdivorce home life is excellent, happy, a dramatic improvement over our predivorce situation, and this is true. However, there are some stresses inherent in our way of life: financial pressures, the tiredness that comes from being the sole caretaker of a family while also being involved in a very demanding public relations job, etc.
>
> Also, I find it very hard to speak positively about my ex-spouse, for (I feel) very valid reasons. What I am trying to say is that our life is not perfect; the children and I do feel some stress occasionally, but overall, our home life is wholesome, healthy, loving, and emotionally well balanced, in my opinion.
>
> I also think one strength we have is that, even though we sometimes get tired and irritable and angry with each other in our household, we also are very inclined to apologize, cry a little together, express our feelings about the sources of our unhappiness, and then start over again with each other.

Adjusting to the working world outside the home is difficult for many mothers who have been at home. One explained how she had been extensively involved in volunteer work—school, church, community, scouting—but after the divorce it was necessary for her to earn some money. This generated some anxiety, but at the same time "gave me some feeling of self-fulfillment while being paid."

"Adjustment is slow and frightening!" one mother noted. "There's a very fine line between giving in and keeping your chin up! It's rough!" Another mother, hundreds of miles away and in a very different situation, echoed her sentiments:

> It's tough! I shoulder all the day-to-day responsibilities of child, home, yard, car, business. Relaxing opportunities come few and far between. Socially, a divorcée is a neuter. You don't really fit in comfortably with married couples, yet you don't have the freedom because of your children to run free with single people. In our city it's very, very rare that you meet new people—new friends of any kind, and men especially. Loneliness is a very real problem for me, and I don't think I have adjusted to that.

One young mother honored us by telling in detail the whole story of her adjustment to the divorce and to having sole custody of the children. We would like to recount some of it: "We separated when my oldest was four and my youngest two. There was never any question as to which one of us would have custody. Naturally, I got custody. This was the only suitable condition as far as we were both concerned." She noted that the problem of caring day-to-day for two young children and having no formal business or professional training seemed "insurmountable" at that time, but as time passed, mother and children adjusted to the situation. "We faced every hardship together," she wrote. "I explained to them what we were going through. Not in great detail, of course, but on their level." The mother was on welfare and received food stamps. She supplemented this meager income by baby-sitting, selling cleaning products, and scraping by here and there. When her youngest child reached nursery school age, she enrolled in a business school. In ten months she completed an intensive executive secretarial program. "Three years before that I would never have believed I could do it! I would never have dreamed it would happen!" She gained employment as an assistant traffic manager in an aerospace distributing organization.

"I feel these difficult steps along the way were good examples for my kids of what an individual could achieve, if she just tried and tried and tried." The children helped her study, she wrote, and helped around the house "without too much reminding." She did feel guilty about not being able to be the traditional stay-at-home, cook-clean-wait-for-the-kids-to-get-home-from-school-chauffeur-type of mother, but her guilt passed as she and the children accepted their new status in life. A new mom and family emerged: she was responsible for job, juggling housework, cooking, shopping, and other errands, with the kids' help and understanding. "I made the children a part of all this new life. The responsibility was good for them. They didn't have to grow up too fast at all. They know that their part has helped," she said.

"If you assume a positive outlook toward your particular problem, your children will also feel positive," the mother concluded.

How Children Adjust to Divorce

Many parents, researchers, and clinicians over the years have noted that children often will mirror their parent's feelings about life when a divorce occurs. If a mother is hysterical, the panic will transfer to the children; if she can figure out ways to be positive about her life, the children will be soothed by her calm. If she fakes it and does not have the courage to find help from friends or professionals, the children will see through her mask very quickly.

One mother stressed the importance of communication with the children. She argued that a mother needs to help the youngsters work through their feelings about the divorce. She was quite specific about how to do this, and she wrote with clarity and power about her discussions with her seventeen and nineteen year old:

> I feel that the best I can do is to say to my children (as I have on several occasions): "Look, I do have some unhappy feelings about your father, and this is only natural. After all, we did decide to get a divorce. So, please be merciful. Do not expect me to praise him and speak of him warmly. On the other hand, I do believe it is not so much that he is a bad person as that we were so very wrong for each other. Also, I believe your father loves you even though, yes, I agree he does not seem to show it often. However, he does send the support money more regularly now, and I believe he sees this as a way of showing his love for you. I also want you to know that I was not a perfect wife, and I am not a perfect mother. But I did try to be a good wife, and I do care very much about being a good mother . . .

Not a permissive, overly indulgent mother, but a mother who balances patience and flexibility with rules and limits. But I am not perfect by any means, and so please do not expect this of me. If you will accept me with my faults, I will accept you with yours.

"The main thing is that I love you, and, as much as possible, I will always be available to listen and care and to try to help as you wrestle with the complexities of life.

"Amen."

Coming to terms is essential, another mother concluded. "The custodial parent needs to help herself/himself to come to terms with the situation, and then to help the children do the same." She explained that the children need to know "what is, *is*. And sometimes, while we may not like it, we can learn to see the good things in our lives and learn not to let the negative things ruin our lives." She urged parents to tell their children that it was not the children's fault that father has gone away, both physically and emotionally. "It is important that they do not blame themselves for something that is in no way their fault."

The custodial parent needs to care for herself, so that she can then adequately care for her children. "I think it is important for the custodial parent to try to have as much health and life and vigor and wholesomeness and decency and warmth and closeness and love in the home as humanly possible. For the sake of everyone."

Support Systems: Where to Go for Help

Some single mothers probably try to go it completely alone, but we hope these folks are rare. The more successful single mothers in our study generally had a wide circle of friends and supporters. Many noted that burnout is the almost inevitable fate of the martyr and that every mother has an obligation to herself and to her children to find replenishment. "Keep in touch, and spend time with your friends," one noted.

Many others argued the importance of other-sex relationships. "Don't assume that all members of the opposite sex have the same traits as your ex-spouse."

Friends can be great counselors, especially if you are willing to counsel them in return. "Go to a friend for moral support during low times, times when you start to feel bad about 'how it could have been.' " Finding new friends while keeping track of old ones was also suggested many times.

A number of mothers found lots of help in local support groups, such as Parents without Partners or other mixed-sex groups in the area. Almost every good-sized town should have a group or two, and if it does not, it needs one. "I started a Growing through Divorce group in our town," one mother noted proudly, "and it's kept me alive a lot of times."

Extended family support, of course, is essential for many single mothers. Generally, grandparents are willing to help if they are financially and physically able to do so. Researcher Linda Bader found that the divorce of an adult child is a difficult crisis for most grandparents.[3] Should a grandparent take the adult child back home? Offer child care? Send money? Feel like a failure as a parent because of the adult child's divorce? Each family decides these issues differently and in a different manner. But none of the questions is easy to answer; if a single mother thinks the reply will be cut and dried and finds out that Mom and Pop feel differently, she really should not be terribly surprised. The issues are complicated. In general, most of the mothers we corresponded with concurred in saying "I greatly appreciated my family's support."

A professional counselor was a key to the healthy resolution of a number of difficult situations:

My ex-husband and I went to counseling immediately upon recognition of the marital problems. Counseling helped us immensely toward reaching an understanding of what happened and why. We still attribute our good relationship to the fact that we did go to counseling and were able to really understand each other and the problems. Without this understanding, I think I would feel very bitter and vengeful.

Many responses like this one came back to us. Counselors in these cases did not miraculously save a sinking marriage. But with a split inevitable, the counselors helped to ease the pain and make life better for both parents and children.

A final support the mothers mentioned was reading. The list of good articles and books on divorce and custody is probably quite long by now. A good writer can observe and distill a lot of wisdom on how to cope with life's troubles, and curling up in a comfy chair with a good book on a cold and lonely night can be a wonderful experience. We will not plug the books of any particular writers here because we believe that it is really a personal matter. But any library ought to have a dozen or more good books on divorce and related topics, and if your town is big enough to have a drugstore, bus depot, or bookstore, you will undoubtedly be able to carry off a good pile of paperbacks for no more than three or four dollars apiece. In our own counseling we often recommend reading; a book can never be a substitute for a good therapist, but it certainly is a lot cheaper!

Dating and Sex

Some of the mothers, of course, were back in circulation quickly after the separation or divorce. Our general impression, however, after reading hundreds of questionnaires and interviewing many, many single mothers is that thoughts of romance and love often take a backseat in a divorce situation to more basic needs. As one young mother noted, "How am I going to survive?"

Many are gun-shy. They are zero for one, or zero for two or three in the marriage game, and they are not likely to jump quickly into another relationship. Money problems, continuing hassles with the ex-husband, worries about finding a job or surviving job stress, and feeling guilty for allegedly neglecting the children all come up.

Some ex-husbands still try to treat the mothers like cattle to be herded, to be owned. One mother told of how her ex persisted in harassing her new boyfriend: "He put sugar down Tom's gas tank. He harassed him at work. He let the air out of his tires and threatened to shoot him. It all culminated when they had a fistfight on my front lawn." She concluded that dating almost was not worth it.

The children also can make a mother's dating situation difficult. Most children harbor desperate hopes that somehow Mom and Dad will miraculously get back together. These hopes may last for a number of years. Any new boyfriend coming around can be a threat to Dad's chances of returning home, and teenagers, especially, can unleash venom on the new suitor. "They swear at him and call him names," one mother told us. "Lola even phoned him at work once and told him off." A divorcing mother's parents can also act as if she should wear black and be celibate for a century or so after the marriage ends.

Many mothers succumb to some or all of these pressures and to their own internal pressures that say to them that it is impossible to be young again and fall in love.

Other mothers have more rational reasons: "I don't recommend dating for six months or a year. Later, when you get to know yourself and what your goals and needs are, that's a better time to date."

But in the long run for possibly the majority of mothers, dating and marriage will be a key to future happiness. Not the only key, of course, but an important one. The vast majority of divorced women remarry. Most have concluded that some men are OK, even though at least one other man was not. Feelings of loneliness and despondency can close in. At 3:00 A.M. on that cold winter night it is often nice to have a warm body to curl up next to in bed. Not for sex alone, of course, but mostly to fight off the grinding feeling that life can be dark and that we are very small by ourselves.

For many single mothers dating can build self-esteem:

I didn't think of myself as being attractive anymore. My husband before we married thought I was a knockout. But after ten years he told me when I walked around in my housecoat and slippers that I looked like a dying Carol Burnett.

I began to believe him. And then when we got divorced all of a sudden a lot of men were chasing after me. Some of his friends from work and, fortunately, a lot of new guys we hadn't known before.

I feel silly saying this, but it sure helped my self-esteem.

Personal Advice for Mothers from Mothers

The advice offered by hundreds of mothers is as good as any we have read or heard from many excellent and well-known family therapists. We would like to present just a smattering:

Take time to get to know yourself:
    So you can understand what happened in your marriage.
    So you won't make the same mistakes.
    So you can rebuild self-esteem.

So you can set up some short- and long-term goals because you have taken the time to know your true feelings.

So you can develop new ideas and interests that strengthen your identity and purpose.

So you can learn to enjoy the creative aspects of single living.

The divorcing parent must have some time for herself to rejuvenate. Remember that, yes, one is a parent, but one is a whole person first. Often if one is unhappy then those feelings of unhappiness can transfer to everyone else in the circle. Simply take time to enjoy your children, and allow time for yourself.

Don't rush into new relationships because it's a very vulnerable period in your life. Don't just transfer dependence to a new relationship. Let go of the past and move on. Realistically face what happened. Learn from it; don't repeat it.

Don't succumb to feelings of failure and worthlessness. Look at divorce as a growing pain necessary for a new stage of growth. Growth that was not possible in your previous marriage.

Don't date for six months or even a year. Get to know yourself and your true feelings and goals.

Don't be alone until you can handle emptiness.

Don't indulge in self-pity. Make the best of the situation.

Don't blame yourself completely. "It takes two to tango."

Don't torture yourself with memories. Look ahead, only remember the lessons you learned. Don't dwell on how.

Don't shut the world out. Don't give up no matter how much it hurts inside. Hang in there. The pain will somehow subside. It may take a good year, but it will happen. I almost gave up, but thank God I did not. It hurt so much I wanted to die, but I made it. You can, too.

Don't be afraid to grieve. I think divorce is a kind of dying. Grieve for your loss awhile, and then get on with life. Don't be bitter or blame.

I was married for twenty years, from age eighteen to thirty-eight. At first I wanted to die and sometimes still do. But, little by little, self-confidence and self-like come back. Just keep telling yourself you can do it, and handle one thing at a time. Don't bury your feelings. It just takes that many more months/ years to begin living for yourself and thereby being a better parent for your children.

—This mother had three children, aged twenty, eighteen, and fourteen. Her husband was overseas when he had his attorney contact her about the divorce. The father then wrote a letter to the children explaining his need for freedom and happiness, but the children never understood. No further communication followed that letter.

You may think the sun will never shine again, but it will. One day you will be alive and thank God for it. When I was first divorced I soon learned to get up, put my makeup on, and the most important thing, put a smile on. At first I really had to hunt for something to smile about, but not now.

Don't blame yourself in too harsh a fashion if your children exhibit some tensions and problems that stem from your unhappy marriage or your divorce. After all, every family, divorced or not, has some problems, and for you to expect that you can offer your children a perfect life is unrealistic. Try to minimize the trauma, of course, and then be merciful to yourself. Even couples with good marriages have children who sometimes get into trouble, struggle to "find themselves," and occasionally have to go through some very bad times along the way, particularly in adolescence.

The noncustodial parent should never be used as a baby-sitter. It would seem to breed resentment on the part of the baby-sitting parent.

Talk with friends, especially those who have been through the divorce experience. You'll find your feelings have been felt by everyone and that those feelings are all a normal part of adjustment.

Take the initiative. Don't sit back and wait for the world to fall at your feet. It won't happen.

Keep busy, do constructive activities.
Listen to others, but always make your own decisions.

Take up new (or old) activities you have always wanted to find time for.

Take one day at a time; set small goals at first.

Consider going back to school.

Be flexible and adaptable.

Be independent.

Rely on yourself again, not your ex-spouse. Many women who are suddenly thrown out into the cruel world after being homemakers have to face this.

Get a job.

Have confidence in the decision made.

Have a positive attitude.

Work on improving your sense of humor.

Allow yourself the luxury of crying on someone's shoulder. I tried to be so strong, and that's really self-defeating.

Get in an exercise program.

Take good care of yourself.

I would say you must, first and foremost, keep a sense of balance—balance between rest and activity, between quiet introspection and active "let's forget it all for awhile and have a good time," between work and play, between self-indulgence and self-discipline.

Immediately pick yourself up. Especially if you are a woman, begin to take charge of your life.

It's time for new beginnings. New clothes, a hairstyle, a new skill all make you feel new.

In any relationship, I think a person has the opportunity to learn or gain. If you have gained or improved yourself from the parting relationship, you haven't lost. And the opportunity to learn from someone else still awaits you.

I have no idea what advice to give other mothers. My adjustment to being single and divorced is wretched. I have economic and emotional needs that make me a void at this point. The hurt of being replaced by someone younger and energetic and full of life is such a hurt that I cannot give advice to anyone.

Learn the legal and tax implications of any divorce decree. Have it reviewed by a competent professional in this area so you know the implications prior to signing. (Particularly regarding the tax to be paid on alimony, joint dependency for tax purposes, etc.) Often both are too emotional or concerned about the psychological repercussions of the divorce on the child when these things can have a long-term impact on custodial parents' ability to support physical necessities.

Learn, if you don't know, how to manage your own financial situation. Go to stores and ask for credit in your own name; check with the local credit bureau to see if you have a rating. If not, ask for advice on how to get it, and work toward getting it.

Keep a daily journal. You'll be amazed how you cope when you read back over it and see how far you came in days and months.

Advice for Mothers about Children

Many mothers with sole custody noted that joint custody of the children with their ex-spouse would be ideal. But they qualified this statement with numerous warnings from their own experience:

> Joint custody is ideal for those equally concerned with the children's welfare and well-being and for those who desire equal responsibility in their care. However, if one parent is closer to the children and is better equipped to provide the emotional security, then perhaps that parent should have custody, with the other having visitation privileges. Above all, on-going communication between parents and between parents and children is essential.

Another single mother said that joint custody would be great if the children are used to being around both parents, but her children were not.

Yet another noted that joint custody seemed "healthier" to her: "I think the trend toward joint custody is healthier. I don't know too many men who want the responsibility, however. Many of my friends' husbands no longer even visit their children on any regular basis."

Other mothers noted that joint custody would be great:

For parents who both truly love their children.

For the father who wants joint custody and can take the responsibilities and do the nurturing.

Because single parenting is "overwhelming" and should be shared when feasible.

As long as the father is not abusive.

Because there would be "less need for either parent to spoil or buy the children if the stress is removed by reasonable custody arrangements."

Among single-parent mothers there was little disagreement with the notion that two good parents are better than one. This is the idea that motivates the joint custody movement. "Optimally, children need two healthy parents who care about them," one mother summed it up. Such an ideal, however, is far from the grasp of many families, and to try to promote it for all families as some kind of panacea is pure and simple nonsense.

Some mothers get pretty steamed up when writing about these issues. For example: "I don't believe in joint custody or split custody. I think one parent should have custody. I would not have it any other way. He gets the kids over my dead body!"

A very common argument against joint custody goes like this: "I am really opposed. If you can manage the communication required for joint custody, you could stay married." A lot of people who believe this type of argument assume that divorce always follows a hostile or aggressive type of scenario (which is often not the case) and that people who cannot have a satisfying marriage cannot be satisfactory co-parents (which also is not always true). The arguments and counterarguments on joint custody are difficult to resolve because many people carry a lot of emotional baggage into a discussion on divorce.

Children Will Benefit Most By Seeing Both Parents Often. One mother stated that her children were allowed to see their father anytime they wished, and because of this they did not feel as insecure as some other children of divorced parents.

"Children should know their parents in daily life, not just as guests," one mother cautioned, while another added that "both parents should try to locate in the same geographical area."

The majority of the sole mothers wanted their ex-spouse to participate in their children's lives. They felt that it was important for the children and it gave the mothers time for themselves. "Keep in mind that your child has two parents. You may be divorcing your spouse, but your children are still entitled to a mother and father, regardless of your feelings toward each other," a mother of one noted.

There Are No Pat Answers. In deciding custody arrangements, one mother noted that parents need to consider the emotional bonds the children have to each spouse and the amount of time available for the children after job demands are met.

Another mother said that custody determinations should be based on the kinds of relationships the parents have or used to have with their children. "If a child is old enough to have preferences, then I think parents should welcome his or her input while making the decisions."

One mother cautioned that parents sometimes "lose sight of what they're really trying to do. Their own inconveniences and needs and desires sometimes are put before what's best for the children. I think a combination of both results in what's best for the children."

The best solution causes the least pain for the children, another argued: "I would think that a trial period of at least a year would be necessary to work things out. How can they decide what would be best until they've tried it? I think custody arrangements should allow leeway for changes and adjustments as circumstances change over the years."

A List of "Don'ts." The mothers generated a long and healthy list of warnings for other mothers to consider:

Never "badmouth" the ex-spouse, because that will end up hurting not only the ex but also the child.

Never use the children as pawns.

Do not let the children make the final decision about custody, because it causes too much guilt for them.

Do not let the children think that they caused the divorce.

Minimize the opportunity for the children to manipulate parents against each other.

Do not be vindictive and allow your feelings to interfere with what the child may need from your ex-spouse.

Do not let the ex-spouse play "Santa Claus."

Do not use the children as "pseudojurors" and attempt to sway them into thinking that you are right and your ex is evil.

Do not inflict guilt on your children.

Do not think you own your children. "God owns children. We are only short-term caretakers!"

A List of "Do's." The mothers were at their level-headed best when they began generating some of the positive things a mother can do to help children:

Share with the children hopes and fears, the good and the bad. Children are smart, and in attempting to shield them in their best interest, we help them become more confused.

Communicate with them. Imaginations conjure up things that are far worse than reality.

Make sure the children know that they are loved.

Be positive about the other parent when talking with the children. You do not have to express love or undying devotion, but at least make an honest attempt to work together without overwhelming malice.

Make sure the children know that they were not to blame for the divorce.

Listen to the children. Be very aware of their realities and their needs.

Laugh with the children.

Have your children share in your life and its daily routines and responsibilities.

Encourage calls from the noncustodial parent. It helps the child
keep the relationship together, even if the child has difficulty
speaking on the phone or just will not.

Parents must decide custody arrangements. Do not trap or manipulate a child into the decision making.

Sorrows

Millions of words have been written about divorce and single parenthood in the past decade or two. Is it a terrible experience? Is it a
good one? Where are we to find balance in our views? Much that is
written focuses on the trauma of divorce, for undoubtedly there is a
large element of trauma in divorce, which is labeled by many as the
most difficult of all family crises. In response to the "trauma of divorce" material another body of literature has arisen: what we could
glibly label the "divorce as challenge and triumph" literature. A book
or article in this genre describes the problems and calls the reader to
action on the assumption that a crisis is also an opportunity for
growth and future happiness.

We are not so sure where we as authors fit on this spectrum. The
process of divorce can be good, bad, ugly, and sublime. Most divorces seem to be a mixture of many emotional elements.

In our final two sections of this chapter, we will look at the sorrows many single parents report and then finish with a note of optimism by listing the joys.

First, the sorrows.

There is just not enough time. "It's very difficult to be a full-time
provider and homemaker, have responsibility for the children 97 percent of the time, live on 50 percent of the income we were accustomed to, and find time to meet everyone's needs on a day-to-day
basis." Constant child care without relief is a tremendous strain.

The dream of "Mom, Dad, and the kids" is for the moment shat-
tered. "We are no longer a traditional family," and that hurts. "But
we are still a family."

Another woman added, "The only real sorrow I feel about the
arrangement is that her father isn't with us to share in the daily
goings on of family life." Who do you share the artwork with? The
first tooth that falls out? The birthday parties? Oftentimes there is
no one.

"It's good for a child to see working relationships where two people love each other, and it hurts that she can't see this with her father and me."

Another mother lamented the lost stability of positive grandparent relationships. Yet another said, "I bleed for my children when I see their loneliness in being away from Dad and former friends. I regret seeking more conversation and support from them in my own loneliness than they can give me." Her children were fourteen and twelve.

Holidays were especially sorrowful times for mothers when the children were away with the father.

Other mothers were sad because the children's desire to see the father more was not to be granted: "The day may come when they will feel that they do not know him at all."

But frequent visitation causes other problems for some mothers:

Because their father sees them as often as he does, they're put in a heavy loyalty dilemma. Consequently, they return home feeling confused by guilt and wanting to blame or hate. This is all happening because their father is trying to get them to live with him. I will never have total peace as long as he's alive!

There were several episodes where my ex was refused visitation by the courts (he never returned the children and took them to California without notifying me, for one). When the time came to resume his visitation, the children did not want to go (for fear of not coming back), and I was forced to have the courts make them go. Having your children leave you crying and screaming "I don't want to go" is a horror, and the courts should be more understanding about them. Children over five are capable of deciding if they want to spend a "visitation" day [at their father's] or go to a friend's party instead. They should not be forced to go under any circumstances.

The future concerned another mother, who worried about being alone when the children were grown and gone. "I know they will soon be gone from me, responsible for themselves. I will be alone for a brief spell, and that unknown is frightening."

The list of sorrows seems endless, and for sheer despondency it is hard to beat the words of this mother: "I think the breakup of our marriage should be voted a classic case of what not to do. Father is

gone, thinking the children don't care for him. The children believe
Father does not care for them. Everyone lost."

Joys

And yet . . .

And yet there is a good deal of joy in the lives of many, many
mothers with custody. Though the list of things causing despair and
despondency may seem to be endless, the list of joys can go on and
on and on.

The joys include:

1. Freedom. Mothers often have the freedom to make decisions
without interference from or battles with fathers.

2. Grandparents. In many families, when a spouse leaves the
grandparents do not also automatically disappear. "My ex-spouse's
parents are extremely helpful. They take my preschool daughter
some weekends, and the space is wonderful."

3. Responsibility. The burden of responsibility is almost unbearable to some mothers, but other mothers seem to thrive under
it:

> The joy that is unique to being a single parent is the all-engulf-
> ing satisfaction when things are going well. You not only take
> all of the responsibility, but you receive all of the joy of their
> growth and new discovery that the child is experiencing. The
> feelings are simply heightened because there is no sharing with
> another human being. It's more concentrated!

This responsibility kept many, many mothers going:

> The sole responsibility for these three lives has kept me from
> giving up completely three times since the divorce, when I've
> been too tired and drained to get out of bed to go to work or
> call the lawyer to set up a court date, the five times I've gone
> to court to try to extract money from my ex and to have our
> names changed to my maiden name.

Mothers spoke of the special bond they now have with their
young: "I can be me all the time with my children. No one else
interferes. I feel a special closeness with them."

Many were thankful for the father who stayed involved. Former spouses oftentimes remained friends, and this contributed to the health, happiness, and adjustment of the children. Both Mom and Dad in these types of families would attend the band concerts, Girl Scout meetings, and open house at school. "The girls are always excited to see Dad. Dad is excited to see the girls. And I'm glad to be alone for awhile."

Another wrote of how important the father had been:

> The kids are happy, with no feelings of guilt about staying with either parent. The children have been given the responsibility of making their own arrangements with their father. I don't have to deal with him. I feel good about myself for being fair. I have learned to enjoy freedom after many years of thinking always of others. Their father, as a result of the continued closeness, has been no problem as far as paying for education, colleges, and alimony. The three oldest have all finished college. The fourth is a sophomore studying to be a biologist. The fifth is an honors student in a scholastically tough private school and he wants to be a scientist. All are very good athletes. The two youngest are fun, laugh easily, and are self-confident and responsible. None of them would have turned out so well without a father present and active in their lives. I am convinced.

A few mothers, sadly, could find nothing to be thankful about. But the vast majority were finding good things in their lives, and some were outright ecstatic:

> There are so many joys it's hard to condense them. During my marriage I was always the outsider. Being able to have time alone with my children is a wonder in itself. We talk, we listen, we explore new things. There is no one to contradict decisions I make. We are a unit, a whole, not parts separate from each other. It is not easy. I had to learn to make decisions and to stick by those decisions. I also had to learn how to say I didn't always know the answers. I think the biggest thing is we talk to each other. I am not just the cook, I am part of the family.

4

Fathers with Sole Custody

One Father's Story

Authors' Note. An Oklahoma father describes the long struggle with his first wife over custody of their children. The man is now remarried and believes that life is "far better than I ever could have hoped."

My former wife and I were married when she was seventeen and I was twenty. We had been "high school sweethearts," and she was pregnant with our son at the time of our wedding. We separated for a short while about five years into our marriage. Through professional counseling and the urging of our families and friends we reunited. Our second child, another son, was born two years later.

My wife chose to work outside the home. Throughout our marriage we shared domestic responsibilities, including caring for the children. My own profession demanded long hours and, at that time, a fair amount of travel. However, I managed to spend a great deal of time with the kids, and developed close relationships with them both.

I feel my relationship with my wife was always strained due to the early ages at which we married and to becoming parents only five months after our wedding. Also, the pressures of two demanding professions in one household added to the strain. I'm certain other factors influenced our situation as well, and we separated again when our children were ten and three.

At that time my wife took the children to her parents' home and moved in with a friend from her office. I stayed alone in our home. I tried to communicate with her to determine what she intended to do, but she would not discuss her plans and did not indicate a desire to accept any responsibility for the children.

After about three weeks it was apparent that my wife was perfectly willing to continue living where she was, away from me and the children, and I then made the decision to bring the children back home to be with me.

My older sister and I drove to my wife's parents' home to tell them of my plan. They agreed that the children should be with at least one of their parents.

We returned home that night and spent the remainder of the weekend contemplating our new situation. On Monday I took the kids to their Bible school and went on to work.

My sister called me during the morning to tell me that my wife had come to the Bible school and taken the children. Three days later my wife called to tell me that she had rented an apartment and was going to keep the children with her.

I went to the apartment, which was located in a run-down section of town. It was unfinished, and the children had no place to sit or sleep. My first impulse was to take them back home with me. I knew that if I did, she would only take them away again. I offered to move out of the house and let them move back there with her. She refused saying she wanted to be "on her own."

The next day I had a friend help me move some furniture and some of the children's toys and clothing to the apartment. Later that day I went to visit an old friend who was an attorney. After relating the story of the situation I told him I wanted custody of the children. He spent a great deal of time explaining the problems I would encounter but did not attempt to persuade me to give up my goal.

The next day he called me to his office. He had prepared a petition cross-filing my ex-wife's petition for divorce and one asking the court for temporary custody. I signed the petitions, and they were filed that day, along with a request for a hearing to determine temporary custody.

The hearing date was set approximately one month later, and my attorney and I began to build my case for custody.

By the date of the hearing we had accumulated a large base of facts to support my case for custody. At the hearing my wife's attorney had little evidence to support her position; instead, he spent his time attacking me. The judge finally asked him to sit down and personally directed questions to me concerning our family life and my plans for the children should I be granted custody.

At the close of the hearing the judge indicated that his decision would be handed down later. After two weeks of agonizing waiting, I was notified that the judge had granted me temporary custody, and I moved the children home with me.

My attorney cautioned me that obtaining temporary custody was not any type of guarantee of permanent custody. But at that time it was a fantastic improvement in my position.

I had hoped that after the hearing we could proceed immediately to finalize the divorce and custody situation. My attorney, however, explained that it was to our advantage to proceed slowly in order to establish my ability to care for the children and our home and still maintain my career.

My ex-wife and I worked out an informal visitation arrangement. The children and I settled into a comfortable routine that included returning them to their former day care provider and resuming their activities, such as Cub Scouts and preschool.

My attorney instructed me to keep a detailed log of the children's reactions to our living situations and events that occurred that might have a bearing on the judge's final decision. The log later became an important source of information to support my request for permanent custody.

My ex-wife terminated her original attorney and retained another who had a reputation for excellence in domestic relations cases. At that point the case became more complex, with private investigators hired to determine my competency to retain custody. Two attempted break-ins at our home seemed suspiciously related to the case.

Several meetings were held with my ex-wife, our attorneys, and me. These sessions usually produced few tangible results, and often served to deepen the bitterness between my ex-wife and me. During these meetings it seemed that my ex-wife and her attorney were more concerned with the financial aspects of our divorce than with the custody or welfare of the children. Her attorney tried to convince me that we should settle the case financially and split the children, with my oldest son living with me and my youngest son living with his mother.

After several months of these types of discussions, my attorney and I petitioned the court to set a trial date. A date was finally set nearly a year after we separated.

In the months that immediately preceded the trial date, we

started the deposition process. Her attorney requested depositions from my family and some of my friends. At one time she threatened to bring in a witness who purportedly had damaging information concerning my background. As the trial date neared, the witness admitted that her information was false and faded from the scene.

On one occasion her attorney met with the children during my ex-wife's visitation period and questioned them at great length concerning our living situation. She went so far as to try to persuade them to make a choice between their mother and me. It was that type of tactic that finally led me to call my ex-wife and ask her to try to work out some type of settlement with me.

My ex-wife would not meet with me at my home, so we met at a neutral location and discussed all of the aspects of the case. I made it clear that at all costs I would not give up custody of the children, short of a court order.

I asked her to think about it and call me in a week to discuss our options further. When we met again she stated that she knew I had a strong case for custody due to some things that had occurred prior to our separation and due to her actions toward the children during the separation.

She said that she knew I had given the children a good living situation during the temporary custody period and that she felt comfortable with this as long as she was entitled to reasonable visitation.

She continued that she did not want me to obtain legal custody by having the court declare her an unfit mother. She finally agreed that she would drop the custody fight in return for not being declared an unfit mother and for an immediate lump-sum financial settlement.

We took our "agreement" to our attorneys and asked them to work out the details. A week later when our trial date arrived we went to court and finalized our divorce. I was awarded full legal and physical custody of the children.

I have little doubt that I would have obtained custody if the case had been determined by a judge. My attorney and I had spent our time preparing a solid case. I had done what I set out to do, providing the children with the best living environment I possibly could. My ex-wife and her attorney on the other hand had not prepared well, and she had done little to establish herself as a concerned, caring parent.

Now, several years later, my ex-wife's position is even more clear. She seldom sees the children and takes no interest in their schooling or activities. She and I have both remarried and established new lives that have taken us in almost opposite directions. The children are very close to my current wife, and things seem to have worked out far better than I ever could have hoped.

Challenges and Accomplishments. Can a divorced father with custody of his children do an adequate job rearing them? Can a father with custody do as well as a mother with custody?

If you are uncomfortable with the contentiousness that politics and religion generate in a discussion, then do not bring up issues regarding fathers and custody, especially with divorced fathers and mothers, for blood pressure is almost guaranteed to rise. We are convinced that there is much more emotion on the topic than information, more adrenaline than data.

The arguments for and against fathers with custody tend to pile up high at the extreme ends of the range:

"Fathers can do just as well as mothers. Maybe even better!"
versus
"Baloney!"

When we initially began looking for objective data on the subject in 1978 with Rod Eirick, we must admit to a measure of eagerness to prove fathers capable. After several more years of research and clinical experience, we find ourselves to be more sober: some divorced fathers with custody are great, some are good, some are terrible. On the average, we have demonstrated in this research and in the previous study that as a group they match up to mothers, statistically speaking at least.[1] And the large-scale study we report here makes fathers look, statistically, pretty good. But our clinical experience makes us much more cautious in our assessment now: a father (or a mother, for that matter) may be quite capable of looking good on a questionnaire, but not so good in the reality of day-to-day family life.

We now believe, almost on a gut level but with a great deal of data to support our beliefs, that millions and millions of fathers are very capable but that on the average mothers are somewhat better at rearing the young than are fathers. Fortunately, children are not reared by statistical averages. Each court decision must be made on objective, individual data gathered specifically from each individual family. Many fathers, in this light, outshine their ex-wives and deserve custody.

Furthermore, human beings are amazingly fluid in their behaviors. They are capable of learning and growing and changing. Mothers learned to be mothers by modeling themselves on their own mothers and by watching other people nurture the young. Likewise, fathers are perfectly capable of learning nurturant behaviors, even though as children and youths males are not usually encouraged or expected to learn to care for the young. Signs that this social attitude is changing slowly make us happy, of course. Maybe in the future, society will see that having nurturant males is just as important as having nurturant females. When that day arrives, fathers on the average will be just as capable as mothers.

We began looking at these questions in a rather happenstance manner. Our research on androgyny gained a small amount of local notoriety in Madison, Wisconsin, and divorcing fathers began calling up, beginning in about 1974. Perhaps the best phrasing for their questions was this: "I need to know, I guess, if fathers can be good mothers."

Our answer back then was, "Yes, of course!" Our answer today is: "Yes, of course. Some can. But some can't, and don't delude yourself into thinking it's easy to tell who is good and who isn't."

The fathers called because they thought they could do a good job with the children after divorce. They had been helping rear the children throughout the marriage, so why wouldn't anybody believe them that they could do it after the marriage ended? Why, indeed?

Of course, many fathers can. In this chapter we will share with you the experiences of the 114 divorced fathers with custody who participated in our latest questionnaire research. We will add to this the information gained in our earlier questionnaire study of 33 fathers.[2] We will also add impressions and insight gained from interviews with another 50 or more fathers over the years in seminars, counseling sessions, and from our experiences as an expert witness in court investigations. All in all, we will weave together the experiences of at least 200 fathers in nearly every state. Their collective insight and counsel is astounding to us.

The chapter will discuss six major issues: the best interests of the children: how to decide custody; custody arrangements: when does mom get the kids?; how was custody negotiated?; personal advice for fathers from fathers; sorrows; and joys.

In the Best Interests of the Children: How to Decide Custody

A few years ago John DeFrain sat down with a father who was fighting for custody of his daughter. His lawyer had suggested that we meet.

"What can you do to help me?" the young father asked after outlining his story, a case that seemed airtight.

"Nothing," was John's immediate and customary response. "I will interview your daughter at length. I will interview your ex-wife, your parents, and any other important people who may shed light on the situation. And I will probably come to a conclusion. But I won't and can't do anything for *you*, personally, because I see my professional duty as trying to determine what is in the best interests of the child."

The father was taken aback by the candor of the reply but quickly saw the logic and strength of this position. The question is not what Mom wants, or what Dad wants, but what can be done to further the child's development?

No easy task, of course. And probably a foolish and presumptuous one in which to engage. But necessary.

Many fathers suggested this kind of approach when we asked them about how custody decisions were made in their family.

Seek Professional Help. "Seek qualified professional psychological guidance, and get at least a second opinion. It is an emotional time and it is difficult to think clearly," one father argued.

And be honest with yourself, a second father added:

Be honest in your feelings about the children's needs and your own needs. Don't fight to get the kids just to support your own martyrdom. If you don't want the children or don't feel you can handle having them, don't take them, even if your ex-spouse doesn't want them either. They will adjust to not living with either of their parents, but if they are forced to live where they

are not wanted, they'll never get over it. However the arrangement ends up, be prepared to live with it. Keep in mind that
circumstances could change in the future.

This point cannot be stressed too much. Many fathers are so
frustrated and angry about losing their wives that they confuse their
emotions for genuine interest and ability in caring for children. Alcoholic and drug-abusing fathers are especially good at deluding
themselves in this way; they may have been abusive to their families
and jobless for years, but when the wife leaves them they plot to get
her back by holding on to the kids. It is a tacky ploy, and judges are
particularly adept at seeing through it.

A professional counselor can help a father look at his motives in
a tough, clear-eyed manner. This examination can save a lot of
money and heartache in the long run. If one does not like the results
of the interview, one can easily gain a second opinion.

Consider the Child's Welfare. A few more eloquent echoes on this subject need to be heard:

> Going through a divorce is very hard on everyone. Children are
> often hurt the worst. Put some of your own feelings aside and
> think of what is best for the child. Be honest with yourself and
> your child. After all, you have choices and options that they
> don't have the freedom to make.

and

> The children's interests and needs must be paramount.

Professionals are usually extremely skeptical about people's abilities to reason things through when they are under the pressure of a
family in collapse. Some divorces, of course, are not consummated
with a bang but a whimper. All emotion drained out long ago from
a devitalized or burned-out marriage, and many people are capable
of being quite rational. But this situation is not necessarily the rule,
by any means, as one father noted:

> Hopefully, both parents should be adult enough to make their
> arrangement in the best interest of the children or to get coun-

seling to help. But being a parent doesn't make a person adult and mature, and I feel that many times the children end up the losers.

A judge we know once told of how he sat mystified in court for nearly an hour while a divorcing couple argued vociferously over who got to keep a 10-foot-long iron pole. Professionals accustomed to seeing such behavior on a regular basis are naturally going to look at proposals with a great deal of skepticism.

In sum, the goal should be "to reach agreement as peacefully as possible, with the welfare of the children the primary concern," one father concluded.

Communication between Parents. Open and honest communication is essential in a discussion of the children's future. Many fathers stressed this point. Poor communication is a major reason many marriages fail, of course, so it may be beyond many people's abilities to work things out sanely. But other marriages died in spite of good communication; people can talk clearly with each other and still disagree, or agree that there is nothing left to hold them together. Furthermore, sometimes people "grow up" while going through a divorce. Irrationality may have wrecked the marriage, but some people can use the occasion of the divorce crisis and make the best of a bad situation by agreeing not to use the children as weapons against each other.

In one father's words:

Important decisions regarding the children should be shared, if possible. When the attitude is right, I feel joint legal custody should be attempted. When this is not possible, the parent without custody should be encouraged to visit or take the children as often as possible, preferably in a regular routine.

Another father urged parents to rise to a spiritual level when trying to solve some of life's most difficult problems:

The parents must sit down together and discuss the matter. Priorities must be established, along with goals and also available resources. The welfare of the children must be in every decision they come to. The best advice I would give any parent

would be to give "God" a chance. Troubles sure seem to be of
lesser importance with Him by your side!

Other fathers urged that *all* the pros and cons of a custody arrangement be discussed before reaching an agreement. Do not go in
with a totally preconceived notion of what is right, for your ex might
have some very good points you simply overlooked in the heat of the
moment.

It is of course hard for many people to be this reasonable. Some
bring such a rabid will to win into the divorce discussions that you
would think that they were playing professional football in the Super
Bowl rather than worrying about the welfare of their young. For
example, one father said that he had spent $100,000 in lawyers' and
counselors' fees trying to win custody of his children. Does this
make good sense?

Another father countered: "Forget about lawyers and courts.
Settle amicably, then go through the legal proceedings." There is a
certain amount of wisdom in such an argument. The "system" often
makes matters worse by adding to the miscommunication and confusion. Having attorneys act as go-betweens can complicate dialogue. The process often comes to resemble the old circle game we
played as children: whisper something in the ear of the kid next to
you, and by the time it comes full circle back to you, the message is
gobbledygook. Attorneys, and counselors too, for that matter, can
add to the gobbledygook. But usually the situation is so mixed up
when the professionals show up on the scene that they can offer some
good advice. The professional then is a necessary evil.

A handful of other fathers' opinions about communication bear
repeating:

Never belittle the other parent.

Be adult. Be objective. See an unbiased professional if objectiv-
ity is not possible. It's best if a mutual agreement by the parents
can be worked out. They're the only ones who truly know
what's best for their children. An arbitrary decision by a judge
is the least desirable. Whatever way it comes out, though, both
parents must support the decision and help the kids adapt to
it. Using kids as messengers or trying to get the kids to undo
the agreement and live with the absent parent is a trauma the
kids can't handle. Don't force them to choose.

Although divorce attests to the fact that a marriage is ended for personal, private, or other reasons, the kids do not initiate the legal procedure. They are not dissolved when the decree is finalized. So a cool-headed custody arrangement should be worked out. If this can't be done, then let the battle begin, and hope there's enough humor in it to make it worth a chuckle or two when the kids grow up.

The Child Needs to See Both Parents. Single fathers were generally as firm on this point as mothers: "Let the children see as much of the other parent as possible. Don't try to turn the children against your ex-spouse. Try to forget your own anger toward your ex if there is any."

Another father added:

First and foremost, consider the effect on the children. If hatred is felt by one parent for the other, that hatred is going to be expressed vocally around the children. Consequently the children learn to hate one parent or the other for disrupting the home. If at all possible, try to part as friends and explain to the children, in tones of compassion, that the life-styles of the two parents were so totally different that divorce was inevitable.

Fathers Can Be Capable Parents. Many fathers had been through bitter court battles and firmly believed in their ability to rear the young:

The woman is definitely not always the one who should get custody. Consideration should be given to the father. In our case, the mother was alcoholic, having affairs with other men. Father was an educator and did most of the upbringing of the children.

Another father concurred:

I think custody should go to the most capable parent and the one who is willing to do the best job. I don't think it's right that the mother has an edge over the father. My son was fourteen and a half at the time, and he decided for himself. His decision was worth about 80 percent of the court decision.

It is interesting to note how many fathers believe that in society's eyes the mother has an edge when a court proceeding is begun. The fathers argue that mothers automatically have what it takes in the judge's eyes because that has been the so-called traditional pattern of childrearing. It is equally interesting to note how many mothers believe that fathers have the edge in court because of all the recent interest in changing male roles. From an objective standpoint we see no valid way of finding out who is right on this question. It would be, of course, an extremely myopic judge who would be swayed by tradition alone in such an important issue. And for that matter, we doubt that many judges are persuaded that current trends are producing more nurturing males to the point that they do not examine the merits of the individual father in the specific case.

We should all probably give the average judge more credit for intellect and action in good faith.

Stability and Change. Many fathers stressed the importance of stability in an unstable world:

> The children should have a stable home. Generally it is best to encourage sibling relationships, as these are more permanent. Children should be encouraged to discuss their problems with other children to realize that their problems are not caused by divorce but by the nature of life itself.

and

> I feel that custody should be given to the parent most likely to give the child a stable home and much love.

But others cautioned that adjustments in the custody arrangement would be necessary because circumstances can easily change: "Arrange in advance for visitation adjustments if either parent begins to engage in unfit behavior in the children's presence: sex, drugs, excessive use of alcohol, abuse (physical or mental)."

Custody Arrangements: When Does Mom Get the Kids?

People often accuse behavioral and social scientists of confirming the obvious in their impeccable and seemingly endless studies. This is often the case, but actually most people are quite skeptical of research findings that contradict common sense or some hallowed social stereotype.

One of the sweet benefits of research for the researcher is to have the data rub a little egg on his or her own face. It is somewhat exhilarating to be surprised and perplexed by the results of the investigation; the game is more interesting this way.

One stereotype we bought into in 1978 when we began the study of fathers with custody was that of the divorce scenario itself. We expected to find a good number of families in which the mother left for career reasons: *Upper-middle-class mother, tired of the burdens and tedium of motherhood, goes off to law school so she can work in a ghetto legal aide program and save the world. Liberal, white-collar, androgynous father understands perfectly and is actually rather pleased to have the chance to spend even more time with the kids.*

Looking back on this figment of our imagination that seemed so obviously real at the time, we can only chuckle at how ludicrous our unresearched assumptions were. There may be a few mothers like the one just described, but many more follow different patterns.

Fathers, we found, generally tend to get custody of the children under very trying and troubled circumstances:

The mother may be incapacitated by disease, alcohol, or other drugs.

The mother may have completely broken down emotionally, been labeled mentally ill, and placed in a hospital or other institution.

The mother may have become extremely violent and tried to kill the children, her husband, or herself.

The mother may have fallen in love with another man or woman and left the children with the husband for any number of reasons.

The mother may have been emotionally and/or physically abused by the father and fled the family, feeling that if she pacified him by leaving the children he would not hunt her down for vengeance.

The mother may be fed up with marriage and parenthood.

The mother may feel that the father is the superior parent.

The burden, joy, and responsibility of parenthood generally still falls on mothers in our society. Mothers do not easily, thoughtlessly, or joyfully forsake this responsibility. We do not want to reinforce a stereotype, but it is probably based on fact: fathers generally can get out of parenthood with less social and emotional cost.

Therefore, when you ask the question, "When does Mom get to see the kids?" you do not get many people who reply, "Never" or "Rarely." But a small minority of fathers do respond this way: "My ex-spouse wished to have nothing to do with our daughter." Or: "Mother hasn't seen the kids since she left a year before."

Scheduled Visits. What follows is a potpourri of schedules. All seem to have pros and cons for the families:

> By mutual agreement my ex-spouse is supposed to have the children every other weekend, every other holiday, one week at Christmas, six weeks in the summer. Through no fault of mine, the children rarely see their mother. Maybe she comes to get them once a month for one day. This has been her procedure since the divorce.

> Ex-wife has children on Wednesday nights and brings them home for bed. Usually has children on Saturday, sometimes overnight, sometimes not. Alternating every other holiday.

> My ex-wife has our little girl one night each week, every other weekend (6:00 P.M. Friday to 6:00 P.M. Sunday, one week at Christmas, two weeks in summer. Working well. I enjoy the breaks.

> Our ten-year-old boy spends time with his mother on weekends. She seems to prefer it that way. There are times when I feel he prefers not to be away from home, but he realizes she is lonely.

> She gets them biweekly from 6:00 P.M. Friday to 6:00 P.M. Sunday. Three weeks in the summer, Christmas week and Christmas day, and Mother's Day. The children are always upset when they return home because of their mother's male friend, whom she is living with.

Ex-spouse has visitation privileges every other weekend and on Wednesday nights in the week in which she has no weekend visitation privileges. She seldom takes them on Wednesday nights and occasionally skips her weekend visits. While giving the kids a chance to see their mother, the visitation causes problems with their activities and schedules.

Ex-spouse picks up Tuesday evening and takes children to school Wednesday morning. This seems to work well for me, but ex is unhappy with the mornings. Children like it. Ex picks up every other Friday evening and returns them after Sunday school at about noon. This is fine with children. Ex would prefer 9:30 A.M., I would prefer 5:30 P.M. Therefore the compromise.

My ex-wife is supposed to get the child every other weekend. We still have a lot of problems. Mother has spent two evenings with her in the last six weeks.

The mother visits her son two to three days a year, only during daytime hours per court order. One week a year he stays with ex-spouse's parents for summer vacation, and ex-spouse visits at this time, also, per court order. The mother is lesbian.

Again, as we cannot emphasize too much, the arrangements are all extremely individualized because the families are all unique. Common currents through all of them are the theme of continuous change and negotiation and the need for compromise and flexibility.

Living in Different Cities. Visitation is complicated in numerous families by distance. One ex-wife lives in Las Vegas and the father in Los Angeles. "She sees our five-year-old son for two to three days every two to three months." This is fine with the father, and the son apparently does not mind.

Another ex-wife lives in California, while Dad and their daughter live in northern Indiana. "I won't allow the child to live with her mom because of her live-in arrangement. I feel this is very harmful to the six-year-old girl. Things work out quite well this way."

Four thousand miles separate another son from his mother. Distance in this case makes visitation "unlikely to happen."

We always encourage divorcing spouses to think through residence issues before signing the final papers. No matter how you slice it, long distance can be deadly to a parent-child relationship.

Several fathers expressed dismay after their ex-wives moved away:

> My ex-spouse is attending school in a city two thousand miles from here. She is welcome to see her children at any time. They may visit her at any time. Although two children live with me only one is under age and thus in my custody. Legally, I'm to allow my ex-spouse "reasonable" visitation. Under the circumstances regular or scheduled visitation is impossible. The situation is working OK, although both my wife and children miss one another.

> I have the children 100 percent of the time because my ex-wife has moved away from the area and has a personal need to pursue. Down the road she intends to have the children spend time with her. The arrangement is difficult for me because it consumes all of my time. It is difficult for my ex-wife because it isolates her.

> When first divorced (five miles between us), my ex was to get the children every other weekend, but no pressure was to be put on them to go. If they had activities to go to or friends invited in, they were to go only if they wanted to. The children were free to spend time with their mother whenever they wanted to. When their mother moved to Arizona, one of the children (now eighteen) moved out there also. When her mother started dating and spending nearly all her free time with her boyfriend, the child suffered extreme trauma. After six months the child (fourteen) moved back with the rest of the family in Alabama. Because of distance and money the children only see their mother once or twice a year.

Unscheduled Visitation. This approach tends to signal sporadic contact between mother and her children. One father who won the children in a court fight said, "My ex-wife takes the children on the average of two weekends a month, and that is the most she ever asks for them. Sometimes she does not even call or take them for a month." Another father explained, "I am an accountant, and during the tax season my son stays with his mother. Other than during this time, my son sees his mother approximately once a month at her convenience."

Unlimited Visitation. As in all the other categories, there is here a lot of diversity. In some cases it works well, in other cases it does not work, in some cases it guarantees a good deal of contact between mother and children, while in other families visits are few and far between.

One father expresses the complaint we hear so often from mothers with sole custody: "My ex-spouse has unlimited visiting rights to the child. But she only sees the child every ten days to two weeks. I would like her to see the child more often."

Another father has agreed to unlimited visitation but feels compelled to put some strings on the deal:

> My ex-wife can see our son whenever arranged. We have been separated two and a half years, in which time she has called and arranged to see him all of about eight times. I don't know how often I would let her see him if she was so inclined. He's six. This summer she wants to keep him for two months (she lives eight hundred miles away), but I feel I can only let her have him for two weeks. I don't like her new husband.

Two other fathers with unlimited visitation were pleased with the arrangements. "My ex-spouse has visitation rights at any time with my permission. There is no set time. This arrangement works well," one explained. The other added, "I have custody. The mother has reasonable, agreeable visitation rights. This seems to be a frictionless, working arrangement."

Another father's story demonstrates the mistrust, bargaining, and strife that can cloud issues:

> My spouse may see the children whenever she wants. She has thrown the two oldest boys (fifteen, thirteen) out twice when they stayed with her. She lives with another man. She had custody the first year, and I offered her $5,000 to let them see me. She laughed. My lawyer told me a year later to go pick them up because I would get to keep them. I did this the very next day. I believe she kept them that first year thinking we would get back together. But this time it was too late to even consider.

As the reader will recall, mothers with custody often lamented their lack of a social life. A number of fathers echoed these feelings. One mother had unlimited visitation opportunities, but the father said that she only saw their three-year-old one weekend a month. "This is a strain on me," he wrote. "I don't have time for myself. She really doesn't want to spend much time with him, though. She appears too busy."

How Was Custody Negotiated?

The circumstances in which fathers retain custody of their children are incredibly varied. The stories are rich and emotion-laden, and almost defy classification. Because of the uniqueness of each situation there are theoretically as many categories to describe them as there are radii emanating from the center of a circle: an infinite number. However, we can define a few broad groupings in relation to issues that come up time and again in the fathers' testimony.

Mother Moved Away. For some mothers the promise of a career or a new relationship outshines the thought of continuous contact with the children. One father noted:

> There were no problems with custody. The children, aged seventeen and nineteen, wanted to stay here to finish school. My ex-spouse wanted to go to school two thousand miles away. Had she stayed here she would have had custody. Since the children are girls we felt that they should live with their mother if possible. Under the circumstances it has worked out very well. However, the children are older. Had they been younger it might have been another story.

Another father was disappointed in his ex-spouse's behavior. She moved to Florida to be with a male companion:

> The children are allowed to go to visit her, but she must pay round-trip fare in advance; thus far she has not come through on her promises to bring them to visit her. She is also very poor at communicating at all with them. Until she matures or her present male-female relationship matures, it is probably best that the children do not get caught between her and her pres-

ent mate. I only wish she would show them more love. The rejection hurts.

Mother Did Not Want the Children. In other families the father argued it was clear that the mother did not want custody of the children. In one father's words:

The arrangement we have was worked out between ourselves. She left and told me she didn't want anything to do with the kids or me. So, she doesn't. I know it sounds mean, but if that's the way she wants it, so be it.

He cares for the four-year-old by himself now.

Another father charged bitterly that his ex wanted the divorce, did not want the children, and did want to be "liberated" and start dating again. "I said I wanted our daughter," the father of a two-year-old wrote simply. "She said okay." The mother has nothing to do with either of them now.

In other cases early arrangements do not work out, and the father gains custody:

When we were first separated I gave her custody because she already had two children from a previous marriage. After three months she called and asked me to take our four-year-old. I had him and the other three children every other weekend during the three months. She has not fought the present situation, nor does she pay child support. She has since remarried (to an ass). That is why I won't let her have the boy for two months this summer, only two weeks.

Some fathers are very analytical about the situation, disarmingly intellectual in their recounting of the story:

My ex-spouse seems to have a difficult time relating to the children when they start to show some independence (eleven to twelve years old). She has no tolerance for stress and at times appears very disoriented. While she claims to love her children, she resents the responsibility. At the court hearings, she did not request physical custody. In short, she wants them when she is in need of their companionship.

The mother he described had five children, ranging in age from seven to twenty.

Some people can see a divorce coming a mile away, while others are completely shocked:

> My wife left me and the kids one year ago. In February. She didn't tell anyone where she was going, nor did she leave any notes. I came home from work one day, and all her clothes and her were gone. I reported her missing to the police. After their investigation, which took about a month, they told me she was alive and living in another state, but they wouldn't tell me where. Since then, I have contacted an attorney, and have filed for and have been granted a divorce and custody under the abandonment law in the state of Massachusetts. I still don't know where she is, and she has never contacted any of her family since she left.

This father, age thirty-one, was raising a ten- and a six-year-old. Another father's experience was similar: "The flavor was bitter. One minute she was here, the next she was gone. She left explaining up to the oldest child. She could not say good-bye to anyone. All responsibility was left up to me." She moved 1,200 miles away and sees the children rarely, but when she can, she does.

"Absence makes the heart grow . . . cold," a wry philosopher has remarked. Fathers who watch their ex-wives move away from the children often share this notion: "I believe she'll be only a memory in six to nine months," one lamented.

The Mother Is Unable to Have Custody. Many fathers told us that they received custody of the children because their wives were unable to care for the young. The reasons for this alleged inability differed dramatically.

Emotional instability was mentioned a number of times. Some mothers tried caring for the children at first but could not handle both the problems of childrearing and the problems of personal life. Some were committed to mental health centers or homes for therapeutic group living; in these situations occasional visiting with the children was possible.

A few fathers wrote simply that their spouses had changed sexual preference. On the face of it this is probably no open-and-shut argument for a father's custody, but many fathers and judges believe that it is. One judge of a more open-minded orientation found nothing particularly dramatic about this: "That's just an affair with someone of the same sex. I've heard of plenty of affairs in court." He needed more convincing evidence of the mother's alleged lack of fitness for childrearing.

Several fathers cited alcoholism as the reason the mother was unfit. Alcoholism among mothers is less common than among fathers, but it certainly surfaces, just as the abuse of other drugs contributes to divorce. One diminutive mother with a 5 foot 2 inch, 110-pound frame downed ten free drinks during ladies' night at a popular dance-and-mate hall. When her husband asked pointedly on her return home whether she was "messing around," a mean knife fight ensued. The father fled from the apartment with the baby, chased by the mother, who was wielding a ten-inch kitchen knife. He jumped in the car with the daughter and locked it. The mother jumped on the hood as the father drove off and rode for a mile and a half holding on to the windshield wipers for dear life, before the father stopped and fled through an apple orchard with the daughter.

Such craziness is not uncommon when people mix drugs and anger. In this case the mother spent a year with Alcoholics Anonymous, went back to school, and regained custody from the father, who had retained it on a temporary basis.

The Father's Persistence. One theme that surfaces continually is that of the persistence of fathers.

> I told my ex-wife I didn't think she was financially or mentally prepared to have the children. When we both feel she is prepared we will renegotiate. We had no help. It took five months, and the "flavor" was push-pull. The hangups were what people would think about traditional roles being switched; this was difficult for her. The process was gradual: arguing, talking, and crying. I was firm and unyielding because I felt the children would be better off in this environment. [This father is thirty-nine and has four children, sixteen, fifteen, fourteen, and nine.]

Many fathers used money and material possessions as leverage in their arguments:

I decided I could take best care of the child, a girl, age four. I tried to convince my ex-wife of this. To help her make up her mind, I gave her all the equity in our home, all our furniture, all our silver—everything. I kept nothing, moved in with parents. Told ex-wife if she fought custody I would fight property settlement. She agreed I could have custody.

Some fathers exercise a good deal of cunning. A thirty-year-old father of a three-year-old wrote:

I was going to take her to court for the child, but she signed the custody papers at the last minute. I had to be sly to work out an agreement with her. In all it took about three months. She felt she could work and go on with an extra social life and it would not affect the child for a year when she would then settle down. She loves the child, but didn't want to look bad for the relatives and friends to give up custody. She still wanted to be single all over again. She understands now after ten months that we came to the right decision about our child.

Other fathers are adamant about the rights of the breadwinner to the custody of the children. One forty-five-year-old Ph.D. father was married and divorced from the same woman twice:

The first time around we hassled for a few weeks, but since she kept the house, the children went with it. The second divorce, after seeing the life-style and the way she handled the responsibility of child care, I told her that I would live in hell and she would never get a divorce if it meant she would get the kids . . .

The parent who pays the bills should have 80–90 percent custody if he or she wants it. There should be no child support payments. If the parent who pays the bills does not want the responsibility of the children or the children refuse to live with him or her, then he or she should be made to support them.

Fathers, in general, tend to be more persistent in arguments over custody. They often have to be persistent because they are bucking the time-honored traditions that hold that mothers rear children. Also, fathers tend to be more persistent because boys and men are socialized to be more assertive or aggressive. This can have positive and negative results in child custody matters: men who would do a good job with the children tend to hang in there and fight it out; but on the other hand, men who have no business rearing children are often too hard-headed and angry to realize this. In these situations we are thankful as professionals that society has the legal ability to step in and adjudicate. Many mothers are bowled over by fathers who are little more than grown-up bullies.

The Court Battle. Given society's predisposition to award custody to mothers, and men's generally more aggressive nature, it is not surprising to find many fathers—both rightly and wrongly—in court fighting for custody of the children.

One father wrote laconically of a brutal process that must have emotionally short-circuited both parents: "My ex-wife filed for divorce. I countersuited. We separated six months. I moved out. We reconciled. I filed for divorce. She countersuited. We divorced. It took two and half years." The mother has unlimited visitation with no time limits. She rarely visits the children, even on holidays.

We meet few people really prepared for divorce warfare. In the early stages they talk eagerly of how much they love the children and how committed they are, and it is good that they have commitment, for the battle they begin is likely to be one of the fiercest they will ever fight. It will last months, usually a year or more. It will steal money from people who are usually already financially overwhelmed. Three or four or six thousand dollars per parent is nothing. Twelve or fifteen or forty thousand is not unheard of. It will dangerously split parents, grandparents, other relatives, and friends over who should win. It makes the objects of adoration, the children, miserable. The games played are ugly, involving: deceit, half-truths, spying, subterfuge, lying, secret tape recordings, private detectives, and Mata Hari episodes in which ex-spouses seduce and counterseduce each other into bed so that they can uncover great truths to parade in court. And ultimately, the judge's decision rarely if ever satisfies anyone. Both sides usually remain frustrated and angry. They continue to feel wronged, and the battle often continues after the court rests. A few months or years later the combatants may be back in court for round two or three or four.

Listen to this:

After several long discussions we both decided the children would be better off with me because of the schooling plus the proximity of all their friends. But we went to court anyway. After a long court battle the custody was given to me. She still confuses the children by giving me a bad time, talking negatively against me. I receive no support from her at all. Yet she continues to harass us, which leaves a very bad relationship for us to contend with.

Or this:

No negotiating. No quarter asked or given. I demanded sole custody. She did also. Law required each to "prove" the other unfit, but this judge remarked that most cases have no parent as fit as either of us. Eight months maternal custody followed, awaiting court and during the first trial, which lasted two months. Regular, strict, grudging visitation during this period. First decision: joint custody. The first such decree in the state: child spent two weeks with me, two weeks with mother, two weeks me, etc. Two homes, two sets of everything: two "Baby Alive" dolls, etc. This went on for fourteen months. Appealed to Supreme Court, which threw out first trial and threw second trial into district court. Child completed kindergarten and most of first grade on joint custody. Second trial gave me sole custody and control over visitation. I swore that visitation would always be liberal, spontaneous, and pleasant for her mother.

This father is a professional and earns $90,000 a year. His child is nine. Now, the mother takes the child to dance class and dinner Thursday night. The child is with her mother for church, horseback riding, hunts, and so on each Sunday from 8:00 A.M. to 8:00 P.M. On one weekend per month the mother has the daughter from 5:00 P.M. Friday through 8:00 P.M. Sunday. Though the father provides memberships and tickets, the mother takes the child to the symphony, opera, and plays. The father takes her to aquaria, zoos, woods, and fossil hunting. The mother buys most of the clothes. The father supplies cash advances and charge cards. He encourages them to "flee" the heat of the South on vacation each summer. Last year he paid for two weeks for them in Seattle, the year before, in Maine, and before that, in San Francisco, and so forth.

Here is another case:

> She wanted joint custody, but the son would live with me. A legal clinic (Virginia) lawyer advised against it. The divorce is finalized. I have sole custody. She has reasonable visitation. Three months after the divorce she goes to a lawyer and wants to set the divorce aside. She wants joint custody and wants the house (one half) to be deeded to our son. In the original agreement I took the house and debts in lieu of child support. The only communication at this time is through lawyers. I refuse joint custody but deeded half the house. I feel she wants joint custody as a manipulative device and also fear she'll take the child to Australia where she is from.

And another:

> My ex-wife and I worked out the arrangement after it became obvious that the court would not grant her custody. Our attorneys assisted us in the process. These negotiations evolved over the thirteen-month period from the date we separated to the date of our divorce decree. Initially I filed for and was granted temporary custody. The kids and I moved into a new house. We lived there throughout the process, and still do. As it became evident that the court would not award her custody my ex-wife agreed to award me custody. Her family did not agree with her and placed a great deal of pressure on her to change her mind. She did change for a while but went along with our arrangement finally on the condition that I pay her a lump sum property settlement. My ex-wife pays no child support.

We could have chosen almost any of the hundreds of stories people have written or told us. The standard story has a number of common elements: tears, anger, frustration, vast amounts of money needed from a financially strapped family, endless negotiation and bickering over seemingly minor points, abysmally poor communication, and enormous amounts of time.

   In the graphic words of one divorce lawyer who had seen his fill and declined to do any more custody disputes, "What I saw made me want to vomit. I just couldn't take the madness any longer, especially seeing the kids caught in the middle."

The Parents Agree That the Father Would Be Best. At the opposite end of the spectrum are those divorcing couples who for a number of different reasons reach an agreement without a court battle that the children would be better off with the father.

> When we discussed child custody I was in a much better position and frame of mind to handle this responsibility. My ex-spouse agreed, and there was no problem. Neither one of us hired an attorney. We worked out the arrangements together. I did get some advice from an attorney friend. The child custody and property settlement were discussed and agreed upon about three months after the separation after meeting about two or three times. There has never been a dispute involving custody since the separation. My ex-spouse takes the kids when it is "convenient" to do so for her—approximately two days and one night, on a weekend per month. I feel that she should for the kids' benefit have them more often and more regularly. It would work better if we were all in a routine.

   Another divorcing couple had a similarly rational approach to the situation:

> I stated that I wanted custody, and she agreed with my arguments—that is, she wanted out so I stayed in the house; the children should not move or change friends and schools; I earn more money and so can afford a housekeeper ($55,000). She volunteered taking children on weekends and when she was not working; however, she went from a four-day work week to five, so weekends were left.

Sometimes, this father added, having the children on weekends interferes with her social life, so the father gets them. Also, she sometimes travels with her boyfriend.

A situation like this, in which a father cares for the children while his ex goes off on a holiday with a male companion, makes many men livid. The jealousy and insecurity that helped poison the marriage continue after the divorce. Other fathers seem to take it in stride.

The following account is also remarkable for the smooth way the parents are handling custody:

> My ex-wife felt I would be the better parent for our six-year-old daughter and did not contest my custody. I prepared my own divorce and represented myself in court. I received neither advice nor physical aid. My ex-wife does not pay child support, nor does she offer any help in clothing. This was agreed upon before the divorce. My ex was completely cooperative in all the proceedings and in fact did not even appear in court for the divorce. My ex-wife sees our daughter about one day a month and has gone up to six months without any visitation requests or inquiries. There are no problems at present. The child does not ask when she will see her mom next, and there appear to be no adjustments to be made when going to see her mom or upon returning.

Perhaps the prize for amicable divorce and custody discussions goes to this father and his ex: "Custody was arranged calmly and intelligently with complete agreement on all parts. The complete arrangement, including property division, was completed within ten to twelve hours. The child can see the mother whenever wished."

Outsiders on hearing such accounts often sigh, "If they can be so rational, why don't they stay married?" The fact is, though, that the ability to communicate, while essential to a sound marriage, is only one important element. We may communicate perfectly well with our electrician without being in love with him. These ex-spouses have managed to replace marriage with a sound partnership for the task of co-parenting. Hats off to them!

The Children Preferred to Live with Dad. In many families the children are clearly more comfortable living with the father. Dealing with this situation is difficult, for one must avoid hurting the mother or putting the kids in a painful dilemma, pitting their needs against a desire not to cause pain.

Sometimes remarriage of the mother makes it easier:

My ex-wife is legal guardian of my fourteen-year-old daughter (youngest of nine kids). However, when she remarried, my daughter, the last at home, wanted to come and live with me and finish high school. We both agreed to this. She goes home to Colorado for Christmas and will go back for as long as she wants this summer. At the time of the divorce, my ex had custody of eight kids. We get along very well about all arrangements.

This father charges that the mother's venom literally drove her boys away:

Actually my ex-wife was legally granted custody. However, she lived such a bad life, my son left her when he was twelve and refused to see her except perhaps once a year for a couple of hours. Then, it is mostly to visit his stepsister and stepbrother, whom he is very concerned about. I felt mothers should have the children; however, I could have taken him from her. I didn't want to do that because I wanted him to love and respect his mother. But it got so unbearable he left. She tried to teach him to hate me, but it didn't work. It only made him hate her. I still try to get him to try to understand his mother and to treat her with respect. He says he tries to understand and tries hard to respect her. My eighteen-year-old son also lives with me. His mother treats him very coldly, falsely accuses him of wrongdoing, and never calls or visits him. She has since married and divorced about four or five times and has had many live-in boyfriends.

Life takes many interesting turns and is a rich and varied tapestry that makes the most wonderful novel pale by comparison. The following story was told to us by a man who was married sixteen years and then underwent a sex-change operation to become female. He went from "Mr." to "Ms." It is an unusual story but not so unusual that we all cannot understand. We report his story at length.

My ex-spouse gave the child the ultimatum of making a permanent decision on whom he wanted to live with. I suggested that he try living with his mother. Regardless of my feelings, I felt he would be under less social pressure with his mother. He stayed with her for three weeks last summer in Philadelphia. He threatened to hitchhike back to Albuquerque, so she put him on a bus and called me two days later to tell me he was coming back. Since then, the random phone calls only seemed to upset the child and me for a few days. There were occasional letters, the content of which I don't know. Sometimes he would get a card with two or three dollars. The no-fault dissolution which I started on July 14, 1978, was held up by her Philadelphia attorney for whatever reasons. They had a little hearing on February 13, 1979, in Philadelphia, which they notified me about later, and she divorced me on the grounds of cruel and abusive treatment. My ex-spouse took custody of my new Dodge and elected that I support our son and pay her attorney $1,900. Our child had no idea of this action until the week before my court session in December 1979. He kept insisting things would be all right if I didn't go to court. My attorney had already told me that I had no chance of custody. My court date was kept; the session was interrupted by a long-distance call to the judge from the Philadelphia attorney, and I do have custody of our boy, age fifteen. There seems to be no end to the harassment from all directions. I had no idea that people could be so cruel. The financial problems seem to make things worse. My son wants to stay with me, and I feel that in some way things will work out. One day at a time. My therapist has been a lot of help, but I only call her on difficult things. I can't afford regular sessions. She has had sessions with all three of us and says that I'm doing fine.

An accountant tells a more common type of story. In this recounting a stepfather plays a major role in the adolescent daughters' decision to live with their father. Remarriage is an important step for most divorced people in the healing process. But children, especially adolescents, very often do not welcome the new adult into the family. The person is seen as an intruder and signifies that, in spite of the child's hopes and dreams, the old marriage between Mom and Dad is finally and completely dead. We would hazard a guess that most stepparents are good and conscientious people, but adolescents question this notion and put the interloper to the test.

Read the father's perception of the family's story, and remember that the mother and stepfather would have an entirely different viewpoint.

There were two girls. The oldest was living at home while going to college and was not subject to the agreement. The youngest was in grade school and was to stay with her mother. My visitation rights were spelled out in general terms, as my ex would never have gotten away with denying me visitation. I was on the road and later got transferred, but I was able to see both girls and have them visit me in my new location. This worked very well for me but would not work for everyone. The ages of children are a big factor.

After the ex's remarriage there was no room for the eldest daughter, and I transferred back to make a home for her. The youngest would then come over for the weekend. The oldest daughter has never spent one night in her mother's new home since July 1975. She would go for supper and leave as soon as possible. Neither daughter likes the stepfather at all. The youngest stayed with her mother until last spring when she could no longer get along with stepfather and moved in with me. She has been back for a couple of meals but has never spent the night.

She felt bad at first about leaving her mother, who got her into counseling, which lasted three visits and was terminated at the daughter's request. The ex has accused me of stealing the girls, which is not true. I feel she will have problems some time down the road, facing up to the fact that both girls chose to live with me. I run a traditional family, and both girls have spent Thanksgiving and Christmas with me since the split.

The arrangements were made by mutual discussion. The ex was more concerned with the material things than the children. I am an accountant by trade, and as indicated I did most of my reading about divorce before the split, which I knew was coming. I resigned myself to keeping my emotions out of the negotiations and was successful. I gave up a great deal of monetary benefits to ensure the children's welfare. Other women accuse me of being taken, but I feel the end results vindicate my approach.

Never negotiate when either party is tired, depressed, or drinking. My lawyers drew up the first separation agreement, and hers the next two. It was solely over wording. The lawyers were not involved in the negotiations, and it is best to keep them out if possible. The whole process took about three months, and there have been no problems over the agreement. Custody was worked out the only way it could have gone at that time.

I told the youngest from the first time she expressed her unhappiness over her home situation that I would never take her mother to court over the custody. I told her she would have to make the decision herself. I knew the trauma that would come from such a battle.

I quietly monitored her situation to ensure that there were no serious problems I was unaware of and simply told her that I always would have room for her. My devotion to my children has been the cause of the breakup of several romances.

The youngest is sixteen. She could not watch TV at night with her mother, could not talk on the phone, had to do her laundry before the stepfather came home from work, could not have girlfriends over for the night, and was confined to her room at night. One time they said she was not talking to them, and so they allotted her fifteen minutes to talk before supper. For a sixteen-year-old girl this is ridiculous. She indicates that when alone with her mother they got along well, but felt that she was the cause of trouble between her mother and the stepfather. The ex told her one time that if she and the new husband split, it would be her fault. Now is that not a guilt trip to lay on a sixteen-year-old?

The Bitterness Lives On. We have advised enough parents on custody issues to know that the words that follow are not unique or uniquely angry.

My ex-wife does not consider the feelings of our child. Billie is afraid of her mother. Her mother lies to her and gives her a hard time, both emotional and physical. When Marge left, Billie stayed with me three months. The ex got mad at me, went to school, cussed everyone out, got Billie. We went through the standard divorce: not right or wrong, but "You're female, you get the child. You're male, you get the shaft!"

From the time our child was taken out of school, through the divorce, etc., about six months, she spent approximately 75 percent of the time with me. After that time she came to live with me. I paid child support for almost a year with her living with me before I got custody. Our child was and still is at times put through pure hell. Things happened I don't even like to think about much less put in writing. Judges, etc., must learn that fathers are parents also. Some men are very good parents.

Personal Advice for Fathers from Fathers

No one likes advice, at least on the surface. We listen politely and occasionally acknowledge that our mind was not totally turned off. Sometimes we even say thank you. Some advice is better than other advice. Some advice costs a lot of money. The advice offered by our sample of about two hundred fathers in nearly every state is just about the best we imagine could be given to a father contemplating taking custody of his children or already into the thick of things.

Some of the advice may be contradictory, of course, because the individuals have different worldviews. Most of the advice is usable, but some may not work for you at all. In fact, the advice some of the men give may not even work for them, or they may be deluding themselves into believing that they follow it when they really do not. As with all advice, take what you need and see if it can be adapted for you and your family. Remember: These men have been there.

Keep Busy

Keep busy doing productive or goal-oriented things. Don't dwell on sorrow, but face it as an emotional experience that is part of life.

Try to keep yourself busy doing something positive to ensure some satisfaction of accomplishment and self-discipline in a positive manner.

Don't sit around and feel sorry for yourself. Stay busy growing and being self-stimulating.

Live from day to day.

I wish I had a good answer. You just have to live from day to day. Don't give up. Don't do foolish things that you will regret later. You have to live with yourself forever. It's not the end of the world, you just think and feel it is.

Do Not Feel So Guilty

Try not to feel guilty. The children will adjust fine . . . perhaps better, much better than the parents. I respect marriage very much, but if life becomes unbearable, divorce and try not to look back. We all can endure more than we sometimes think. Life is too short to be negative.

—*This man's child lived with the mother until age twelve, then ran away to the father. The child is now eighteen.*

Remember you are not the sole cause. Guilt can be very destructive.

Family, Friends, Counselors, God

Don't dwell on what you went through. It's too easy to do. Hold your head up and go on living. There are a lot of bridges to cross, but you can make it if you think positively about it. It's easier if you have support from family and friends, but even if you don't have them you still have yourself, and always remember God is with you at all times, and he will help when no one else seems to want to. Just don't feel guilty about anything. Go on living and be happy.

Find a friend to confide in. Stay busy. Keep as good a relationship with your ex as possible.

Don't be afraid. Have a good friend who can keep you stable when you are not actualizing yourself properly and your brain is not in control of your body.

The best thing to do is find a good friend of the opposite sex and enjoy her company.

Don't be afraid to discuss feelings with friends and relatives.

Make friends with people in the same situation (preferably platonic relationships.)

Good and regular counseling should be available. (The court family counselor is a farce.)

CIRCLEVILLE BIBLE COLLEGE

Seek professional guidance, even if you feel you don't need it.
Learn who you are. What are your strengths and weaknesses?
Build on your strengths and improve your weaknesses.

Seek professional help. It's tough to do it alone. It gives you
moral support and confidence.

Read

Read books that help with the children.

Read *Creative Divorce,* by Mel Krantzler.

Read all you can about assertiveness and Transactional Analysis.
Read everything by Dr. Wayne Dyer.

Establish Goals

Forget the past. Set new goals and work toward them. If you
have custody of the children, all work together for the good of
the family. Above all go to church and bring the children regularly. Don't go anyplace without the children. Let them enjoy
the good times with you (vacations, movies, camping). Also,
share the work. Give each child (depending on age) a chore he
or she can do to help out so all the work is done, and the parent
isn't worn out so that he is too tired to go anywhere together.

One must keep a proper perspective of himself and the action
he is going through. He is not the first or the only one to be
experiencing the pain and feeling of not belonging. Establish
immediate and long-term goals, with a positive expectation
that these will be fulfilled.

Look to the Future

Don't sit around feeling sorry for yourself. Discuss your feelings
with close friends or a counselor. Try not to look back. Just look
ahead to the future. Be positive. A counselor can be extremely
useful, even if there is no chance for a reconciliation, because
you will learn about yourself and how not to make the same
mistake again.

Try to leave the past behind you. It's over and nothing can be done to change it. Look to the future and all the new opportunities it will bring. Above all, try not to repeat the same mistakes.

Due to the heavy shock of my situation, as she walked out and announced she had changed her sexual preference, totally unbeknownst to me, I'd say finish the divorce proceedings rapidly and move on to new horizons, as soon as possible.

Do your best to make it a positive solution without guilt or feeling sorry for yourself. Keep busy. Develop new friends and interests. Don't carry the hurt and anger. Face up to it and go from there.

Take Time for Yourself

If you have ended up with custody, give yourself a safety valve. Provide for a way to get away, especially at first. Suddenly being both father and mother can be a drain and requires getting used to. At the same time, learn your new responsibilities as quickly as possible. Don't put off learning how to make ponytails.

Be sure and take time out for yourself, to get out and relax. I haven't given enough time to myself in the past year. As a result, I have not dated in a year and have lost contact in that respect.

Get out and meet other people in the same situation. It helps to be able to talk to others with the same problems. Do not harbor anger, as it only hurts you and sets up a bad environment for the children.

I'm still adjusting. I take it a day at a time. This too will pass. Take time to read, reflect, know self.

Personalities are so different from one person to the next that each individual needs to look within himself to know himself before an adjustment can be made.

Be Yourself

Be yourself, don't be adversely influenced by the views and opinions of others.

Accept, adjust, go forward, be yourself, don't stop living. Life is too great to waste.

Try being yourself, since you may not have had the opportunity while married.

Don't try to be two parents for your children. Just be yourself and do the best job you can.

Some people can handle marriage, some can't. The bullshit society gives those who can't is sometimes too much. The best advice is to stand firm, look the world in the eye, and say, "To hell with you. I know what I need. I know what I can handle, and all these stupid rules don't work for me. Maybe I can handle a marriage, maybe not. Maybe I can handle children, maybe not. Don't condemn me for being me. God put me together with my unique chemistry and needs. Get off my back."

The Emotional Battle: Handling the Hurt

I am far from an average person: extremely rational with a high desire to control my environment; an introvert, self-sufficient and with extremely high abstract intelligence. I would recommend all, however, to use the emotions (generated in the divorce battle) as a catalyst for self-improvement.

—*This father fought for his children in court and won. He claims his wife abused them.*

A divorce is an emotional severance as much as it is physical. A life dies, but the body remains to perform the autopsy. Living, healthy, functional emotions are questioned as to their contribution to the death. The only advice I can give is: first accept yourself and know yourself. Realize that any decision made by you, you are totally responsible for.

—*The words are from a forty-six-year-old American Indian, the custodial father of four children, ages twenty-one, sixteen, four, and four. Both parents agreed to this arrangement.*

One must travel through the emotional valley of hate/rejection, etc., to a positive point of benign apathy and from that point reassess one's priorities and attitudes. There must be a rediscovery of who you are and what values are required to achieve the contentment necessary for a meaningful existence. The pain will go away, but you have to experience it, and no one else can do it for you.

I would think it would be important to rationalize the whole situation, past and present, and to put things in their respective places. Have a good look at self, reevaluate, and set new goals in life.

After nineteen years of giving myself to one person only, the hardest adjustment is the hurt. It is lonely and painful. Is this what the rest of my life is going to be like, will things change? The only thing to believe in is God and myself. I feel that to adjust successfully, one should hold self-confidence at top priority.

Ensuring optimal adjustment is impossible in the short run. As bitter as my feelings are, I would still be open to reconcile under the right circumstances. But that internal battle makes it hard to adjust.

If you had any good type of marriage to begin with, I don't think there is any advice to give except to let time take its course. Divorce is a traumatic experience, at best.

You Are Better Off Apart

Hopefully each can realize that they are better off living separately than they were together. From that point on, everything they can add to self-appreciation and self-respect will pay dividends in permitting them to relate to the children.

Do Not Change Your Environment

You need some time alone. Don't change your environment too drastically. Divorce is very difficult. If you separate yourself from other things too soon—friends, community, job, etc.—it is really tough. My ex-spouse has had a real struggle. (She moved two thousand miles away to attend school.)

Dating and Remarriage

Don't feel obligated to date, to be unnaturally social because of the divorce.

Do not jump right back into another marriage until you've had time to control your own emotions and can think clearly without your emotions clouding your judgment.

Children

If you are even halfway sure of yourself, don't let others influence your decision to have custody of the children.

Sorrows

The results of any decision or any road taken in life are always a mixed bag: good and ill abound. In our final sections on fathers with custody we will explore the joys and sorrows fathers perceived in their situation. We will end the chapter on a high note, the joys, because survival requires that fathers keep the faith that life gets better and that all in all, it is worth living.

The list of difficulties that the fathers generated was very long. Keep in mind that each father had his own unique list, with a few major items. Fortunately, no father had every item on the list to contend with.

The Family Unit Is Broken. Even though the single-parent family is seen as a family by virtually all professionals and probably by most people generally today, it is not a complete family in the eyes of many of the fathers: "I feel sorry for my children (ages seven and five) because they don't have their real mother anymore, and their family unit is forever broken." Mom, Dad, and the kids are no more.

Single parents can certainly do an adequate or excellent job rearing children alone. There is little question of this, for millions of families function perfectly happily with one adult. And, as more single parents—both male and female—will tell you, family life generally got better after the marital separation. Not in all cases, of course. But in the majority of families the healing process began when one spouse left. Tension and conflict began to dissipate.

But this is not to say that a single-parent family is the ideal. Few single parents would argue that. A team of two happy, loving parents who get along well are going to be better at homemaking than is one happy, loving parent. In this sense the fathers who lamented "the lack of complete family life" are indeed correct.

Parenting Is a Two-Person Job. Before the reader gets angry about this statement, read the father's explanation:

> Raising children is a two-person job. One person is not always available, not always feeling well, not in the mood, etc. One parent cannot be totally responsible for another person (child) or feel that another person is totally dependent upon him. If that's the case, he'll go crazy. He must rely on friends, neighbors, relatives, etc.

We are indebted to this father for the pained honesty of his words.

This is not an attack on single parenthood or single parents. They do not really need any more nonsense heaped upon them, for social stereotypes—worthy foolish ones—abound. But there is a poignant truth in this father's words: "At times, I feel my son is missing the beauty of a mother-and-father relationship that could aid his growth. I do at times need more time to develop myself."

Father Misses His Ex-wife. Marriages end legally in the split second of the judge's gavel falling. But the emotional shock waves reverberate across a person's psyche for a time: "At first, I really missed my wife. I just sat around waiting for her. But I've gotten over that. So I can't see any sorrows with my situation." The mother had walked out and did not want the children.

Letting Go. "I have occasional lonely periods," one father wrote. "This bothers me, and the knowledge that the children will continue to grow and not require the care that you give them." This father's feelings almost sound like a foreshadowing of the so-called empty nest syndrome. We note with pride that some fathers are able to get so intensely involved with their children. Fortunately, empty nest syndrome is well publicized but almost never terminal. Parents survive the children's leaving home and learn to love their subsequent freedom from the crushing responsibility of childrearing. But the gradual letting go does cause some pain: "It becomes hard to let go a little at a time. The dedicating that one develops to give them the emotional stability necessary for growth soon becomes unnecessary, and one must adjust constantly."

No Time or Money. The list of problems fathers generated sounds remarkably like the list mothers came up with. Though fathers on the average make several thousand dollars a year more than mothers, money can be a problem for many of them. And time is a problem for almost all. "I don't seem to have much time or money to do the things that I would like. It is difficult for me to meet women, and when I do, getting time to go out or being able to afford going out is just about impossible."

A forty-four-year-old father of two teenagers making $42,000 a year added: "At times I want more freedom to live my own life. The financial burden is becoming very difficult. My ex-spouse should at least be able to take some responsibility for herself. I'm afraid to get involved in another relationship."

Constant Pressure—No Relief. Many fathers added this related notion:

> The bad thing is the constant pressure, seven days a week, twenty-four hours a day, with no relief in sight.

> Time management, having the whole load, not being able to go when you want.

> I am with my kids too much, twenty-four hours a day, seven days a week, etc. We need a break from each other. My social life is virtually nil, because I don't like to leave them alone or with strangers.

Sharing the Joys. As one father said, "The problems of raising a child alone, I can handle. But there's no one to share the joys with." Someone to care for, and someone to care for you . . . children can be loving and kind, but children are still children. The deep longing for adult contact wells up in the hearts of many, many fathers. And some worry, along with single mothers, that they will not fare well on the remarriage market because they bring an instant family with them. "Another woman may not want to accept both me and my children plus her own. Most women I've met have their own children or are older and their children have grown up."

Mother's Loss. Some fathers feel sad that their ex-wife is missing so much. "Mother is two thousand miles away, can only visit on the phone, doesn't get to see growth, joys, sorrows, accomplishments, etc., of the children." These fathers are divorced, remember, but still sorry for their ex-spouse's loss.

Another father told of his ex-wife, a recovering alcoholic: "Mother has recently dried out and has missed many enjoyable experiences with her youngest daughter."

The Children Are Upset over Mom's Behavior. This bothered a number of fathers. One mother, for example, apparently "was the perfect mom, and we were the perfect family." The father charged that she was leading a double life, however, a life foreign to the perfect facade she put on. Finally, she ran away and took the children with her into a life of "smoking, drinking, immorality, selfishness, and brutality, until I received custody."

Another mother apparently wants nothing to do with her son. "That left some emotional hurt when on Christmas there were no gifts from his mom. Also, when it came time for her to pick him up at 8:00 A.M. for the weekend she wouldn't show up, leaving him in tears."

Other fathers charged their ex-wives with being self-centered and abrupt toward the children and with leaving without saying good-bye or explaining why to the children. (One father could not bear to describe what his ex-wife had done to his daughter: "She put her through hell . . I doubt if I will ever trust women again.")

Father Cannot Give Motherly Love. Though some might charge sexist attitudes, a few fathers felt sad that they could not provide their children with motherly love, supposedly distinct from fatherly or parental love. Their words explain what they mean quite well, though: "In my case, having a young daughter (five years), I probably don't have as much patience as I should. Also, being a father I'm not able to provide the motherly love that I think is important for a young girl to be given. Also, it is difficult when she asks, 'Why doesn't my mom call me or want to see me?' "

"I wish my son had more of a motherly influence," another father added. "We live with my parents so my mother fills the gap temporarily." A third grieved that since the marriage broke up when the children were very young, they might never "know what having a mother around really meant."

So very eloquent. The sadness is not because the fathers, as single parents, cannot adequately care for the young. Most fathers apparently can, as far as our research indicates. The sadness remains, though, because there is a beauty that is missing—the beauty that another parent can add to the family. And maybe, just maybe, motherly love is different and is special, just as fatherly love has its unique aspects.

The Children Miss Mother. Many fathers expressed sorrow at watching the children's sadness over not seeing Mom enough:

> My son would like to see his mother more often, but he understands that she has her life and that he can't be included in her life at his will. He gets a little sad when he calls and wants to see her and she has already made plans, but his sadness is short-lived as he is a very active child (age ten) and has a lot of friends, and therefore he finds other things to do.

In this case the custody was amicably decided.

Another father's eight- and nine-year-olds sometimes cry when they do not get to see mother enough.

Many children hoped to see their parents reunite. This persistent dream lasts months, sometimes even years.

One father was obviously frustrated by his ex-wife's behavior:

> She lives with a surgeon, and my son is not free to call her sometimes. This is the fourth person she's been involved with in two years. My son would like to see her more often, but she just doesn't have the time for him. I think she must have a mental problem that she feels this way. He has not heard from her in seven weeks.

Yet another father worries that his son may have difficulty handling the mother's apparent rejection in the future, but so far so good.

> My son has a problem somewhat (I think) with seemingly wanting to reach out and love his mom. Yet she acts as if she doesn't want him. It hurts me to see he has no mother to (who will) accept his love. He has difficulty sometimes being able to express his love. I do believe he may have trouble later in life with this. So far, he handles it extremely well. He's very mature for his age. Now eighteen.

Joys

After reading the lamentations of the fathers, it is clear that the single-parent experience is not all hearts and flowers. But the good times are plentiful, and we believe that it is best to leave the reader on a positive note, for the lives of the vast majority of fathers are, all things considered, happy and fulfilling.

The joys of sole fathers are remarkably similar to those of sole mothers. In fact, our research over the years has demonstrated that the similarities between the fathers and mothers far outweigh the differences in almost every area under investigation: relationships, stress, strengths, weaknesses, joys, sorrows, discipline style, whatever.

A brief look at the joys of fathers with custody follows:

Being Able to Watch the Children Grow. This was the most frequently cited joy:

"With the right moral convictions," one father added, a bit sourly. In this case he was peeved by the mother's live-in boyfriend.

On a more positive note, one father came up with reasons for joy that read almost like poetry:

> Watching my kids become independent and self-confident.
>   Helping them reach their full potential.
>   Recognizing their separateness yet enjoying the warmth and love of oneness.
>   Observing the innocence and honesty of a child.

Another father told of how the mother has gone through a total of four or five divorces. "To see my son's mind develop" is a great joy, he wrote. "He is quite intelligent, and his ambitions are much greater with me. The environment around his mother is extremely negative, shameful. I see him blossom like a beautiful flower."

Other fathers' joy over watching life unfold can be read almost like a litany:

I witness the growth patterns of my son, and it is a joy to be able to see the little things that are involved in his growing and maturing.

Watching the kids grow, helping with their dreams, and hoping they'll achieve a start toward those dreams.
— *This father has four children, ages twenty-one, sixteen, fourteen, and fourteen.*

Watching the growth as they become adults and the little things that they do as acts of appreciation. One enjoys their successes and shares in their disappointment.

I have my son. I can go fishing, to the movies, and on trips with him. I can watch him grow up.

The Love Between Us. One father has truly found that love; it causes him great joy "to see that my children truly love me and are willing to help so much to make us happy in this situation." Another father acknowledged the challenges he faced without a partner: "Now there are only two in our family, and it's much harder on me but well worth it. We have more love and a stronger bond now. It's funny that I get words of encouragement and praise from women, not men." The men may think that this man is a bit crazy for stepping out of his traditional, well-defined role. The women know what he can gain from his new role, if he is smart enough and strong enough.

As authors, our egos demand that we put more of our own words down on paper to edify the reader. But our good sense suppresses this egotistical desire. The fathers describe their lives so much better:

> Joy is knowing your children love you and allowing them to make their own decisions.

> The joys are evident inasmuch as I'm raising two sons who are my very life.

> I enjoy my children. I love them and could never part with them except by their choice.

Having Custody, Having Control. Many of the fathers were involved in a good deal of storm and stress with their wives over childrearing and custody issues, and finally getting custody is seen as a great relief.

> Control! The months of maternal custody while awaiting the first trial date were intolerable. Visitation each Wednesday 5:00 to 7:00 P.M. and Sunday noon to 5:00 P.M. The child was not permitted to leave the house one minute early. A lawyer was called if I returned her one minute late.

Other fathers seem simply to thrive on the responsibility that control brings, and the children apparently are doing well also: "The obvious joy is that I have custody of my kids, and they appear to be very well adjusted living in a single-parent family. They do well in school and are well adjusted socially."

One father was ecstatic over the situation, probably overestimating the positive influence he would have in his children's development: "I have sole custody of my kids, so I alone will shape and mold their futures."

Another father reveled in the fact that "I don't have to share. All of his joys, accomplishments in school, in sports, and so many others are mine alone, consequently the rewards are twice as big."

These fathers may seem to be gloating a bit, but the reader must recall that some of the men have been involved in some fierce court battles, and the thrill of victory after a long and intense bloodletting can unsettle even the calmest individual.

Becoming Closer to the Children. This is one of the major pluses the fathers report. "I feel I have become very close to my son, and have really grown up with him and involved him in a lot of areas where I am interested as well," one father reported. Another father told us that he became closer to the children after adjusting his priorities, putting the children before his job and the housework.

One father felt very special: "I believe the opportunity to get this close to my daughter is one that even very few happily married fathers ever have or exercise. This has been one of the very few benefits of the divorce. Sorry it had to come this way." And, like many single mothers, a lot of single fathers go above and beyond the call of duty to make their children's lives fulfilling: "My son and I are terrifically close. We get along and communicate extremely well. Many people who know me say that I have done more with my son by myself than they have done with their children with the help of a spouse."

Enjoying the Children. For most divorced men, contact with the children is woefully reduced. The poignant picture of the Sunday afternoon father buying his daughter cotton candy at the zoo sticks in our mind. He sees the little girl four synthetic hours a week, and they visit a different attraction each time, but genuine parenting is impossible. He cannot nurture, teach, or discipline much. He is left to be a tour guide or an uncle who brings presents.

On the contrary, many single fathers with custody are pleased to be really able to enjoy their children. "Being able to share with my son, especially as I see so many men become separate from their children." Another proud father added, "I get great pleasure from being with my son. I know of no other divorced man who even considered taking custody of his children. This gives me a sense of accomplishment since I do have him and am making it work."

Doing Your Best for Your Children, and Doing What Is Best for Them. "I know that my child is being taken care of as best I can," one father told us. "And my child cares a lot for me, otherwise he wouldn't be here." Another felt good knowing that he had created a stable environment for his daughter. Hearing her say "Daddy, I love you" was all the thanks he needed.

One big-city father was relieved and proud that he had taught his children to stay away from those "who ran in gangs, got arrested, and raised hell." He explained that he raised his boys alone and that they all turned out well, to be hard workers. "I never had any money to spend on them, but I did spend a lot of time with them." He is justly proud.

There is great satisfaction in knowing that your children need you and that you can provide a stable home for them in which to dwell. "I feel real good that I could keep my son in the same home and area he grew up in and that he could keep his same friends and same school."

The Satisfaction of Being Able to Handle Custody. We again have to let the fathers speak to this issue, for they are quite eloquent:

> The look on people's faces when they find out you have custody of young children. The respect and admiration. Nothing compares to the joy of having custody of the children.

> I have the opportunity to show that a man can raise a happy, loving child as well as a woman. I am no chauvinist and am the first to put in place those who are. Just being able to share in my daughter's life has been a special job and blessing to me.

> Single parenting has been, is, a joyous education. The responsibilities have matured me. I feel more confident, as a parent and in myself in general.

Getting Along with the Ex. One fifty-four-year-old father caring for nine children was especially happy "that my ex-wife and I get along so well. If there is a problem—and we have had few—I get on the phone, and we talk it out and resolve it. Something we didn't do too well when married."

There Is Nothing to Be Happy About. As with the single mothers, a minute percentage of fathers felt so boxed in by circumstances that nothing looked good to them. One father explained that the mother was not financially or mentally prepared to have the children. The father felt that they would be better off with him, but the decision brought no joy, only resignation. Another father without joy in his life works seventy hours a week in a semiskilled job, and the mother rarely visits the children.

In Conclusion

It is terribly difficult to draw any general conclusions about these fathers. Some are doing extremely well, while others are in the depths of despair. On the average, we have evidence to conclude that the fathers compare rather well to mothers with custody. Though it could be argued that fathers—being male—could be guilty of over-estimating their expertise in parenthood, it is probably more likely that fathers who end up with custody of their children after a divorce in general tend to be the cream of the crop. They are probably on the average more interested fathers, more involved, more adept.

Some of the fathers were thrown into raising the children alone almost by accident, but most apparently were active in pursuing custody and were genuinely interested in the children's welfare.

We do wish them all the best, because like all single parents, they undoubtedly have their hands full.

5

Split Custody

Two Parents' Stories

Authors' Note. "Split custody left neither child dealing with the idea that one parent was alone. This helped the boys because in their own way, they felt a responsibility for us, too." In this narrative, a New Hampshire mother with split custody describes a relationship that she and her husband have developed for their two boys' sake. It is difficult, but it works.

We have split custody of the boys. I have the younger boy, and my ex-spouse has the older one. We have *no* set rules. The children determine when they go to the other parent, and we baby-sit for each other whenever the need arises. The boys usually exchange places at least one night a week, and we each visit with the other child almost on a daily basis.

Child custody was never a struggle with us. We discussed with the boys before we separated what was happening, and they were given a chance to state whom they wanted to live with. The older boy chose his father, and the younger wanted to go with me.

This is basically the way we had lived our lives anyway, so no one was really surprised or crushed. However, I felt I would put no restrictions on the son I had in seeing or being with his father when he wanted to, as long as it didn't interfere with school, etc. That is also the approach my ex took with the older son and me.

We no longer loved each other, but we both love our children dearly, and they had to know this above all. We never fought over them, and child custody was no negative issue in our arrangement.

For the benefit of the children, always let them know they are loved, and don't play get-back-at-spouse games, using them as go-betweens. Split custody left neither child dealing with the idea that one parent was alone. This helped the boys because in their own way, they felt a responsibility for us, too.

Split custody really helped my ex and me adjust to divorce better because neither parent was left feeling like a total failure, as we each continued to have a part-time parenting job. I think it's important to remember that everyone is hurting and that healing takes time. Try to conquer the guilt right away, because it can be very destructive. Pray a lot and believe that God forgives and loves you as an individual. Seek support from a group, a counselor, and friends. Don't fool yourself into thinking you can handle everything alone. Let yourself feel the hurt and other emotions, and *deal* with them *now*.

Because of our split-custody arrangement, each child has more individual attention and is praised and encouraged more in his special interest fields. I have more freedom and less frustration with one child than two, which I feel makes me a better person and mother. I also have a good relationship with the son I don't have living with me.

My biggest problem with the arrangement is a daily hurt deep inside for the son that I left behind. I really love him and would love to have him with me. I had to adjust to leaving him at age twelve as most people do when their kids are eighteen. However, I really had to accept him as a person and where he was. I know if I had forced him away from his father that I would have lost him completely.

I would like to have less association with my ex but feel that the door has to be kept open for the kids' sake. I will be glad when our lives can be separated more. I won't do anything to jeopardize my relationship with the son I don't have, so I don't create waves with my ex.

Authors' Note. A Florida father tells his side of the bitter two-year war he waged with his ex-wife for custody of the children. The court decree apparently used the term "joint custody," but the arrangement is clearly that of split custody because the boy now lives with the father and the girl lives with the mother. The father's anger is difficult to evaluate without corroborating testimony from his ex-wife. Is it justified? We cannot know for sure. The fact remains, though, that he is still very angry at his ex, the lawyers, the judge, the psychologist, the social worker. Residual anger is common in custody scraps and can poison relations between ex-spouses for years to come.

I have spent $10,000 for a split custody situation. My son now lives with me; my daughter has chosen, after two years, to live with her mother. The arrangement with both is as follows: either child is free to do whatever he or she wants to with either parent at any time. It's the child's choice. The boy is twelve, and the girl is seventeen.

In my opinion, my former spouse exploited the children and her position by manipulating the court-appointed guardian and the court for personal and financial benefit to herself. Absolutely no cooperation came from her in regard to settling the matter of custody. She refused to consider anything other than her having the children 100 percent of the time. It was impossible to have basic visitation rights, even though these were given as "liberal" by the temporary order.

As a result, a two-year custody dispute raged, and all of this time both children wanted to live with their father, realizing that they would be better cared for.

The twelve-year-old son finally could take no more and moved into my apartment with me, refusing to go back.

The seventeen-year-old daughter at that time chose to remain with her mother. I believe that during the long court process, and being at that age, she discovered that the flamboyant life-style of her mother provided her with all the freedom she could want, and she was enjoying it. Mother was never home to cook, clean, or supervise her.

After almost two years of my own pleas for the kids falling on the deaf ears of the legal guardian and county social services, it was actually my son who finally settled it. He realized where he was, and wanted to go, and then did something about it.

It was rough on me, fighting the court system, but being able to save one of the children was well worth the effort and expense.

As long as both children accepted this arrangement, the

custody was set up as follows: daughter and son are under a joint custody arrangement, giving them two parents. Daughter has physical living arrangement with mother. Son has physical living arrangement with father. Visitation with the other parent is unrestricted, and at the discretion of the children.

After spending almost $1,500 on a court-ordered psychologist for all family members, it is my opinion that it is nothing but a big joke. He did more harm than good, particularly with the children.

During the last three years of the marriage, I was in the position of being both father and mother to the kids, as well as doing most of the daily care and cooking. Through this, I feel that no outsider would be anywhere near qualified to make any improvements.

The representative of Social Services was completely useless, and the legal guardian found it difficult to get out of his chair at all. Both were under thirty years old and had no children of their own or even the slightest idea what life is all about. They just didn't care!

I am a believer in letting teenagers develop at their own pace, with proper supervision and restraint. Their own individual personality is developing, and a good atmosphere is important at this time in their life.

The mood they create for themselves can be complemented with parental guidance and participation, giving the right atmosphere at home. I found this very beneficial to both child and parent's happiness.

I rarely find it necessary to discipline, or even criticize him. Through the years I'm convinced that he knows where I'm coming from and has learned to some extent that his own input into life, or lack of it, determines what type of life he will have.

I must admit that many times I think he is trying "too hard" to please me.

Relatives have been naturally supportive of our family, and I found friends and virtually all of the neighbors, being family people, very understanding and supportive of my efforts to maintain a continuing relationship with the children. They all were aware of how close the kids and I were, all along.

The custody arrangement, through the actions of my son, materialized rather rapidly and forcefully.

After experiencing a two-year legal battle, it is my feeling that the court system leaves a lot to be desired. In addition, the

Social Services Department is a big waste of taxpayers' money, staffed with incompetent and unconcerned employees. This tends to generate a state of indifference and even arrogance in our system.

My daughter has developed what I believe to be serious emotional problems, resulting from the extremely long and traumatic experience.

Any split custody arrangement is definitely contingent on the cooperation of both parents. This case was not the ordinary, inasmuch as my former spouse was acting in her own best interests, not those of the children.

A definite "feminist" attitude developed in the later years of the marriage, along with her extremely flamboyant lifestyle, which developed through her "newfound freedom," and caused many problems for the children during the separation period.

The biggest problem was the court system in general:

1. The guardian *ad litem,* with no regard for the kids' well-being or desires, refused to do his job, by total lack of concern or investigation. He represented the ex-spouse more than the kids. (His law office is located directly across the street from my former spouse's attorney!)

2. An unqualified and incompetent twenty-five-year-old social worker, who was only interested in getting the case off the books.

3. A court-appointed psychologist did more emotional damage to the kids than any number of family problems could create (especially the daughter).

As long as both parents want an active part in the children's life, there should be no doubt in anyone's mind that this is the way it must be, for the children's best interests. The parents, agreeing on the divorce, will have to work out the details. No court should be allowed to prohibit a parent from a relationship with a child, that both parent and child desire—no matter what!

It undoubtedly will be uncomfortable for one, or both parents, to varying degrees, when the children are involved, but nothing can change the fact that these are the only two parents the kids will ever have.

It is difficult to accept the fact that legal people thrive on a family's traumatic experiences, and I can safely say in this case that they even prolonged it to their own financial advantage.

After living two years of sheer hell, and after the smoke clears away, no one will ever convince me that a decision made by obviously unconcerned individuals in our court system must be final, and having to do it over again, my ideas and desires would not be any different—only the method I used.

My advice to other parents would be that parents' problems should not involve the kids. Parents must realize that kids have two parents, not one. Children cannot be used as pawns for personal or financial gain. Work out custody arrangements as quickly as possible, before court, and if possible without lawyers and court involvement. It will be less costly and less traumatic, as well as faster.

Against overwhelming odds, a prejudiced legal system, and prevailing court orders, a fourteen-year-old boy got what he wanted all along: to be with and to maintain a relationship with his own father.

A Unique Option. A curious-sounding term, and not yet generally recognized, split custody is simply a traditional child custody arrangement for *both* parents.

Both parents have almost total responsibility for the care of at least one of their children. Both parents have an opportunity to feel the joy of shepherding a child's growth. And both parents feel simultaneously the strain of solo parenting without battling another adult over form and style.

As far as our research can determine, split custody is the rarest option of all four. Only 6 percent of the parents in our study (forty people) participated in a split custody arrangement. But as we reported in chapter 2, our statistical analysis of the data revealed that split custody was a workable option for parents—probably just as workable as any other option.

And as in all the other approaches, split custody is a unique option for unique families with individual needs. For some families split custody will work well, for others it will be a disaster. For most of the families who have opted for split custody, it is probably the best approach available for them at the time.

Studying the testimony of forty split custody parents reinforces the conclusion we have come to again and again in our investigations: time passes, circumstances change, and people change. Many split custody parents started out with another custody arrangement that

evolved into split custody, and many change again over the months and years. A legal divorce comes and goes quickly. But the *process* of dissolution, divorce, and rebuilding lives goes on and on through many phases.

In this chapter we will be looking closely at: negotiating split custody arrangements; logistics; advice on what is best for children; adjustment of the parents; sorrows; and joys. .

Negotiating Split Custody Arrangements

How families happened to find themselves in a split custody arrangement is a fascinating and intricate subject. All the stories are different. We will share a few somewhat representative stories with you. First, fathers speak:

Open Communication. One father's wife left with both children:

> After being with Sarah and Nancy in Colorado for two months (April and May), Nathan told me he wanted to come back to Arizona with me. I visited Sarah, Nancy, and Nathan in July, and we discussed it. Sarah was hurt but loved Nathan enough to let him come back with me. I loved him enough to take him. The split custody derived or evolved from this. Nathan was the generator, as I would not have wanted to split the kids. We just did what *he* wanted.

The parents evidently had an open enough relationship with the boy that he could honestly express his true feelings without fear. And split custody probably could not have been worked out if the parents had not been able to sit down and talk straightforwardly with each other.

Another father wrote a cryptic explanation of his side of the story:

> Uncontested divorce wanted by father, agreed to only if mother got daughter and most of furniture. Mother running around, father couldn't afford to prove it in court. Southern Alabama judges could have given her all kids just because it is the South. Mother didn't want all kids anyway. Best decision under circumstances was to split family. Not what father

wanted, but wanted wife out now. For the most part negotiations were friendly. Wife had been hitting the bottle and running around for a couple of years.

The Sons Choose. A number of fathers told us how sons wanted to live with them, especially adolescents:

I don't have legal custody of my oldest boy, although he has lived with me for over two years—since a month after my ex-wife moved from my home. My oldest (fourteen) told her he'd rather live with me. I told him it would be all right. She brought him to my house and asked if I said he could stay. When I told her yes, she said, "Good, you take him. I can't handle him anymore." Later (about six months) she wanted him back, but he refused to go.

Adolescent boys can be spirited young animals, and many mothers are intimidated into submission.

A Family Decision. Several parents noted that custody was a family decision, involving input from all involved and a good deal of experimenting to find the best solution to a difficult question:

Ever since the separation we have tried to do the right thing for the children and put aside our own differences. Therefore the decision on custody was negotiated among the four of us, with no outsider involved. The decision was made shortly after separation.

and

Over a two- to three-year period we worked out the age split for the children's best interest, determining that the oldest/ youngest were best together with father and the middle child with the mother. Only hang-up was the determination of this and the shuttling back and forth of the kids to find the proper "mix."

A father of a sixteen- and a seventeen-year-old describes in detail

the changes he and his children have gone through over the past several years:

> I let her set the arrangements. Children should never have to enter into the decision-making process. The mother, since she was with them, set the rules. She knew them better than I and what their needs were while young. They set the limits on what they want now. Daughter is with me during weekends and all vacations and has been the last seven years. Son moved in three years ago. Up to then he spent all vacations and weekends with me if their mother was working. Otherwise, they would be with the one who was going to be home. At first, the first year I was in school or living in odd places and working in a bar after teaching during this time, I would have Darren and Alyssa on some days and nights at least two days or nights a week.
>
> The second year, my ex-wife worked for a U.S. Representative and had to be gone more. I then kept Darren and Alyssa more and picked them up from school and worked only on weekends. At this time I wanted to be closer to them. We did spend the special holidays as a group. I bought a house about a half-mile away from their home, and since their mother still worked in Tallahassee, I took them to school and they came to my school and we went home together (my house). Some of the time I would have them on weekends. Their mother and I tried to work it out so that they would be with one or the other of us when possible. Their mother remarried two or three years ago, and because they were moving to the mountains above Knoxville, the oldest stayed with me. Alyssa went with her mother. Now Alyssa stays the weekend with me and all vacations, for she has the same days off that I do.
>
> I believe they both are better off than to hear people fighting with words. I have had some very bad days in the past but not anymore. The last seven years have been good.

Persistent Fathers. It is amazing how persistent some fathers are. Listen to the following story, a unique one indeed:

> My particular custody arrangement involves six children: two from my first wife and me; three I adopted with my second wife; one five-year-old by my second wife and me. The first two live in Oregon. I see them one to two months in summer. The

three who were adopted live in Arizona, and I don't see them at all. The five-year-old daughter lives with me in Kansas. Her mother has seen her once in the last four years.

My second marriage broke up when my daughter was nine months old. I made a deal that said my ex-wife would get: a car; about $6,000 proceeds from the sale of our home; half of all the furniture; and her three children. I was to get custody of my daughter and would also assume responsibility for all the bills, about $10,000 worth.

After about a year my wife and I remarried. It lasted about two months. When I left the second time she would not agree to give me custody. After about six months, in exchange for $150-a-month alimony, she returned custody of my daughter to me. My daughter is now five years old, lives with me, and never sees her mother, who lives two thousand miles away.

Lawyers and Court. Many families simply could not come to a decision without legal help.

"Our lawyers handled it," one father told us. "The judge ruled visitation rights through convenience to each party. This is fine with me because I wouldn't want it in print that I would have my son on certain times. No way, because I could see it would be to his mother's benefit in some way."

In another case the court decided, giving all three children to the care of the mother. Time brought considerable changes, and the oldest daughter was moved in with the father to finish out her senior year in high school.

Lawyers often help parents fight fire with fire. The intricate maneuvers may be legal and "part of the game" of law, but they certainly do not do a whole lot to smooth things out in the family:

As long as I would have agreed with my ex-wife everything would have worked out nicely. The only hitch, I would only have been able to see the boys (nine and seven) at her convenience, and they would have lived with her. So I countered, asking for complete custody of both boys, and the whole process slid downhill. She wanted the divorce, the boys to live with her, but I could see them when her work interfered. Her lawyer drew up the papers, I contested with same.

The hearing was very brutal. I was accused of many untruths. On my part, I did not dispute her ability to be a mother at her convenience, but that both boys spend more time with me and that I was the better parent. In the end, the judge split the boys. I did not get custody of the youngest because of his "tender age."

I was a no-good according to my former wife. The preliminary posturing spread out from June through December. Then I was summoned back into court when I moved, but the court agreed with my decision to move after the fact. I had a lot of legal advice, but very little *help*!

I have been accused of keeping one boy from his mother and forgetting the other boy completely.

It is obvious that each scenario is a bit different from all the rest. Let us look more closely at what the mothers with split custody had to say. Most of the stories defy categorization because they are a complex mixture of many interrelated elements. A few themes do emerge, though, which we will highlight:

A Free-spirited Son. Split custody often occurs in the teenage years when a youngster begins to feel his oats. One mother of a seventeen-year-old boy and fourteen-year-old girl explains:

There was no negotiating. He did not fight for custody, and I agreed readily to weekend visitation. One year later my son elected to move with his father. He wanted to have a "free life-style" of no rules and regulations. It has been extremely trying for me to see a young fellow waste his life. His father has allowed him to "drop out" of school and have a permissive life-style. As a result of this I rarely see him—he chooses not to visit due to parental pressure from me. My daughter visits her dad on Sundays. This works out fairly well.

A Rebellious Daughter. Mothers told of "losing" not only sons to ex-husbands but also daughters. It is probably almost inevitable that this switching around will happen in many divorced families, for the teens have to find out that their fantasy of life with the other parent is a lot better than the reality.

A forty-one-year-old mother told us:

We have two *adopted* children, a girl, sixteen, and a boy, ten. Legally I have custody of both children; however, approximately seventeen months after the divorce my daughter "rebelled" and wanted to live with her father, who is remarried. By mutual agreement and for ultimately the children's wellbeing, she now lives with her father and my son with me. Of course, my child support (again by mutual consent) is cut in half. I am unhappy about "losing" my daughter but feel she is happier.

A mother with three children, ages sixteen, twelve, and two, wrote:

When my husband and I decided to separate (he is large, intimidating, and has used violence on me in the past; consequently, I'm physically afraid of him), he told me that since he pays for the house, HE would continue to live there and I would have to be the one to move. I didn't argue. However, I could not find something I could afford and that would allow children in the same small town.

At this time, my husband and I agreed that since the first two children were older, they should be given the choice of the parent they wanted to be with. Because they are both very active in sports and other school activities, they chose to remain with their father since they didn't want to change schools or friends. Since this was their choice, that's the way things went.

However, the smallest child, being two years old at the time, was too small to make a choice, and there was no way in the world I would leave him behind.

I find the arrangement heartbreaking since I believe they should all be together. Also, because he's said it in front of them so much, the two oldest children, especially the oldest boy, are all hostile toward me since I "left" them. My husband does nothing whatsoever to help the relationship, and I feel he secretly delights in their negative feelings toward me. It is my only hope that, given enough time, they will someday understand why I had to do what I did.

Professional Intervention. Professionals played important roles in many split custody negotiations—both lawyers and counselors. The reviews on the professionals were mixed, of course, but in many cases professional intervention was necessary, for the family was trapped in a quagmire of its own design.

A mother of a two-year-old and a five-year-old wrote:

We discussed what we felt would be fair to all—the children and us—and decided on split custody. I was upset at giving up custody of my son but decided that it was best for all the way we were working it out. There were some problems at first, as I was not sure about giving up custody and he didn't want joint custody. The lawyers helped, plus a counselor. It took about two to three months.

First, we discussed the divorce and what to do about the children. He said no divorce unless he was awarded custody of our son. I decided this was probably fair and he is a very good father, so we went to a lawyer and had the papers drawn up. Then I became upset and went to another lawyer to see about changing it, and he said there wasn't too much chance of changing it without a court battle. So after a lot of discussion and visiting with a counselor we agreed on the final decree.

One mother lost the daughter to the father for mysterious reasons. The son stayed:

Daughter indicated she preferred living with father. Consulted child psychologist—both parents and child. I gave my permission for her to leave. Never knew the reason for her leaving.

I said youngest son stays with me. No discussion on this— my decision! Never have gone to court about anything.

Many custody fights never really are resolved:

It was not worked out. There was tremendous emotional conflict with my son, and eventually he went to live with his father. His father made no attempt at ameliorating the situation and even encouraged the conflict.

I was under tremendous emotional stress at the time and couldn't handle what was going on (in essence, he took over the role of his father toward me).

I went into family counseling with the children, but my ex refused to participate, and when my son went to live with his father, he did not encourage my son to take part in the counseling, so he stopped coming.

In some cases people are happy with the professionals and happy
with the result:

> Occupational change caused ex-husband to forfeit a custody
> fight. Legal advice on both sides was beneficial. General mood
> amiable from point of settlement. I had both children for seven
> years. Last year ex-husband took son back. Although difficult at
> first, I feel impact on everyone has been positive.

"Wooing" the Children. Several of the mothers accused their ex-husbands of unduly influencing the children. A thirty-one-year-old
mother with ten- and eight-year-old children told us:

> I was awarded custody. There was no contest. Several months
> passed before their father showed any interest in visiting them.
> Then he began "wooing" the younger of the boys—he was
> then five—to come live with them when they got married. It
> created much friction between the boy and me, and after sev-
> eral months I agreed to let him go live with them. After several
> months his father contacted his lawyer, and I received papers
> to sign to give him custody of the younger son—which I signed.
>
> I felt then that his father was "game playing" and his going
> to live with him was never in his best interest but that he was
> an "acquisition" on the father's part.

One mother who "lost" her son to the father was very methodical
in outlining the terms of the arrangement. Note that she uses the
term *joint custody*, though we would call the arrangement *split custody*.

> The final custody arrangement in my case:
>
> 1. Joint custody of the minor children
> 2. Open visitation
> 3. Child support from the father given me for the children
>   that lived with me
> 4. I gave no child support to the father for the children living
>   with him, due to his income being much, much higher than
>   mine
> 5. At the age of thirteen or the end of the eighth grade any

child living with me could go and live with the father without an objection from me, if they so desired

The loss of the son caused her a good deal of grief:

I had been a child of divorce at the age of nine.

I wouldn't want any child living with me that didn't want
to. A child loves both parents in most cases.

Our son, who was thirteen and in the eighth grade, was
persuaded by his father that living with him would be the best
"Father and Son, Mother and Daughter" thing. He took him
out of a school he had attended all his life—this was in November—and entered him in another school district to finish up
eighth grade. He graduated that following June. When I
agreed to item number five in the custody arrangement I
surely felt that he would let him live with me to at least graduation. I strongly objected when this came about but could not
fight it.

We lived in the same house for four months after the divorce was granted. The divorce took ten months from start to
finish. We had been married for seventeen years when the divorce was granted.

I remarried after one year of being a divorcée. My second
husband died two years later; no children were born to that
marriage. I've been alone for three and a half years, being a
one-parent family. However, eight months ago I began to date
again.

Life is good and full, and I'd do it all over again to be the
person I am today! My divorcing allowed me to find myself and
who I really am.

One final story of the father's persuasive powers over the children. In this case, the mother of two children, eight and thirteen,
tells of her ex-husband's alcoholism and how she is still distraught
over the "loss" of her son. At first, the children spent weekends with
the ex:

The children were in my sole custody originally, as I maintained
the home. When my son was thirteen, his father pleaded for
his custody (through him). After consulting with minister,

school, his doctor, my family, I agreed to it, primarily so that he could be enrolled in a vo-tech school.

I regretted it then and still am sorry for letting him go. His father did not live up to promises he made. (I kept our daughter.)

After my son went with him to live I rarely saw him, except on Sunday mornings when we attended church.

His father continued to drink after he vowed to quit, and my son had less and less supervision. I was unable to get him back.

The Court Battle. A thirty-five-year-old mother with split custody told of a vicious court fight that still rankles:

The thirteen-year-old son lives with his father. The nine-year-old daughter with me. The children spend one weekend with me together, the next with the father. Both children are with their father on Tuesday nights, and Thursday nights with me.

At the time of separation, we mutually agreed to split custody. After a few months I didn't feel he was upholding his part of the arrangement. I was working part-time, and when the children got out of school, they both came to my apartment. I never knew when or if their father was coming to pick up one or both or neither child, and he was not assuming any parental responsibilities, i.e., washing clothes, cleaning house, buying clothes, doctors' appointments.

At that point my attitude was that if I was going to have the kids most of the time, I would get custody of both and put a stop to the constant upheaval I felt my ex-husband was creating by his noncooperativeness.

At that point he hired a lawyer and fought me bitterly for custody. All the while he had custody of our son he assumed his share of the responsibility and became a model father.

After an eleven-hour court battle, the judge determined that the children were both doing very well in their respective situations, and he could see no reason to change the custody arrangement.

I felt betrayed and angry and had to deal with those feelings, which took me some time. (I still can tune in to those angry feelings from time to time.)

I have, however, dealt for the most part with the negative aspects of a nasty court battle and my ex and I have made our peace. We get along fair to good and are both dedicated to making the situation good for the kids. We have purposely remained in close proximity with one another in order for the kids to be able to walk back and forth. Neither of us has remarried but not because of the children. Each of us was engaged but didn't follow through with marriage for reasons other than the children.

Another mother with three children described two visits to court, six years apart. The first was relatively simple and straightforward. Six years later, it got hotter:

After twelve years of marriage I left my husband and my oldest daughter (then age thirteen) and moved across the state with the two youngest children. A custody hearing granted him custody of the oldest and me custody of the two youngest children. Last year our other daughter (then age fourteen) who had lived with me for six years expressed a desire to live with her father. The court awarded her custody to her father. The youngest (age twelve) remains in my custody.

Our youngest daughter visits her father approximately one weekend a month and for several weeks in the summer. We alternate Christmas visitation. I don't see enough of the older children.

The mother goes on to outline the court sessions:

1972—The first custody arrangement was made entirely in the courtroom, and no one helped. There was no negotiating, and the entire process took two months.

1978—The second custody arrangement was negotiated through the family court commissioner with the help of social services. An outline of the process was given to us, and we spent several hours with the caseworker. The flavor of the negotiations was accusatory, and the hang-up was our entirely different attitudes toward the child involved and her education. The entire process took one month.

Time Flies, a Father Mellows. As amazing as it may seem to angry mothers, many divorced fathers do change for the better over time (and many fathers apparently do not). In the long narrative that follows, a forty-four-year-old mother divorced eight years tells how desperately her son wants a father and how the boy's father has risen to the occasion, finally:

I got the children, then sixteen, thirteen, twelve, and nine. Father had visitation every other weekend but rarely planned this. He asked to see them perhaps once a month. He was busy playing at being single.

Three years later he remarried, and a year or so later our son, then fifteen, went to live with him, as the boy was getting into minor problems and we talked it over. He stayed with his dad for three years, was back with me about nine months, and then enlisted in the Navy. That son came often to see me each week, for supper or with friends—all very casual, as he had a job, etc. We took no legal action on that, as he would soon be eighteen.

The girls never wanted to live with their dad; the older girl never got on well with him. He was most unreasonable with her for eighteen months or so before he sued for divorce. She was never as a result close to him, and now that she is twenty-one, the relationship is strained—there is no genuine fondness there at all.

The younger boy (thirteen in June) had spent the summer with his father. In early fall he (the boy) asked me if he could live with his dad. He really needs a father badly, always had, and now his dad seems ready to take on some responsibilities. So since the boy was just starting high school, his dad and I had the legal papers drawn up and put through the court. The boy had been held back in fifth grade, the year of the divorce, as he was so withdrawn and just wouldn't try in school.

The youngest child, now seventeen, a girl, lives with me, likes to visit at father's *elegant* home but not to live. We have a loose arrangement for her—perhaps one weekend a month, in summer and fall two weeks here or there, and time at Christmas. It's not cut and dried.

At the time of the divorce I got the kids. No way did he want that responsibility. However, after eight years he's mellowed and in particular toward our son, James. James is a delightful teen, nice manners, good humor, a fair student, not an athlete, just a nice kid. So we talked over the custody arrangement *very friendly, for the boy's sake.* I realize James needs a man's influence now very much; he's wanted his dad to notice him for several years.

The first hang-up was mine—emotional. I took it very hard when the boy decided he wanted to live with his dad. I felt rejected, very sad, cried a lot when by myself. But I did get over it. It took three or four weeks, and we did *talk civilly* about legal custody, which his father felt strongly about. Jim spends every other weekend with me. I'm *firm* on that. And time at holidays and vacation. A lawyer (his) drew up the new custody papers with my approval.

Here's another wrinkle: After I got over my sadness at Jim's choosing to live with his dad, then I felt guilty because I enjoyed not having the responsibility of raising a son alone through the difficult high school years. These feelings of sadness and guilt are with me at times even now.

For instance, Jim got a driver's permit (beginner's), and I was really relieved that he can't drive my car. My insurance doesn't cover him as I don't have custody. I thought, "Let his dad have that worry and problem of a teenage male driver. I've done my bit with three other children."

Logistics

We would like to get down to details now. Just how do split custody parents manage time with the children? What are the logistics of all this?

Three major themes emerge from the parents' discussion of the issues: unlimited visitation; the problem of seeing the other children; and scheduled visitation.

Unlimited Visitation. We believe that flexibility is the key to a satisfactory arrangement. Families who have some kind of schedule that is very open to change as circumstances come up seem to be the least burdened by conflict.

One father told us, "My children, that is, the ones I have custody of, spend as much time as they desire with their mother. I really leave that up to them. This works okay for me."

A mother described how the arrangement evolved over the

years. With five children she obviously could use some help, and the
father stepped in to offer it:

> Originally the arrangement was set up for alternate weekends
> and holidays—with all five children going at the same time.
> That helped me. I had some freedom, yet I also could under-
> stand how he felt about not seeing them for several days at a
> time. He was allowed reasonable access on weeknights. After a
> period of adjustment the custody has evolved to the point that
> the children have the freedom to see their father whenever
> they want to. In 1976 I took the fourth child to Spain for the
> summer. Their father took care of the other children that sum-
> mer. He is able to take the youngest child whenever I can't be
> home, and it is super for everyone.

Another mother was very businesslike in describing relations
with her ex-spouse and the logistics of split custody:

> Each child makes his or her arrangements for spending week-
> ends with the noncustodial parent. Since they are teenagers
> and have social lives of their own, they visit the other parent
> about one weekend a month, with phone calls initiated either
> by the parent or child during the week.

A mother tells of the logistics in her situation. She has custody
of the youngest son; the father has custody of a daughter:

> One daughter lives with her father all the time. I see her occa-
> sionally for lunch, dinner, shopping, travel, etc. She calls, I call.
> Youngest son lives with me. Sees father every weekend he is in
> town. If I have plans to attend concert, plays, travel, etc., that
> include son, father stays home. So far this has worked out well
> (one year). I expect change when the ten-year-old is preteen
> and wants to do more with his peer group.

Another family defies the traditional logic of separating children
on gender lines:

> Daughter lives with father. Son lives with mother.
>   Every weekend I have daughter, and my ex has son. Summer
> vacations usually spent with father—holidays, vacations ro-
> tated and very liberal.

Many parents choose to ignore details of the divorce decree to fit day-to-day realities of family life. A thirty-two-year-old mother with three children explains her situation, which is legally defined as split custody but is so flexible that it almost defies categorization:

> In the decree we split custody, with visitation rights for each parent to have both children together every other weekend and every other holiday, plus two weeks each year.
> We do not follow this as we work out each day—if one of us has plans the other baby-sits and vice versa. If both of us have plans, we hire a sitter together. He takes the kids to day care and school each morning, and I pick them up after school. Some evenings they are with me, some with him, and some he has my son and I have my daughter. Since we are as of now on a friendly basis this works out very well. Weekends we also work out as to who has plans, as to where they are. We also only live two miles apart so transportation is easy.

One daughter goes to her father's on the weekend, but the two other adult children do not reciprocate by going to their mother's to stay:

> "Open visitation" is stated in the divorce papers. The fourteen-year-old girl living with me spends most weekends (Friday night until Sunday evening) with her father, and the twenty-one-year-old brother and twenty-three-year-old sister live with their dad.

Split custody can be worked out without vast amounts of communication after the fact, as we infer from this mother's testimony:

> My ex-husband has our daughter on Thursday evenings and every other weekend. This is a feasible arrangement, and there are times when she spends other time with him. She and I find this arrangement fine. He does not communicate his feelings. I see very little of my son—he works three nights a week and spends a lot of time on schoolwork. In the end, it just worked out that my daughter would stay with me and my son would live with his father.

A forty-year-old mother with twenty- and eighteen-year-old adult children described her situation to us. She had vowed that if she "couldn't *make* marriage work, maybe I could make divorce work." We believe that she, her children, and her husband have found the key, and we report her story in detail:

> The children have been free to go back and forth as they wish. Both parents are happy to accommodate the children's needs and desires over and above their own. The only time this varies is when there is behavior that one parent can handle better than the other, i.e., if the boy did not cooperate with the mother, he would have to go back to the dad, who had better disciplinary control.
>
> When the divorce was first decided, the dad was very depressed at the thought of losing the experience of childrearing. He was always very involved in that process, although our ideas and methods often clashed.
>
> Nevertheless, when he expressed in a heartrending manner his sense of loss, I did not hesitate to consider an "open custody" situation, hoping to put him at ease as best as possible. From that time on, there was little or no argument, especially over the kids (that alone made the divorce "worth it").
>
> This level of cooperation took only a few minutes to develop, probably because emotions were expressed and respected. There were no hang-ups, except in the beginning; the dad came over to the house every weekend (to see the daughter) and to keep a hand in with household chores (which he wasn't so eager to do before).
>
> I often felt it was as if we weren't even divorced—I wanted to be free of many of the daily irritations that these visits prolonged.
>
> Finally, he remarried, and I left the state. This relieved the problem for enough time to allow me to heal and forget.
>
> When his second marriage ended in divorce, he moved out here, one state away to be closer to us. Since then, there have been happy and successful visits back and forth for him, me, and the kids. We have a good relationship, all of us now, with a surprisingly healthy feeling of family, despite the situation.
>
> He is currently courting another woman, who has a young child by another marriage. Our children found this difficult at first but have learned to accept it pretty well, especially because we all are able to get together (including her and her child) without any problems, but actually with an ever greater feeling of family.

I never thought it would be possible, but it can and does happen, with unselfish love and devotion.

I always wondered why one couldn't *make* marriage in the same way, but that's not so easy. I vowed if I couldn't *make* marriage work, maybe I could make divorce work. It has! So essentially, there is no divorce, at least between hearts.

One professional woman, forty-seven years old, lives 1,725 miles from her ex-spouse. Her outline of their split custody arrangement illustrates how complex it all can be and how the situation can change so quickly:

First year—three children lived at home with mother; spent Wednesday evenings and alternate weekends with father.

Second and third years—son with mother; one daughter with father; one daughter at university; one weekend per month exchanged.

Fourth and fifth years—son with mother; two daughters in university; holiday visits.

Sixth year—son with father; two daughters in university; holiday visits.

These arrangements met their needs and mileage restrictions. These parents have maintained a co-parenting, businesslike arrangement that has lasted over the long haul. The relationship works to both parents' benefit.

Another mother, age thirty-six, told us of the complicated changes her family has gone through over the past three years in terms of arrangements. This family is interesting because it defied conventional wisdom by splitting up twins. The story takes an unusual turn at the end of the mother's narrative:

Sixteen-year-old girls (twins). One lives with mother; one lives with father. They spend nights at each house whenever they wish. No set dates observed *now.* The girls are free to spend nights with mother or father whenever they want to.

Child custody was decided by the judge at the time of the divorce when the twins were thirteen. One was to live weekdays with the father, the other to live weekdays with the mother; then rotate every other weekend so they could spend weekends together; also rotate holidays. This lasted less than one year when *both* decided to live with their mother. This arrangement lasted over one year, and now the daughter I have custody of lives with her father, and the daughter he has custody of lives with me (mother).

One mother described an enormously challenging situation: two sons, age fourteen and nine; split custody arranged with the paternal grandmother; an income of $8,000 per year; and a "mentally ill" ex-spouse:

My oldest son lives with his paternal grandmother and does not care to see me. My youngest son lives with me and does not care to see his father. At this point, it works out fine. The father is mentally ill, which does not allow for reasoning on any situation. Until mental illness is improved, I do not see any other way of handling this. Visitation rights were not set up at the time of the divorce, just that children were undergoing counseling and visitation rights will be set up at another time.

The courts set up the child custody arrangements. Due to my ex-husband's mental illness, he was not allowed custody. Temporary custody was given to the paternal grandmother for six months. My oldest son kept running away to be with his father. Father lives with his mother. The hang-up was the mental illness. My son wanted to help care for the father.

My youngest son lives with me. I have total custody and care of him. I do not receive child support or help of any kind. Ex-husband cannot work and is on disability at the present. My attorney made all the arrangements with the courts.

The oldest son is under psychiatric care because of the divorce. I believe he blames me because I left his father when he was ill. But he would not accept help from me. He had three girlfriends that I knew about before I left him. The son feels I should have stayed with him because he was "sick" even though he had girlfriends.

I was all for my ex-husband taking the kids whenever he wanted to for a day or more or even in the evening. But because the mental illness was involved, normal visitation became impossible. He would keep the children sometimes twenty-four hours past what the courts had set up for visitation before we were divorced.

I am totally for the children having a relationship with both mother and father. I believe that to be the best situation for children involved in a divorce. But like I say, my situation is not a normal one. I have been harassed from the day I left my ex-husband, and because of this, my youngest is very afraid of his father.

The Problem of Seeing the Other Children. A few parents complained that they did not get enough time with the children who are in the ex-spouse's custody. Sometimes it is easy to see why:

Up to now I have not been able to see my ten-year-old daughter much because I have refused to talk with her mother. I feel that my asking my daughter to visit, etc., and her asking her mother should be sufficient enough. But her mother says no, she can't visit me unless I talk with her personally. I have our son. He in no way cares to visit his mother or have anything to do with her.

In other families hostility is not a problem, but distance is.

Surprisingly enough, no parents complained that siblings did not have enough time to visit each other.

Some judges are skeptical of split custody because it separates the siblings. Split custody parents, by having at least one child live with each parent, are implying that maintaining strong parent-child bonds takes precedence over maintaining sibling bonds. We concur with this view. And split custody parents often go out of their way to ensure that sibling bonds can be maintained.

In the parents' view, at least, sibling contacts in split custody families are adequate. We do not know how the children feel about this issue.

Scheduled Visitation. Most split custody families seem to thrive on flexible scheduling. That is probably due to the nature of split custody itself: often split custody is a flexible response to a changing situation—a son who cannot get along with his mother; a daughter who really misses her dad and is afraid that he is disappearing from the family altogether; a young adult who wants to go to the state university in the father's hometown; and so forth.

Since split custody is often devised as a creative response to a tough situation, it stands to reason that few split custody families will have a lockstep approach to scheduling. Almost every split cus-

tody family has a schedule of sorts. Very few families fit into what
we would see as an inflexible mold, however, or a highly structured
and basically uncooperative, unhelpful design.

A typical, very workable schedule goes like this: "One child lives
with me, the other one with my ex-spouse. One weekend they are
both with me and the next weekend they are both with her. Works
well for both of us. Gives us a free weekend every other week."

This design ensures sibling interaction. A father with a fourteen-
year-old daughter and a twelve-year-old son described a similar
schedule: "Son is with me all week. Daughter is with her mother all
week. We split weekends—usually with mother having both Saturday 6:00 P.M. to Sunday afternoon; I have both Friday 5:00 P.M. to
Saturday 6:00 P.M. She takes both when I travel on business, and I
do the same for her (though less frequently)."

Another father felt that he gave his ex-wife a good deal of relief
from the burdens of solo parenting, but the relief was not
reciprocated:

> My oldest boy lives with me, the youngest with his mother. The
> youngest is dropped off every morning at 7:30 A.M. for school
> at my home and goes back home to his mother's at 5 P.M. He is
> with me just about every weekend and vacations. The oldest
> rarely sees or talks to his mother. She doesn't call him or visit,
> and he doesn't like to go to her house. This arrangement is
> sometimes hard on me. [The boys are thirteen and nine years
> old.]

Very tight scheduling often goes hand in hand with parental conflict. Is it a cause of conflict or an effect of warring personalities?

> Two children, both girls, one with each parent. Oldest girl to
> spend each spring school break with her mother, plus one-half
> of summer break. The girls are to be together with each parent
> on alternating Christmases. Youngest girl to be with her sister
> and father other one-half of summer.

The father speaking above was unhappy with the arrangement and
reported a good deal of conflict with his ex-wife. She alleged that he
is keeping one girl from her and forgetting the other girl completely.

Regardless of distance, split custody can work if both parents are willing to try to make it work. Though a thousand miles separate these parents, the arrangement has lasted six years, and there are no clouds on the horizon:

> We live in California. Our thirteen-year-old son, Tom, lives with me, since his sixth year. Our ten-year-old daughter, Betsy, lives with Karen [the father's ex-wife], since her fourth year. Betsy visits a month or so in summer, then she and Tom go north (Washington state) to visit Karen, and Tom flies home or I'll drive up and pick him up and visit.

The details of scheduling are far less important than the inherent kindness and heart of the parents who make the schedules.

Advice on What Is Best for the Children

The forty split custody parents in our study had a great deal of good advice to offer. All suggestions must be judged carefully, of course. What works for one family could fail miserably in another.

First, from the fifteen fathers:

Be Objective. "The kids come first," one father cautioned. "Seek dispassionate third-party advice. Try to be objective. Stay interested in your kids regardless of who has custody."

Fighting only hurts the youngsters, another father noted: "Look at the children's needs and your needs. Cooperation should be the rule. Don't fight. The children pay a big price for adult incompatibility. They should not suffer through hate."

Some mothers were not as evenhanded as these fathers would desire: "My advice would be to think of the children and who would be more capable of raising them. Don't take custody of a child to hurt the other person. My ex-wife's favorite quote was, 'Don't forget I have legal custody.'"

Keep the Children Together. "Don't split them up," one father advised, feeling split custody had been a mistake in his case. Other parents, of course, disagreed with this. And many felt that they had no reasonable alternative to splitting up the kids.

Children Should Help in the Decision-making Process. One father urged, "Talk to the children and find out their feelings and let them be a part of the decision making." But another father countered that "every effort should be made to settle the custody arrangements without involving the children any more than can be helped." He qualified this statement by saying that this "of course depends on the age of the children; if they are old enough they should be allowed to have something to say about whom they live with."

The key is finding a subtle way to learn the children's true feelings without putting them in the middle of a dogfight. Even the best of parents has been known to chew out a child remorselessly for honestly saying she would rather live with the other parent.

Do Not Use Children as Weapons. As all the other groups of single parents also state, this is widespread and "stupid."

Maintain Contact with All the Children. "Make decisions that benefit all. Kids are smarter than you credit them for. The ones who are with you, fine. See the others as much as you can, give them love as you never have before. They need it." Another father complemented this thought when he wrote: "Let the children know that you love and care for them, and try not to become a weekend father. See or speak to them often and let them know that even though you are not there you are still their father. Do not badmouth your former spouse in front of them, and try to be supportive of the ex-spouse's decisions."

Honesty. "Be honest about each parent's psychology. In our case, the wife determined that more than one child would be too much by herself." That takes enormous courage on a person's part.

Know Your True Feelings. "Be sure of your true emotional attachments to the children, and if you truly want to be a parent with all the responsibility it entails, then stand up and fight for yourself as well as for your children!" The converse of this is, of course: If you aren't sure, don't fight.

We really love how one father put it all together:

I believe you should mingle:

1. What's best for you with
2. What's best for the kids.
3. Don't be afraid to change it if you did it wrong.
4. Don't fix it if it's good.

Now let us look at what the twenty-five mothers with split custody had to say about what is best for kids:

Go to School. That is what one mother of two teenagers advised. Her logic was excellent: "Go to school if necessary. Give your children responsibilities around the home. Get a job even if you do not need the money. It keeps you from feeling sorry for yourself. Find single friends of both sexes—single people help each other."

Another mother with four children also argued that a little selfishness can be a very unselfish act:

> Think of yourself. You will have a whole new set of problems to handle as a single person. Can you really take good care of your kids and leave time for your new identity? You are important, too. If you don't have a good self-image during this time, what kind of a parent are you going to be? If you were not the main wage earner in the family, you will have a major adjustment. A woman will have to work, and if it's for the first time, it's really hell.

She added,

> Think of the kids. Don't take custody just to prove you are the best parent. Maybe your ex-spouse is a rat or worse, but maybe he also is a good parent and better able to provide than you are.

Children Seem Happiest When Parents Live Close to Each Other. A mother of two teens told us this. She continued, "When the children do not have to move, change schools, etc., the more contact they have with the parent who leaves, the more secure they are. They don't feel abandoned."

The Best Interests of the Child. How many times have we heard this refrain? Split custody mothers were no different than any other on this issue: "For the children's sake, try to have a happy divorce if you couldn't have a happy marriage. Since the marriage agreement is over, perhaps you could be friends—the pressure is off and there's no need to hate forever." Go to a counselor or a lawyer and that very same advice would cost you fifty to seventy-five dollars!

While trying to keep hostilities minimal, one mother advised against the other extreme. "*Don't* try to be *friends* with the 'new spouse.' And don't socialize together (with the ex, either)." A businesslike arrangement is best, she concluded.

All of this, of course, can be "an extremely difficult hurdle for feuding parents to overcome, but a very essential one for everyone involved."

"Any custody arrangement could be beneficial if both parents keep the peace of mind of their children at the forefront," a mother of three children, ages sixteen, fourteen, and thirteen, pointed out: "They should be able to separate their personal feelings for each other when it comes to parent-child relationships, since this is what causes feelings of insecurity, hostility, negativism in children toward parents, regardless of who has custody!"

Ah, but how do we get some people to understand this important truth?

Talk with the Children. A mother advised. "Don't just arrange things and then tell them. Even small children need to feel consulted." But do not go overboard, another mother added: "I feel that thirteen years of age is too young for them to choose where they would like to live. At the age of sixteen, I think, a child should choose where he or she wants to live and will be the happiest."

Never, Never Agree to Separating the Children. A mother urged. "*Never!* If they are brother and sister, etc., they should be reared together— no matter what!" This woman was forty-seven years old and had twenty- and eighteen-year-old adult children. No other parent in our sample of split custody parents was this firm. We do not know why she has such strong feelings.

Try to Keep from Divorcing the "In-Law Family." That is advice we heartily endorse, also. The move by grandparents' organizations to ensure some modest grandchild-grandparent contact after divorce when the relationship is a healthy one makes a lot of sense. Children deserve to have grandparents; a parent who wants his or her child to divorce not only the other parent but also grandma and grandpa is way out of bounds.

Sometimes the Unconventional Approach Makes Sense. "Don't fear making the best arrangements for the children—even if it deviates from 'societal' expectations." This mother challenged parents to stand up for their convictions.

Adjustment of the Parents

Let us more closely examine the notion of the virtue of (limited) selfishness. First, our fifteen split custody fathers offer some "words to the wise" on how they have struggled through divorce and kept themselves together while engaged in a rather rare custody arrangement.

Take Good Care of Yourself. "Believe in yourself strongly, and be satisfied with yourself," one advised. Another father added, "Build your *self.* Then you can give to your children and the ex-spouse. Don't turn anger inward (upon yourself). Try new things, but stay away from drugs and alcohol, even if the drugs are prescribed."

A father who almost smothered in loneliness has a few ideas on how to prevent this: "Do not seclude yourself. Loneliness will get you down more. Occupy yourself. Before I got the kids I was alone for eight months. I didn't go out much and almost went nuts coming home from work to my one-room apartment. Maybe, too, I had a hard time adjusting, because I didn't want the divorce."

Acceptance. Men are socialized to do battle with the hounds of hell. This aggressiveness can be quite useful at times, but it can be disastrous in a divorce, which often calls for more subtle behavior. It took one father a long time to figure this out, but he now advises: "The best thing one can do is accept whatever the situation is and do the best you can to continue."

Honesty. This can be a bitter pill, but "honesty is what each person wants in his or her single life. If you're just not 'parent material,' admit it."

Read. "Read, read, read. Things like *Creative Divorce, How to Be Your Own Best Friend,* and so forth." Some people have gotten the idea somewhere that reading a self-help book is a sign of weakness. If you are worried about this perception, you can always sneak the book home between the pages of the *Wall Street Journal.*

Support Groups and Counseling. Groups such as Parents without Partners can be helpful, some split custody fathers noted. Talk with other divorced parents whenever you get a chance—including women, to get a female perspective, which will generally help relations with the former wife. In short, develop a support system of people, "be they family, friends, clergy, a counselor." People "you feel free to talk or weep with, laugh, or whatever." Another father complemented this thought, saying, "Of course some people will need counseling at least for a period of time until they can get back on their emotional feet. Notwithstanding my preparation for the divorce, it still took *time.* I was lucky in that I had a good job, which kept my mind occupied."

Settle Things as Soon as Possible. Given the complexities of the legal system and the confusion divorce proceedings can generate, this may be wishful thinking on the part of the father who advised it: "The greatest problem I have had is attempting to work out community property settlements, which are still not settled after six years of being divorced."

Do Not Feel Your Own Personal Misery Is So Special and Unique. Feeling that way is a luxury you cannot afford. "Take time for yourself and get to enjoy your own company. Get to know yourself again. Enjoy going a little wild for awhile. Hang in there—it will get much easier. There are a lot of people in your situation."

Be Philosophical about It All. Many fathers were quite eloquent in this regard: "Realize the universe unfolds as it should," one wrote. "Read 'The Desiderata,'" he added. "Don't get your ego in the way. Worry

less about others' conception of a good parent," another father said.
And a third summed it up beautifully: "Be gentle with yourself; it is
an extremely difficult time, even for the one who initiated the separation. Remember that time can heal. You won't feel this way
forever."

The mothers with split custody had very similar bits of wisdom
to offer. We separated them from the fathers for two reasons: to make
the point that women cope with crisis in ways very similar to those
of men; and that if men and women have a chance to see how the
other sex copes with the crisis of divorce, they may better understand the ex-spouse's behavior.

The mothers' section on personal adjustment is longer for two
reasons: Twenty-five mothers with split custody participated in the
research, compared with only fifteen fathers; and, as we have seen
in many other previous studies, women tend to be more verbal than
men when it comes to talking or writing about feelings.

Grow. "Get some outside interest—school, a job, a church—something to elevate your self-esteem and reassure yourself that 'we're
going to be all right!' " one mother told us. Others urged those who
will follow them in the divorce crisis to reach out and grow in the
company of others: "It probably would be beneficial to seek the companionship of those in a similar situation; I didn't and had an extremely difficult time adjusting, and still am."

If you can't find a friend to talk with for free, or simple friendship simply doesn't do the trick, "get some counseling—get rid of
your guilt trips." See a counselor if the children are having trouble
adjusting too. A divorce recovery workshop or other positive singles
group could help, this mother added. In sum: "Continue to develop
and grow as an independent, functioning, contributing individual in
society."

Do Not Sit on Your Hands. "Do something—get a new hairdo, lose five
pounds, fix yourself up. Change *something* about your appearance.
Don't try to pretend things haven't changed." As the reader will recall, many of the mothers have advised a change of appearance.
None of the men did, and we think they should have. Women seem
to know better than men that appearance affects personality. Another mother, who repeated the oft-chanted refrain of "go to school,

get a job," added that "if the children are too small, try to do something part-time. It's important to get on with one's life. Have something to think about other than a dreadful ex-husband. It is a mistake to vegetate." Many of us tend to hunker down in a crisis; the impulse to sit in a corner and suck our thumb is strong. But "when you know there is no reconciliation possible, you must pick up your life and keep on going for your family first and then for yourself. Having a daughter to come home to was the only thing that kept me strong. You can't sit back and feel sorry for yourself."

Emote. Explore your highs and lows. Study grief and good times. Learn from them. Cry, all the time remembering that the old-fashioned belief in "crying it all out" has scientific studies to back up the notion that you *will* feel better after crying.

> Expect a lot of changes. You'll be scared and lonely. You'll be joyful and serene. Sometimes all at the same time. Try everything. If you don't like it, you don't have to do it again. This is your time to become more than you were.

You may never feel this *alive* again in your life. Enjoy.

Love the Children. Many parents came close to going overboard on this:

> Try to be as unselfish as possible. If the marriage couldn't work, maybe the divorce will. Devote yourselves to the children as much as possible. Sacrifice for them, if not by remaining in marriage, then as single parents. Enjoy yourselves later, when they're grown.

Such self-sacrifice can be a way of hiding. Single fathers more commonly hide in alcohol and drugs and work and physical fitness. Single mothers more often submerge in childrearing. All these approaches can be addictive behaviors and need to be tempered with reality. "Think of your own long-term goals. Your children grow up fast, and you, too, have the right to a life of happiness."

In the same vein, another mother cautions: "keep being the *parent*! *Don't* try to be 'pals' with your children!" In general, parents who get overwrought with the so-called pain of their children are usually just expressing their own pain in an indirect way.

"The kids will be freaky if you let yourself get freaky." Indeed.

Give Yourself Time. "It takes time to adjust, so don't get in a hurry to find someone else right away. Get to know yourself and feel good about yourself again before entering another relationship," one mother argued. Another concurred, noting how easy it is to get caught up in "the single-parent social world." Is that a euphemism for the world of the stereotypic wild divorcée of yesteryear?

A thirty-three-year-old mother of a fifteen- and a twelve-year-old put it quite nicely: "Divorce is certainly not pleasant, but the eventual outcome can certainly be so. My advice might well be: be patient. It takes *at least* a year to adjust, but by the second year being divorced can become *very* comfortable!"

Forgive. "Heal and forgive," a mother urged. "It doesn't have to mean getting back together, but it does mean establishing a positive relationship. Don't be aggrieved or bitter. It won't help."

Plan. One mother, obviously a very analytical person, had it all planned out:

> To have a plan of action is essential for optimal adjustment. Preferably an overall plan of growth for your life as a single person. To set goals and to know who you are is important to that growth. Flexibility will be necessary, and not feeling guilty about the past is vital to your future.

Or, in other words, "Look forward."

Sorrows

Finally, it is time to sum it all up. What is good about life now for these split custody parents? And what is bad?

Some of the problems relate to split custody specifically, but most relate to the pain of divorce in general. Though split custody parents are rare, they have much in common with all single parents and do not need to feel especially unique or different, for all in all, they really are not.

First, let us see what the fathers had to say.

Cannot See All the Children Daily. The traditional divorced father does not get to see any of the children very regularly, but even for split custody fathers the ache is still there: "Not getting to see my daughter on a day-to-day basis makes me feel that we have grown apart." Similarly, another father was sad because "I can't be with all three at the same time."

Other fathers added:

> I am not able to see my little girl except when the judge said I could. Although the court said that was the minimum time for her to see me, my former wife has seen fit to keep her from me. My oldest girl is constantly hassled by her mother, never giving her a chance to settle down to sort out her own feelings.

> I missed my daughter at first very, very much. It broke my heart to lose my little girl. But now I know her much better and more naturally than I would have otherwise.

Not Prepared for Parenthood. One father was overjoyed at having the kids, and underprepared: "No one really prepares you for parenthood. We study math, English, and so forth. But the one area most important we neglect—raising a family and understanding their needs."

Children Growing Too Fast. "My children grew up too fast," one father lamented. "I missed the younger years of everyday life." Doesn't that sound like a mother talking?

Love for Former Wife. "I am still in love with my ex-wife, and I miss the full family life."

A Broken Home. Most single fathers continue to yearn for "Mom, Dad, and the kids" in one form or another:

> Seeing my children grow up without the additional parent to help with them. Raising children is a two-person job.

My sorrow is a broken home. I would have wanted a better situation, not divorce.

That mom (my wife) did not try one bit to save the marriage, and the children do miss her not being with us. We have a part-time family.

Not having their mother to share in the fun of growing together. I take the kids places, vacations, and so forth, and it would have been nice to do these things as a family.

Courts. "My initial sorrow was the courts and the lawyers."

And perhaps the most unique sorrow a father reported: "Buying shoes for a thirteen-year-old with size eleven feet."

Let us take a look now at the sorrows of split-custody mothers. How similar they are.

Losing a Child. "Six months after our divorce, my younger daughter [age twelve] wanted to live with her father, and I let her do so," a mother reported the familiar story of how a youngster tries to keep Dad in the family somehow, in spite of the divorce. "But after six months it became apparent we had definitely 'split teams.' I feel she was alienated against me. I have seen very little of her, and the daughter with me [age seventeen] has no contact with her father."

Another mother also told of losing a daughter but was hopeful that it would all turn out okay:

I feel I have 'lost' my daughter at times, though I feel that eventually we will grow to be closer than before. Sometimes we play 'shuffle' kids, and I feel badly that they probably will not have any real 'roots'!"

Holidays. And so forth. "The holidays when I don't have the kids around make me feel lower than a snake's belly," one mother wrote. "And when the kids are sick I don't know about it. When they get their report cards I don't know about it."

Splitting Up the Children. Divorce wars often pit one child against another, making split custody a logical alternative to tradition:

Two sisters have been turned against each other. I do not like her not seeing her father, but at this point, it's the way it has to be. Maybe in the future things will improve and a relationship can once again come about. The sisters have completely different personalities, and the divorce brought out even more differences of opinion. I hope that will improve, also.

Even if the youngsters care for each other, they are often split up to preserve the parent-child relationship, which takes precedence. And the subsequent "lack of family closeness kills me," another mother confided.

Loss of Influence in the Children's Lives. "My daughter and my son are both unhappy about their separation," a mother wrote. "My daughter is in a *terrible* marriage of her own, which I relate to her relationship with her father."

Another mother was crushed by the split:

I feel that losing both older children's custody before I was ready to let go has been the greatest sorrow of my life, and not seeing them as often as I would like to is another. I had hoped they would finish school in an excellent school system, but they attended a poor school and have adopted their father's negative attitude on continued education.

Mom, Dad, and the Kids. No matter how many times counselors and single parents say that a single-parent family can be a good place in which to grow for both children and parents, some single parents will still mourn the loss of the "ideal" family, the broken dream: "I believe children need both parents. I would like to have a 'complete' family—husband, wife, and *their* children."

Could Not Handle a Male Teen. Perhaps the most common reason why parents split custody is that teenagers have very definite ideas about what they want to do, who they want to do it with, who they want to live with, and who they do not. Many are masters at buffaloing parents, and "losing" the battle is a frustrating and saddening defeat for many parents:

My son wanted to live with his father from the moment we separated. I objected, and since his father was living with another woman, he didn't want him. Finally the child began getting into some trouble, and since the child still wanted to live with his father, I insisted his father take custody. All through the separation, which lasted three years, the children spent about five weekends a year with their father. He never had any time for them. If he had not accepted custody voluntarily I would have asked the court for help. It was apparent that I could not handle a male teenager.

Games People Play. From toddlerhood children learn that Mom and Dad often have different responses to requests. If you cannot win with one, try the other: "I feel that the girls have been deprived of a 'togetherness home life' by going from one home to the other. If they are dissatisfied with something at one home, they can always move. I don't think this is a good idea!"

Sometimes a parent runs out of steam in the fight over the children. Rather than exhaust herself and further damage the youngsters, she withdraws:

My daughter who left to live with her father has been alienated from me, and I am completely out of her life, and she, mine. I can only hope she will grow up to understand that it was because of my love for her that I refused to pull and tug with her father for her affection. I loved her enough to let her go. I hope she grows to understand that.

Joys

And finally, let us talk of joy. Single parenthood is a mix of joy and sorrow, and to forget the joy is to overdramatize the challenge these parents face. Certainly life is hard, but it is hard for everyone. If we forget this, we run the risk of isolating single parents, of making them somehow different, less capable, less resilient. Most single parents are, fortunately, very tough and capable. They seem to meet life's challenges, sometimes merely getting by, but often they are transcendent.

Let us look at those transcendent times. First, from the fathers.

Better Relationships. Many fathers reported improved relationships with their children after the divorce. This in part could be simply because the children were getting older. But, we believe, it is also because the fathers have learned from their divorce experience that parenthood is a precious commodity, to be cherished as a fleeting, finite time together:

> I have become a better parent. My son and I are friends. I am more sensitive. We support each other.

> The relationship between me and my son has grown to be very strong and understanding. We're not only father and son, we are best friends.

> We are actually sharing more now and have gotten to know each other better.

Independence. The drag of being "father figure," the boss who felt he had to know all and be all ended for one relieved father: "I can do about everything, and I don't need, in a dependent way, another person. I am free to give with no regrets. I don't have to be the final authority."

"Growing with Children. And being there when they want me."

The Ability to Take Care of Children. Pride in this accomplishment, and relief that it can be done without a fight from a spouse, was voiced by some split custody fathers: "Being able to take care or provide for the upbringing of my children as I see fit without having to do so through someone I don't trust."

Love. The eloquence of the parents never fails to move our emotions. These words should be read in a church: "I am a father who shares sick days and teacher visits. I am watching and being part of the good and bad of being a father. My joy is the love I can give and receive from my children."

Companionship. The joy? "Just the companionship of my sons." Another father in a split custody arrangement involving four children noted: "We still do many things together as a family—Christmases, birthdays, graduation. Surprisingly, the kids enjoy getting more attention when they're split than when they were four together."

And finally, one proud father's reply fairly exuded happiness over his children:

> Ted has a 132 + IQ. He's a joy to live and grow with (no ego trip here—he's adopted). I'm a fairly wild person. Lord knows what would have happened without him to stabilize me. Ted and Bobbi (my girlfriend) really enjoy each other when they get together. *I've* got it best. The first half of the summer (with me) they get along well. In the second half, Bette's half [the former wife], they act more normal.

And now for the joys that split custody mothers experience:

Closeness. The benefit most commonly mentioned by the mothers was the close ties that have been developed since split custody was instituted. Does this seem paradoxical? Listen:

> I have come to know and respect my daughter as a person. My home is not an "armed camp" with two children competing for my attention any longer.

> I get to see the kids all together on weekends. We are a family on weekends. I have complete freedom on alternate weekends. My daughter and I, who were never close before, have discovered that we do love each other as individual people.

> The children are as happy as is possible under the circumstances. They don't have to be afraid to talk about anything with either of us—there's no animosity between any of us, something we've all decided to maintain. We are all freer with our love since there are no pressures or expectations to behave as a "family."

> A good relationship with the children by each custodial parent—more time for individual caring.

> My daughter and I have become closer because of the particular arrangement. We are all we have. I spend more time with her than I normally did. I try to be more understanding, and she seems to be very understanding of my needs. We try harder to make each other's lives as happy as possible.

My older daughter—who has been completely rejected by her
father—and I are *extremely* close. There is no conflict from outside sources at all. I would not stop her from having a relationship with her father, but in all honesty, I prefer him having no
influence on her at all!

Cooperation. A cooperative working relationship with the former husband was rated highly by a number of mothers: "We help each other
out so both kids can be with both parents as much as possible. When
one parent is busy the kids can be with the other."

Different Life-styles. In a number of split custody families, different
styles caused a good deal of conflict. But in others the variations
were viewed as a strength. The children had the opportunity to live
in different worlds, and in many ways this was beneficial. At the
top of a thirty-three-year-old mother's list of joys: "The *very* liberal
visitation allowing the children maximum exposure to two sets of
life-styles, friends, schools, and so forth."

No Joy. Only one mother in twenty-five could think of nothing good
to say about split custody: "I was not satisfied, so there was none.
Finances were, perhaps, better, but that was no consolation."

Growth. Finally, watching a child grow up without the competitive
atmosphere siblings bring was beneficial for some children and a
source of joy for their parents:

At the moment, with only the youngest daughter in my home,
she is enjoying, for the first time, the status of an only child.
There are no older siblings to overshadow her or distract my
attention from her. Without constant sibling criticism and put-
downs she has matured and become more positive about herself—much to my delight.

All in all, split custody is clearly a suitable alternative for some
families. Many parents see it as a lesser of several evils type of arrangement, while others believe that if divorce is unavoidable, split
custody is just about the best option open to them in their particular
circumstances.

When comparing split custody families to joint custody families and families with paternal or maternal custody arrangements, there is no clearly superior approach. Split custody for many families is the only workable arrangement, while in other families it might be totally out of the question.

6

Joint Custody

One Mother's Story

Authors' Note. An Illinois mother who shares custody of her five-year-old son with her ex-husband tells of her experience. Her account touches upon many of the issues faced by families who work through the complex process of joint custody. Numerous details have been changed in the narrative to protect her family's privacy.

Alyssa's father has custody six months of the year, and I have custody the other six months. Seems to work pretty well for everyone involved. Alyssa is a pretty "happy-go-lucky" kid, and the unusual arrangement doesn't seem to phase her a bit. I think she just thinks this is all normal. Probably her father and I have a harder time adjusting to going from full-time parent to nothing for six months. It's really hard for both of us, not seeing her for six months.

No one helped with the child custody arrangement, and it took awhile, probably around a month or so of bringing it up, then letting the subject drop ... sleep on it ... try again. It's very difficult to try to work something out like that when you're both hurting. That was the most important issue and the most difficult, too. It's one of the things we disagreed most strongly on.

At the time we were both stuck in a trying situation because I was recovering from a serious car accident that we were both in but I was the only one injured, and we both knew that as soon as I had the doctor's okay, I would leave the marriage. I think those last five months were heartbreaking because we had to continue to live together, and it was so sad to see how things had disintegrated between us.

The big hang-up was that he didn't feel he should pay any child support, and I felt he should. I left behind a house and almost all the furniture, plus when we were first married I finished putting him through school. He's a banker now. Things still aren't equal, and a man has a lot more earning potential.

I didn't ask for anything else. I felt I was being extremely fair. Most people said I was being a fool, letting him have everything. Those things weren't important to me, though, and they are to him.

Anyway, for awhile he was very bitter about it. He said he wasn't going to "pay me to take his daughter away from him," etc. Things were pretty tense for awhile, but eventually we worked it out. I think what it came down to was, either do it this way, or we get a couple of lawyers to fight it out for us, which neither of us wanted to do.

We've only seen each other once since we split up—we're pretty good "long-distance" friends now. Whenever we talk or write, it's mostly about Alyssa or just trivial banter, etc. We never get into anything heavy. He does help out moneywise when Alyssa is with me, but he's often late or the check bounces. Eventually he does come through. I never nag him about it, though.

I think for us it helped not getting lawyers involved. I know we both got free legal advice once before the split, and had we followed their advice, we would probably be enemies now. I think it was *most* beneficial for our daughter that we were able to work things out between us, and we have both kept our word on things we agreed upon. All you can do is trust in the other person's good judgment, too, and then hope for the best. Obviously that will only work in some situations—you really have to put the child first and hostilities, etc., in the background.

I guess I feel really good about the fact that Alyssa has a real strong relationship with both me and her father. I think it's paid off and will only continue to in the future—when she's older. Alyssa knows that both her mother and father love her very much and that we'll always be there—both of us. We're pretty supportive of each other—willing to be flexible and help out.

I guess it wouldn't be so bad if her father and I didn't live quite so far apart. As it is, neither of us can afford to fly back and forth to see Alyssa during the six months that the other one has her. We both get pretty lonesome for her, and it's especially hard on holidays and special occasions.

Joint Custody—The Right Choice? As researchers we are especially adept at manipulating quantitative data. We feed massive amounts of numerical information into our computers, and the machine pumps out the statistical conclusions.

The reader will recall a number of important statistically based conclusions about joint custody families at which we arrived in our quantitative studies:

A positive relationship exists between parental adjustment to the custody arrangement and child adjustment to the arrangement. If the parent is comfortable, the child is likely to be comfortable.

Feelings of being overburdened by the children are significantly less prevalent among parents with joint custody than they are among those with sole custody.

Sole custody parents claim to be experiencing significantly greater stress in their lives than do joint custody parents.

Children's adjustment to the custody arrangement did not differ between the two groups, according to the parents.

Joint custody parents lived closer to the ex-spouse than did sole custody parents, on the average.

Joint custody parents were more likely than sole custody parents to feel positively toward the ex-spouse at the time custody arrangements were set up and more often reported that the process of working out custody arrangements was a mutual, friendly one.

Sole custody parents often wished that the ex-spouse spent more time with the children; joint custody parents were relatively more satisfied in this regard.

The children maintained a stronger relationship with both parents in joint custody families than they did in sole custody families.

Joint custody parents were significantly more positive than were sole custody parents about the importance of children's maintaining close relationships with both parents after a divorce.

Sole custody parents reported significantly lower gross yearly incomes than did joint custody parents.

Joint custody parents reported more positive changes in their social lives since assuming custody than did parents with sole custody (joint custody, in many instances, gave parents more free time to develop social relationships).

But besides being researchers, impelled to produce quantitative conclusions, we are even happier as clinicians, searching out the emotions of divorce and strategies for coping. A number of qualitative conclusions about joint custody families can be drawn from the interviews and questionnaires we have studied.

First and foremost is the very general impression we gained from reading these joint custody parents' responses to our myriad questions: they are simply happier in general than are the parents with sole custody. Life is more buoyant. The stresses are less. This happiness cannot help but affect the children in a positive way.

The second important conclusion we come to when reading the parents' responses is that they are fortunate to have been able to work things out so well. Perhaps they are blessed with personal skills—a calmness, a reasonableness that makes it possible for them to solve all the problems inherent to coparenting after a divorce. And perhaps they were lucky to be divorcing a spouse who is also reasonable and relatively calm. When joint custody works, our clinical intuitions tell us, it works because the parents have a personality makeup conducive to joint custody. And joint custody is also absolutely impossible in many cases because at least one of the parents is bullheaded or hostile or drunk or addicted to other drugs or lacks empathy or is incestuously inclined or is self-centered or all of the above.

Simply having joint custody is not going to solve all the problems of divorce and children. It will for many families, but other families are foundering in such an irrational or combative situation that joint custody would not have a prayer of a chance.

We will dismount from our soapbox and spend the rest of this chapter objectively reporting the words of our joint custody families.

The major sections in this chapter deal with these issues: negotiating joint custody; who decides? The parents, the children, or the courts?; common approaches to joint custody; the extent of coparenting in joint custody families; adjustment of the parents; adjustment of the children; sorrows; and the joys; and one last story.

Negotiating Joint Custody

As the reader will recall, joint custody often evolves out of a much different set of family dynamics than does sole custody. In our research, we found that a significantly higher percentage of joint custody parents than sole custody parents reported feeling positive emotions toward the ex-spouse at the time custody was set up. And 68 percent of the parents with joint custody said that it was a mutual, friendly agreement between parents, compared with 20 percent of the parents with sole custody who said this.

In this section of our chapter on joint custody, we will address two basic negotiating issues: the "flavor" or tone of the negotiations (cooperativeness, anger, bitterness, hate, love, emotional neutrality, and so forth); and we will look at who decides the issues (parents, children, or the courts).

In a Spirit of Cooperation. Remember all the stories of storm and stress you read in the chapters on mothers with custody and fathers with custody? Think of those as you read this story from a father with joint custody of a five- and a six-year-old for a study in contrast:

> My ex-spouse suggested that we try an arrangement where we each have the children every other week. I said, "Let's try it and see how it works." It worked fine. We had no help. It took five minutes. There were no hang-ups.

The decision was quite natural for this divorcing couple also:

> We both felt strongly that the children were our mutual responsibility. It never occurred to us to do it any other way. The difficulty we had was with the financial arrangements. I accepted very little in the way of a property settlement in hopes of having continual child support. This has worked out well.

We were impressed with how well organized this mother was in her efforts to ease the transition for the children:

> My ex-husband simply stated that he thought the children should live with me. There was never any conflict whatsoever as to when he would see the children. Anytime he asked to see them, he saw them.
>
> The flavor of our negotiations concerning the entire divorce was amiable. While our separation and divorce was sudden, certain arrangements that we made, I feel, helped to soften the transition for our children:
>
> 1. I went to each of my children's schools and privately informed their teachers of our separation and divorce, and asked them not only to keep the situation in mind regarding my children's behavior, but also to inform me of any problems or unusual reactions my children might exhibit.
>
> 2. I made a concerted effort to maintain the same routine in our home after my husband left. We ate at the same time, we ate out as usual on Friday nights—the only thing different was that their father was not there.
>
> 3. I was attending college at night at the time, so even though we were separated, my ex-husband continued to come over each week and take care of the children while I was at school.
>
> At first, he even occasionally ate with us before I left. He continued to come each week for about four months after our separation. I feel this was a positive thing for my children and probably for their father, because it gave them a chance to be together in familiar surroundings.
>
> 4. In addition, my ex-husband took care of the children in my home when I went on vacation the first summer we were separated. He has also continued to attend their school plays, football games, graduations, etc., as I do.
>
> The comment I make to everyone, including the children, regarding our custody arrangement is that our children have a mother *and* a father, who just don't happen to live in the same house. I think our children feel the same way.
>
> *—A forty-three-year-old mother with joint custody of a sixteen- and a thirteen-year-old.*

A forty-four-year-old mother kept a cooperative spirit in the negotiations, for she had it clearly noted in her mind that "the child is getting something unique from the other parent that you cannot provide—no matter how much love or time or effort you devote to the child—and it is not fair of you to want to deprive the child of that for selfish reasons."

If parents can agree upon the importance of joint custody, details can fall into line relatively quickly, as this man with a fifteen-year-old daughter concludes: "We both agreed that maximum parental participation and support was necessary for the child. The discussions were very agreeable—no problems. We spent little time on it. We agreed on the need and the methods at once."

This mother has an especially well developed sense of empathy when it comes to her ex-husband's need to see the children:

My ex-husband has the children on alternate months. They spend quite a bit of time with the parent they're not currently living with. If moving every month seems like too much or too often, we'll probably extend it to two or three months with frequent visiting with the absent parent.

In the beginning I wanted sole custody, with liberal visitation for their father. After twelve years of "mothering," I didn't think I could stand any separation from them. Then I began to realize that their father would of course feel the same way. Our personal problems in no way affected his ability to parent. He is more involved with his kids than most men I know and is a very good father. I didn't want to punish him by taking away his children.

Also, because both kids are boys, ten and fourteen, I felt they needed their father at least as much as their mother at this stage. I've never felt that it made sense for mothers "always" to get the children and fathers "always" to get support payments. They're as much his as mine. Another factor was that the boys wanted it this way. As soon as they realized that they weren't going to lose one of their parents but would instead have two homes and two parents, they began to accept the divorce and adjust.

An added benefit that didn't occur to me until later was that, while I love my kids more than anything else, I have been a twenty-four-hour-a-day mother for twelve years, and I have to say honestly that I enjoy sharing that responsibility now. It's almost like having every other month off, I miss them, but we enjoy each other when we're together, and it has given me an opportunity to grow as an individual.

There really wasn't much negotiating. Joint custody was what we all wanted and insisted upon. An attorney friend of mine said it was "stupid and could never work" (a middle-aged male). My attorney (a young woman) was very enthusiastic and said it was certainly worth trying.

Even though it has only been five months, it's working well, and I'm confident it will continue. The main thing, to their father and me, is that the kids are happy.

One Parent Did Not Want All of the Responsibility. While some single parents jealously guard the children and make every effort to keep them from the ex-spouse, others believe strongly that the ex should bear a fair share of the childrearing burden:

My ex-husband had never had any other children, and I had raised two others. We both care deeply about each other and our son, so we would never put stress on him. I resented having to raise another child *full-time*, so we mutually agreed that his father would have custody.

We didn't know we could have joint custody at the time, but we did agree to share financial and emotional obligations. We were always on good terms. No one helped us. It was pretty well agreed from the time I left.

We now not only have our separate times with the child, but we take "family-type" trips to see "our" daughters and spend time together on holidays and on Saturdays when we all play tennis. My ex-spouse is generally included in all family gatherings.

Similarly, another mother wrote:

One of my reasons for insisting on the joint custody arrangement was that I feared their father would be more comfortable without the responsibility of the children. He feared I would try to take them away from him, for they always have been a far more central part of my existence than of his.

Gradually this has actually come about, but he is an extremely loving, proud, supportive father. Most of the difficulties in the situation have to do with his personality rather than the custody situation.

Horse-trading. Parents who arrange joint custody are capable of a considerable amount of "horse-trading" to get what they are after. There is, of course, nothing wrong with this if it smooths the way for a workable agreement. A father with joint custody of nine- and eleven-year-old children explained:

> At the time when the arrangements were made, my ex-wife was planning to remarry. She told her attorney to agree to anything to get the matter settled. The amount of time was set up by me to fit into my business obligations. She agreed to the summer visitation with the idea that it would not work for me. I have changed my work pattern and now travel with my children during the summer. The settlement conference that was held in the family court was just a place for the two attorneys to finalize all the agreements. This took less than one hour.

Another parent wrote in a similar vein:

> It was agreed upon from the first, but I had trouble with getting the first child my share of the time in the beginning. I feel he would never have agreed to the divorce if I had not agreed to joint custody, and we would have had a long battle. My lawyer helped, and we had counseling. Hang-ups were that joint custody is so uncommon that the lawyer had some difficulty in writing up the divorce papers so they would be okayed.

Several parents with joint custody stressed the importance of children maintaining relationships with both parents. Even though parents may not be able to continue in a marital relationship, many seem able to separate the issues of "divorce" and "custody" and to work out a good joint custody arrangement.

Bitterness. Before the reader is falsely swayed into thinking that joint custody is always arrived at in a hearts-and-flowers manner, we need to tell some tales of bitterness. For example, this family tried to engineer joint custody in the early postseparation months but ended up with the father's having the bulk of the custodial responsibilities:

> My ex-spouse has the children during the week. I have them alternate weekends and often one night during the week. We

often meet for short time intervals, i.e., breakfast, lunch, doctor, to play racquetball. I am available 90 percent of the time for phone conversations. The disadvantage is probably lack of long-range planning for the father (the ex-spouse).

He was not much of a father before the separation; I decided to terminate the marriage and wanted custody of the boys. He refused to leave the house and asked for full custody of the children.

I was stunned when he began to show a great deal of interest and to express affection for them. I left and moved across town. Our time was divided thus: Monday through Thursday with Mom; Friday through Monday with Dad; alternating weeks.

The boys (eight and ten) were upset and fought constantly. It was a very traumatic time for us all. After two months of this, we each took one child during the week and alternated weekends with both together. This was a great improvement, but the constant moving back and forth was an upset for the children's sense of order and difficult on their friendships.

Father was still pushing for full custody. I could not do this; however, after much soul-searching and conflict within myself, I let them set up permanent residence with their father, five miles away. They seemed much more content having *one* home.

Father is a high school teacher and able to spend a lot of time with them and is happy to do so. He is not involved with another person; *I am.* The children still fight, and I rarely have them together since it is difficult for me to deal with their fighting. I feel that they need a man's discipline. It is perhaps a jealous ploy (the fighting) for attention.

I would like the oldest son to live with me and let the youngest live with him. He will not consider this arrangement. We do not have to make this decision as long as we both reside in the same town. When (if) one of us chooses to move, we will have to put the question to the boys. This is an uncomfortable thought for both parents to deal with.

The "flavor" of the negotiating process has been one of emotional stress for both parents. We are trying to do what is best for the children. I think we are succeeding so far.

In some cases a spouse will bitterly fight the ex-spouse who simply wants to see the child alone. Problems with drugs, alcoholism, violence, or incest usually explain why a parent tries to protect his or her children from the ex-spouse. Amazingly enough, though, dramatic turnarounds do occur. The troubled spouse may get counseling, go on the wagon, and gain joint custody:

As my husband and his live-in girlfriend were so spaced out on drugs, at the time of the divorce, he had very little to do with the arrangement. I told my lawyer I didn't want my husband seeing the child outside of my presence, and this is what the judge approved. However, after my ex-husband and his girlfriend married, got off drugs, and shaped up their lives, he was welcome to see our daughter at any time and place he wanted.

A father of a four-year-old girl was especially incensed:

A lawyer (hers) acted as mediator during the negotiating process. He pushed for me to grant sole custody to my ex-wife. I refused, saying that I would fight them in court unless we agreed to joint custody and that I intended to continue raising my child.

Our first order said "reasonable visitation," which means what is reasonable to the custodial parent. The order was a temporary order that she obtained after abandoning custody totally to me for over a month. I trusted that she would not try to deprive me of my daughter.

I was wrong. My daughter was used to manipulate in an insidious game of withholding that still goes on, even to this day . . . I feel that it will only cease when the courts of California begin to uphold the laws of custody (joint) that are already on the books.

People in a troubled marriage sometimes almost want to dive into a divorce. Somehow, they seem to feel, a divorce will magically end all the pain and misery. This of course often is nonsense. In talking with hundreds of divorced people and reading hundreds of accounts, we have concluded that the fear, anger, uncertainty, and hurt linger for a long time. Sometimes there is a period of respite, but the troubles circle around, double back, and start all over again. Listen to this father's story. It is very typical:

Before she moved we both met with my lawyer and came to an agreement on visitation: one-half of the holidays for each parent, and every other week for me.

She then moved in with her mother, who turned her

around 180 degrees and hired her a lawyer who fed her head full of possibilities. Her lawyer took it upon himself to hit me with lies and threats.

When she found out what the lawyer was doing, she cooled a bit herself and agreed to let the child [age three] visit me anytime she wanted to after she reached the age of seven years. I was advised that this was going to be the best I could do, so I signed.

I didn't see either one for two years. Last year she moved back into town and let me see the child as much as I wanted—approximately sixteen hours a day. After finding out we were not going to get back together, she moved back to her mother's, and I've seen the child two days since then.

She had lived here for six months, and that was one year ago. I am leaving this weekend to go and pick up the child and bring her back with me for a one-week visit, Monday through Friday. Hopefully, this will start a trend.

Who Decides? The Parents, the Children, or the Courts?

In most cases, divorcing parents take it upon themselves to decide where the responsibility for the children will lie after the divorce. If they are leaning in the direction of joint custody, the decision often comes more easily, for neither parent is as likely to feel slighted. In this section, we will take a look at how parents decide the issue, how children occasionally decide, and the times when courts become involved.

Ideally, we like to see parents themselves making an enlightened decision based upon what is best for the children. (The children's wishes should be clearly known, but in no way should the children be made *responsible* for the decision, nor should they be made to feel responsible.) As a last resort, we recommend court action, but only after attempts at mediation by counselors (not lawyers) have failed. The adversary system in the courts can do as much harm to a family as good.

The Parents Decide. First, then, a look at parents who are deciding the issue. In these first examples, the parents did not get into a big fight over "who the children love more," and so forth. Because the parents respected each other as people, the decision was not particularly painful:

> At the time we decided to separate we decided on joint custody. He wanted six months each. I explained there was no way we could do that—especially if one of us were to move away—because of school. We then went to nine months and three months, which we alternate. No one helped. We just talked it over a couple of times.
>
> *—a mother with joint custody of an eight- and a ten-year-old.*

> We alternate months and weekends. We make modifications as the need arises. It works exceptionally well. Only minor conflicts have arisen. She proposed it, and I readily agreed.
>
> We both worked. Our daughter was in nursery school from the age of three. After school, she went to her grandmother's. After work we picked her up. She attended the same school for grades kindergarten through fourth, following the same routine, except that from the second grade on, depending on the month, either I or her mother picked her up at her grandmother's. In the middle of the fifth grade, we moved close to her mother's residence, and she transferred to public school.
>
> Our goals with respect to our daughter's rearing are the same, and so we have few disagreements. We chose our current residence so that our daughter could walk or ride to school, her mother's place of employment, and her daily swim team practices. She is physically healthy, and there are no signs of abnormal emotional or psychological development. Her ego is strong, and she is nearly an all-A student.
>
> *—a father with joint custody of a ten-year-old daughter.*

> We wanted joint custody, but in our state you can't have it. He begged, pleaded, took me to see a child psychologist, who recommended that the boys be with their dad. I loved them *both*. I decided I was only going to hurt the children if I tried to hurt my husband by keeping the children. I even stayed in the state—bought a house eight miles from the farm so we could share the kids.
>
> It was very painful. I lost twenty-five pounds, which I couldn't afford to do. I was criticized by many people, which

made it *hard*. It took me two months to decide. Hang-ups were:
first, I had just had a baby. He told me when I was seven months
pregnant that he didn't love me like before, etc., and the week
before the baby was born he asked for a divorce and said
there'd be no divorce unless I gave him custody of the boy. I
was haggard and sick from a breast abscess and devastated over
the divorce.

But I gained a lot of insight and support from several close
friends and the child psychologist and the hospital social
worker. It's a very painful thing for me to have to relive—I'm
lucky I have a daddy (ex-husband) who loves his children and
who plays such a part in their development.

But, his constant appearance has made it very hard for me
to get over the divorce. You don't get over a divorce when you
see the ex and his girlfriend every day and watch the girlfriend
move into your "Big House."

> —*a mother with joint custody of five- and one-year-old children*

One father of seven- and six-year-old children told of how he
made his proposal of joint custody to his wife—in which he would
assume almost 50 percent of their day-to-day care—and how the proposal was finally worked out after three months of haggling over
details: "I told her she could accept it or fight it out in court," the
father, who made $50,000 a year at the time, wrote. He reported
that he took the entire lead in their discussions, which were unpleas-
ant. A marriage counselor and a lawyer (a good combination, we
might interject) teamed up to help. Finding correct terminology for
the agreement was difficult, the father told us, but the biggest problem "was getting my passive-aggressive ex-spouse to communicate."

The benefits of parents' successfully working out an agreement
are not inconsequential. One mother reported that her ex-spouse insisted on having 50 percent of the time with the children, not just
weekends. The negotiations were not overly friendly, she noted, but
were always child-centered. She worried that going "back and forth,
back and forth" between parents' homes would be hard on the kids:
"The boys come home to *my* house every day after school—then he
picks them up after supper approximately four nights a week. I was
worried that they weren't here enough nights a week." But her worries were unfounded. Though she would have liked total custody,

joint custody "has been wonderful for the three boys. Their main complaint comes when they leave a baseball glove, etc., at the wrong house."

Involving Children in the Decision. Many families involve the children in the decision for joint custody. They reason that they want to maintain a democratic spirit in the family and/or that the children are mature enough to help in the decision-making process.

In our nationwide study, significantly more parents with joint custody discussed custody options with their children before the divorce than did parents with a sole custody arrangement.

When asked about their convictions about the importance of children's having close relationships with both mother and father after divorce, the parents with joint custody felt considerably more strongly.

Parents must be careful not to let the children think that they "run the show" in a family, however, for families cannot operate completely on democratic principles. A five-year-old's wishes should be known, but his vote cannot count the same as his parents'. Similarly, parents who let their children decide custody may be copping out; they may not want the responsibility for such a momentous decision on their shoulders. They may be lacking in courage.

Though we as clinicians believe that even the youngest child should be talked with about custody issues (even down to three- and four-year-olds), we do not think that a child should actually decide until age eighteen or even twenty-one. Many parents we talked with had strong feelings about this issue. In the words of one mother with two daughters: "I refused to allow either of the girls to make the final decision about which parent they would spend holidays with because I didn't want them to feel responsible for the lonesome parent's sadness on those occasions."

In families in which joint custody has been the option of choice, the problem of children's guilt is generally minimal. In short, the problem is not as great as that of which parent to live with all the time.

Parents Who Listen to Children. We will quote a number of parents who listened a good deal to their children:

Initially the children spent a few days here and a few days there. Often we allowed the child to make the decision to switch or alter the situation if the need arose. We (father and mother) also kept in very close contact regarding what was happening with the kids. Sniffles would rate a phone call from their father saying "What would you do?"

The children decided the stay to be extended to a week at a time, instead of a few days here and a few days there. I missed them terribly but learned to be on my own and to enjoy the empty time.

Beyond that, I took the children on a five-month traveling vacation during which their father joined us twice for approximately a week each time. When we returned, to the amazement of everyone else I placed the three of them with their father and proceeded to be out of touch with them—though I was right here in town. It was my time to grow, and I feared that their father had become far too comfortable with them out of his hair.

Eventually, the boy (youngest) got in trouble due to lack of supervision (and many other complications) at his dad's house, and the court ordered him to be with me. Since he needed not just me, I requested that his sisters remain with me also. The middle child agreed; the eldest opted for her father's house where she has her own cabin. She is not living on campus, and for this school year the boy is in a special school.

One fifty-one-year-old father of two children, ages twenty-one and eighteen, was rather cryptic in his response: "The children decided and we agreed." This pattern emerged in the families with older children in our study—late teens and early twenties. In these families, the children generally decided how to divide their time between parents. When the children are this age, parents who have joint custody often do not have much time with them to divide up anyway. One father of sixteen-, seventeen-, and eighteen-year-old children explained that all three moved out of the house into an apartment together after the divorce: "They moved into an apartment by themselves, and we both never see them."

In many families, agreement on a suitable custody arrangement cannot be reached. This is of course no surprise, for many divorcing couples could not find agreement on other issues either.

The Court Decides. Though joint custody works best in an atmosphere of cooperation and a willingness to agree, many families ended up having joint custody worked out in court.

One father wrote that "our county judge was very much against it." The father added that his ex "dragged her feet" on the issue, but with the help of a marriage and divorce counselor, he managed to persuade the ex-wife, his lawyer, and the judge that it would work. The father finally gained joint custody of his four-and-a-half-year-old daughter, alternate weeks.

Fathers accused of incest by their divorcing spouses still have a chance of winning joint custody in court if the charges cannot be substantiated. One father of nine- and seven-year-old girls wrote:

> Custody was settled by the courts. It was a very hostile situation because my ex-spouse was determined at all costs that I would not have the kids except at those times which she chose as appropriate. It took one year and nine months before the final decree was issued. The attorneys did most of the initial negotiating, which ended in a standoff.
>
> The general overall hang-up was in my ex-spouse being determined to control the situation, not allowing me to see or be with the kids except on her limited terms, and telling the kids how bad I was, to reinforce her position. Near the time for the first court hearing on custody, she attempted to press sexual assault and incest charges against me in an attempt to sway the court or get me to go along with her terms or for some other reason of which I'm not sure.

These kinds of charges are often leveled in court and are difficult to substantiate.

We want to report the following ex-couple's story in detail, because over time a very level-headed approach evolved in dealing with a judge who was skeptical about joint custody. The thirty-four-year-old mother of a six- and a five-year-old tells the story much better than we could paraphrase it:

> My ex-husband and I alternate weeks with the children. It seems to be working satisfactorily; however, I am beginning to feel that perhaps we should extend the time to two weeks, in order to cut down on the amount of moves in a month's time.

Right after our separation, we sought counseling. Within a month's time, I had decided to end the marriage. We talked about coparenting with the counselor, who indicated her disagreement with the plan. My ex-husband then agreed with her and indicated that he wanted custody.

I didn't believe he was serious and thought that I would go along with it, assuming that he would eventually back away. During this time, I was living in the house with the children. We were waiting for the sale of our house, with the plan that we would split the money and each buy a house. (This took from October to December.) As December came closer, I realized that he was serious, and then I said I wanted custody, as I could not see myself as a weekend parent to our girls.

We each threatened to fight it out in court, but I then realized that he did not want to be a weekend parent any more than I did. I then brought up the possibility of coparenting again. We both bought books on the subject, exchanged them, and decided to give it a try.

When we came to this decision, we also decided to share the same attorney as we agreed to the settlement. Our attorney was somewhat discouraging, indicating that there was only one judge who even considered joint custody, and he had recently had one that blew up.

We decided to coparent for three months prior to going to court in order to show the court that we could do it successfully. When we went to court, the judge advised us of some of the problems but did grant joint custody.

Another couple similarly profited from the fact that joint custody had been working a long time for them by the time that they went before a skeptical judge. Rather than criticize judges like this one, we applaud him, for joint custody is still a social experiment today, and experiments can be successful or they can just as easily fail. The judge, as representative of our social institutions, had a duty to be cautious, for the children's sake:

We agreed upon joint custody from the beginning. It was one area of the divorce negotiations that we agreed upon. The judge, however, was against the concept and delayed our dissolution because of it. With the help of both our lawyers, and with the judge having a private interview with our son, joint custody finally was granted.

However, since my husband and I had been separated for four years prior to our divorce and had been practicing joint custody during that time, the judge decided that an interview with the child would give him an indication of the effects. He decided that our son was well-adjusted, understood the situation, and had thrived under the arrangement.

Even though a couple ends up before a judge, joint custody can still work, as a father of two boys explains:

Our custody arrangement was settled through court. Reasonable visitation was decided by the judge, and her lawyer asked for $200/month child support, which was approved by the judge.

The only hang-ups in the divorce were property settlement. Everything was agreed on within the sixty-day waiting period for the divorce to be finalized. The flavor of the negotiating was stressful, but thinking back, everything worked out for the good.

My ex-wife and I communicate better now than when we were married, although once in a while we have small differences. But we work them out.

The differences that separate parents are often not insignificant. Sometimes different but heartfelt philosophical views of life make agreement impossible, and a judge must step in. In one family, the virtues of city life versus country life were argued:

The "flavor" or tone of our discussions went through changes, depending on the present outlook of each parent. It never reached hate; it never reached a love that would allow either of us to relent, either.

The hang-ups were that my husband wanted just the opposite arrangement of what we have. He also felt strongly that he wanted our son to grow up in a tiny town surrounded by nature. Virtually no crime. He looks at any town larger than five thousand as a jungle.

I felt that a larger town afforded more opportunities, and with proper supervision and home life, the bad things could be dealt with.

The mother above went on to outline the court process the family went through:

I decided that I wanted custody arranged as it eventually worked out to be. I told my husband. He argued, said "No way!" etc. Our lawyers finally agreed that our son needed a guardian of the court (an attorney appointed by a judge to interview both parents and the child, if necessary).

Because neither parent has any legal reason not to be awarded custody, no one seemed able to decide who should have it. The guardian interviewed both parents, but not the child, as he (the guardian) was leaning toward me, the mother, having custody. Minutes before we went into court for the hearing to determine custody, my husband gave in and agreed to my wishes.

This mother went on to explain what was to be termed legal joint custody. The reader will note that this looks much like a traditional arrangement, with the mother having most of the responsibility for rearing the child:

During the school year my son lives with me. His father has a minimum of one weekend per month with him (in the father's home)—more weekend visitations if agreeable to both parents.

During the summer my son lives with his father, and I have the same visitation privileges. Holidays are alternated, i.e., Thanksgiving with me, Christmas with father, Easter me, and so forth. Each year is opposite from the year prior. At present it is working quite well.

Our estimate is that genuine joint custody—coparenting or shared responsibility of the children—happens much less frequently in cases in which a court decides. We have a sneaking, gut-level suspicion that some lawyers and judges are allowing the term *joint custody* to be used to disguise a traditional maternal custody arrangement. The advantage of doing this is that fathers can be made to feel not quite so left out in the cold—even if, in fact, they have been left out in the cold.

Sometimes the tables get turned, and the term *joint custody* is used to mask paternal custody, as we infer from this mother's story:

We have joint custody. The children live in the former home with the father. So far I just ask for the children whenever I want them.

I usually have them on Wednesday after school until shortly before bedtime. Then, Friday after school, overnight, and all day Saturday. We have only been divorced for two months, so I'm sure the arrangements will change as we find what works best.

So far it works fairly well, but I don't feel that I'm getting to spend nearly the time I should with a joint custody situation. The children need time with their father, friends, lessons, sports, and some time to themselves, and with working and having some sort of life for myself, this does limit the time available.

Our arrangements were all made through the lawyers, as our communication with each other was zero as it had been for seventeen years. It took us eleven and a half months to agree on joint custody. I wanted either complete custody or joint, and my ex-husband wanted complete custody, period. Our biggest delays came from trying to get into court and from the long process of communicating through the lawyers.

Finally, on the day of our hearing, we both made some compromises due to the fact that we neither one wanted to lose completely. My extramarital affair worried me in regard to the judge's decision. The children's ages and the fact that I had always taken total care of the children worried my ex-husband.

My ex-husband could afford to purchase my half of the house and continue to live there, so the kids could keep familiar surroundings, friends, and schools. At least in a joint custody situation, I still get to help make the decisions and see them as often as I can.

I don't feel the court system is fair in divorce cases, as it seemingly could have made a big difference in my life had we gone ahead into court with the judge we had. It was many people's view that had we gotten the other judge available, that his views were completely different about divorce than the one we had.

It seems there should be a set way to deal with certain circumstances, instead of how a certain judge feels on a certain day. I realize that everyone's case is different, but there must be some way to be fairer to everyone.

We offer the following observation, not trying to sound moralistic. Divorcing couples who have spent years disagreeing in marriage are not likely to be satisfied with a judge's decision. We rarely have witnessed a court order that made either parent resoundingly happy. Judges, first of all, are not supposed to make people happy—they are only supposed to administer justice. And in the process of coming to a decision, the judge will take many differing viewpoints into account. His or her decision will generally take into account the fact that each viewpoint probably has an element of truth in it, as well as an element of falsehood. In divorce wars, individuals are rarely completely right and rarely completely wrong. Spouses who are accustomed to thinking of each other as the Antichrist, however, are unlikely to realize that most of us are a mixture of good, not-so-good, and evil.

A father of a four-year-old girl complained that his "joint custody" arrangement left much to be desired:

I, as the father, am allowed to see my daughter every other weekend and alternate Mondays; alternate holidays if I'm lucky. I have a joint legal custody situation and feel that I have been duped all the way down the line in that I have *no* legal control over my child's upbringing. Even the courts cooperate in deceiving fathers in this regard. In short, I don't get enough time.

Terminology seems to add to the confusion. One judge apparently defines joint and split custody differently from the way we do (we do not imply that he is wrong; rather, it is important that parents know *exactly* how each court defines terms because there is apparently a great deal of disagreement over terms). Listen to this father's story:

For about six years (three before and three since the divorce), the child has lived with the father during the school year, with the mother for two months, and attends a resident camp for one month during the summer. The child "wants" to go to camp.

During the school year the child stays with the mother when the father is out of town, which is sometimes required for his business—at least once every other month, sometimes for as long as a week. The child also spends part of the weekend, either one or two nights, and often Wednesday afternoon and overnight with mother. During the summer the time is reversed on weekends. This arrangement was in operation when the parents lived eight miles apart.

The mother moved in January. The distance between the residence is now about 1,400 miles. Needless to say, the visitation times have changed. The child will visit his mother during spring break in April and two months during the summer:

For a long time, I felt slighted because I was not given equal legal status in the child custody arrangement (i.e., joint custody). However, there are some advantages for me this way. I have limited legal responsibility. There is no child support, which is a source of problems for many parents.

Both parents wanted joint custody and had legal papers requesting it. This arrangement of jointly sharing the responsibility for the child had worked well for the three years of separation prior to the divorce.

However, the judge said joint custody does not work and would not grant it. He then changed the word "joint" to "split" custody. The living arrangement had been outlined in the original papers. It stated that the child would live with his father during the school year and with the mother during the summer when the child is not in school. (Legally, split custody means that one parent is legally responsible for the child at a given time as stated in the agreement. I refer to our custody as a 9–3 split.) Also, it granted "reasonable" visitation rights for each parent.

Quite simply, we do what seems best for all three of us. The child is sometimes given a choice on weekends. There have never been any major problems. The biggest problem ever is needing to make a last-minute change. Example: the child is scheduled to go somewhere with one parent and the child is invited to spend the weekend with one of his friends.

Common Approaches to Joint Custody

After studying dozens of joint custody plans, we have come to the conclusion that each is slightly different and that categorizing families is foolish business. There are, however, a number of common approaches that jump out from the data we collected, and we have organized them as follows.

1. Three and a half days with Mom; three and a half days with Dad
2. One week with Mom; one week with Dad
3. Weekdays with one parent; weekends with the other
4. Three months with Mom; three months with Dad
5. Six months with Mom; six months with Dad
6. School year with one parent (one or more weekends per month spent with other parent); summer with other parent (one or more weekends per month spent with other parent)
7. Kids live in same house all the time; parents take turns moving in and out (one week/one week, one month/one month, three months/three months, six months/six months, or whatever schedule is most convenient for the family's life-style)
8. Total flexibility

In outlining these common approaches to joint custody, we express quite obviously our bias: for us, joint custody has to do with who is caring—physically and emotionally—for the child. We are not particularly interested in legalistic hairsplitting or arguments over who can authorize medical treatment after an automobile crash or who decides what Ivy League university the child is to attend in fifteen years. Rather, we are concerned with a here-and-now, nontheoretical issue: Who is to take care of this child today and tomorrow and the day after?

In our definition of joint custody families, both parents are actively caring for the child. Not one doing the work and one sending a check. The question is, are the ex-spouses genuine coparents in the enterprise of rearing children after divorce?

The Extent of Co-parenting in Joint Custody Families

As we have made perhaps overly clear, the sharing of the children is not always 50/50 in joint custody families. Many parents share legal custody of the children, and this is often called joint custody. But legal joint custody often means that one parent still does 90 percent of the daily caring for the children.

Since there was a great deal of variation in the definitions of joint custody, we decided to come up with some precise, though arbitrary, operational definitions:

Legal joint custody will refer to those cases in which parents shared legal responsibilities for the children.

Physical joint custody will refer to those cases in which parents genuinely shared the day-to-day responsibilities of caring for the children.

How did we as researchers measure this sharing? We used a complicated technique developed for studies of other role-sharing families. The approach is explained in detail in a research journal.[1] Essentially, it involves going through a family's child care schedule hour-by-hour in a "typical" week. When is Mom with the kids? When does Dad have them? When are they at school, at the sitter, and so forth?

We then calculated the ratio of the father's hours to the mother's hours and came up with a percentage—for example, in one family the father might care for the kids 52 percent of the time, compared with the mother's 48 percent.

Our operational definition of physical joint custody, then, is: neither parent has more than 60 percent of the total hours of care for the children, nor less than 40 percent. The 60/40 figure is relatively arbitrary. To us it indicates that each parent is taking a sizable share of the workload. Any range greater than that of 60/40—say, 70/30, 80/20, 90/10—would lean toward the more traditional custody arrangements.

In our study 21 percent of the parents (152 out of 738) described their legal custody arrangement as joint custody. Using our more strict definition, implying genuine shared or coparenting (60/40), only 8 percent (56 out of 738 parents) fit the criteria.

Genuine joint custody, a continuing partnership between ex-spouses for the purpose of rearing the children after divorce, is thus rather rare. We are not arguing in this book that more parents should try joint custody; nor are we arguing that it should remain an option that few families choose. Rather, we are saying simply that if it makes sense to a particular family, they should try it.

Successful Joint Custody Families. In this section, we will take a close look at how a number of these nearly 50/50 parents work things out. We note a good deal of creativity on their part and extreme flexibility—they seem to be able to adapt to many different circumstances.

Listen to this mother, age forty, who has joint custody of her sixteen- and fifteen-year-old children:

> What has evolved for us is that we, the parents, move in and out of the house that the kids *stay* in—the house they've lived in for the past ten-plus years—at one-and-a-half year intervals.
>
> The spouse who is not living with the children lives in an apartment in the same community. The children visit this apartment two times a week, or once a week for dinner in the apartment and once for dinner out. We all have free access to each other and are very flexible. If the live-in spouse has to be out of town for some reason, the out-spouse goes to the kids' house to care for them. Seems to work fine for all concerned.

How did this family work out such an arrangement?

> There was not a question of child custody ever. The one thing we both felt strongly about was that the children should not suffer from our incapabilities. Therefore, we put parenting first, our needs second.
>
> The only time it was an issue briefly was when we put it before the lawyer, who said joint custody was frowned upon. We also dealt directly with it when trying to figure out who would claim whom for tax purposes, etc. . . . and then, too, there was no problem. We were not out to screw each other,

just to be separated from one another in the fairest, least painful process possible.

What kind of advice would this mother give to other divorcing parents?

Keep spousal animosities *separate* from parenting obligations. If you love your kids allow them equal access to each parent without poisoning the other spouse's character with your own material about that spouse. Kids can make their own judgment in time.

Be honest; be really kind and loving to yourself. So you can "be there" for others.

This family seems to have it put together quite well, in spite of divorce. But when asked about advice to ensure optimal adjustment of the divorcing individual, the mother suggested that counseling can help, which suggests to us that a good counselor was on her side at some point:

Seek therapy for yourself and/or your family to weather the rough spots. Give yourself time to heal and forgive. Love yourself. Allow other people their discomfort. They'll live through it all. People (kids, relatives, friends, spouses) are pretty strong. Be true to yourself. Be honest with yourself and the kids. Love them a lot.

The following mother seems to have the advantages of parenthood and the advantages of the child-free alternative wrapped up in the same life:

When living with them, I like the sharing of daily joys and woes with kids, watching them grow, enjoying them!

When not living with them, I have the joys of greatly reduced responsibilities and the freedom of being single (we do consult on major developmental decisions always).

There are definite costs involved in joint custody, of course, as the same mother indicates:

When not living with them, I do not have enough daily contact; I miss out on their growing.

When living with them, I have a *huge* responsibility for kids, household, ground upkeep, pets, regular meals, on top of working full-time—plus social life, etc.

A father with joint custody of his son told us of his concern for the future: "Each of us has custody a week at a time. He is only sixteen months old, so he really does not know what is going on. For us it seems to work now, but I have some doubts about later on." His sentiment was expressed in similar ways by other parents aware that they are participating in an important social experiment. The parents are cautious about drawing conclusions. "One day at a time" seems to be their attitude:

I have my son from Sunday to Sunday. My spouse has him from Sunday to Sunday. Joint custody. Our son seems to manage real well with the arrangement. Sometimes I would rather he be with me all of the time. I know my ex-spouse takes good care of him, but I just feel like he should be with his mother.

—*a twenty-five-year-old mother of an eighteen-month-old boy*

We are dividing time equally. I take care of our son from Thursday afternoon until the following Thursday morning. Our son's father then picks him up from school on Thursday afternoon and takes care of him until the following Thursday morning when he drops him at school. It has worked quite well for the past few weeks that my ex-husband has followed this schedule as it's set up. However, he refused to take care of our son at first.

—*a mother of a five-year-old boy*

My ex and I have joint custody. Our girl is four and a half years old. We each have her a week at a time, with Wednesday evenings the time that we exchange her. This arrangement works very well for the time being. Some other kind of setup will have to be arranged when she enters school.

—*a father*

We share equally Monday night through the next Monday morning with each parent. It works well—she attends the same preschool every day, and so has that consistency. It works better than the previous arrangement—Wednesday night through Saturday afternoon with father, the rest with mother—because it seemed to take her a day or two to become adjusted to the new place. She exhibited more aggression and whiney behavior at first.

—a mother of a four-year-old girl, divorced one year

Unsuccessful Joint Custody Families. Not all joint custody arrangements include such an equal sharing of parental responsibility or as much cooperation between family members as the arrangements the preceding stories suggest. In fact, some legally delineated joint custody arrangements bear little resemblance to the concept of shared parental responsibility after divorce. Some so-called joint custody arrangements may be disasters. The following story illustrates this:

We have joint custody, according to the lawyers. The father is to have the children six weeks every summer, spring vacation, alternate weeks of winter break, one weekend a month, one night out alone with father every three weeks, and special occasions, as arranged.

Father is a psychiatrist and has this time available. When we lived in close proximity, the longest he ever took them was four days—that's four days in six years. The older two girls ran away on many occasions from him. He moved away. One and a half years later I moved from the area. He has seen each child a total of one week in the last three and a half years.

He encouraged the running away of one child who could not deny his request for "love." She returned six months later as an emotionally distraught person (she has been hospitalized 50 percent of the last year).

He has shown no real interest, and when he was in the general area, he refused to come into the state. He would only visit them if I sent them out of the state to visit him. There has been a tendency on his part to have a sexual relationship with his female children.

Joint custody was worked out with one attorney. One week later my ex and a girlfriend had a new attorney, and I was charged as an unfit parent. I kept the original attorney who had been a mutual friend. My ex-spouse's first girlfriend was a successful union—they were super together and with the children. But she later went back to her husband.

The next girlfriend—several years later—had many things in common with me (animals, outdoor interests, even appearance somewhat) but had abandoned her two kids in her own divorce. He said she didn't want kids around—so generally he took the children to his mother's and spent nights himself with the girlfriend. They were married two years ago.

There were a total of seven harassing court scenes, including the children in several hearings. He has told the first child he wasn't a parent anymore, and if she came to visit, it would be his sole option to send her away. He has totally abandoned the third child, who is adopted.

For holidays, birthdays, special occasions—*if* there is a gift or communication, it is small and impersonal. The whole tedious divorce took about three years. Final papers were picked up by me after six years. He had by then left the state.

Joint custody should be able to be worked out by two reasonably intelligent people. My ex-spouse wanted it—I did not. However, his lack of interest (unwillingness to visit and neither emotional nor financial support unless there's an underlying purpose) leads me to believe that I would have been better off with sole custody.

The anger has not disappeared. He never has been willing to participate, although he has made court efforts to "show" his interest. I think divorced parents should get together—with a negotiator if necessary—to support their children emotionally. He wanted reconciliation counseling, which would have been useless at the time. Later discussions for the kids' benefit would have been good.

I believe that the children have the *right* to know each parent and to give/receive love from each parent. An ex-spouse figuring to get even with the husband/wife by denying the children his/her love, emotional support, *and* financial help is not successfully getting even but instead hurting the children by these denials.

In time, the children know that when the peanut butter runs out, it's because we're all waiting for that extra "allowance." (I bring home $1,560/month. He should be adding $615.) The $1,560 custodial parent gets locked into many expenses that are not for her/himself. Generally, from my point of view, they're for the kids: braces, dentists, doctors, special clothing, special occasions, summer camp. An ex-spouse who is able—

mine earns double my salary—should offer to help work out specials for the kids and *try* to help with the expenses.

If there are special medical circumstances, he/she should try to help (not laugh). Mine cashes the insurance checks, and I get stuck with the bills. (On previous occasions I've been stuck with $4,000 when a child got hit by a car; $700 for a child with braces on his teeth; and $8,700 for hospitalization of a child whom I believe he severely emotionally damaged.)

There must either be a willingness to communicate with the other party (and not turn around and harm that person) or a total abstinence from communicating. The arguments over the check or summer camp are harmful to the child and only provide more stress to what they see as an already stressful arrangement.

Don't file for the divorce until you've had several months (or as long as necessary) to see where you are going for yourself. Give yourself a chance to know your kids if you have custody. More important, let your kids get to know you—free of what stress there was before separation.

Still before filing for divorce, get yourself situated jobwise if possible. This allows you the peace of being able to stand alone and not be frightened or threatened by the ex-spouse's demands.

I really took a long time to stand on my feet with a forty-hour job because I had not worked, except part-time. (All positions I had prior to divorce were such as to allow me to be with my children: teaching art classes, running a swim school. They were part-time positions or seasonal positions that provided an excellent second income without forcing me to have outside child care.)

Besides this, I had recent back surgery, so my timing was terribly off. I feel secure today, but it took a good six years. Financially, I was not beholden to him—I was angry that he cared so little for his children.

Our legal custodial arrangement bears no resemblance to what in fact exists. I feel very badly that the children have no opportunity to have a relationship with their father. I do *know* that he's made a choice. When a child is vibrant, happy, excited, looking forward, I feel good because I'm living with the child.

I have at this time a resident "caretaker" (not boyfriend). He's fabulous with the kids and dogs, and they challenge occasionally the authority I've allowed him but show increasing pride in him and in caring for him. It doesn't replace a father—but helps.

I have had the joys of seeing the children grow to achieve in academics, sports, sociability. They have participated, sometimes successfully, but in any case they have the option to participate in activities of their choice.

I would like the comfort/support of a husband/man. It would allow the children to see that people could care for each other—respect each other and still differ—hopefully constructively. Children don't feel support but instead domination when they have only one person at the "top." They don't see that person enter discussions and make decisions but instead hear only one command.

As a single parent, my "cute" ex-spouse informs the children that the custodial parent gets help because she's "stupid" or some equally marvelous term. The near destruction of one child (tried suicide at least three times) was a tragic thing for him to have pushed her into. She was fragile emotionally but outstanding in everything she tried. During the time (six months) that she was with him (she ran away to come back here), she nearly was destroyed. After hospitalization for much of last year, she again is rising and will succeed.

I'm thrilled that my son, age eleven, this year is finally loving himself and succeeding, and he's a very exciting young man. But most of the time he refused to talk on the phone with his dad, which is sad. He needs a dad.

Joint Legal Custody. One mother with joint legal custody gives the reader a good sense of how situations evolve over time. Life just does not seem to want to stand still:

We had been separated three times previously, and I always had sole custody. We always went back together for the kids, and so my ex-husband could spend more time with them.

We jointly decided to get a divorce, with him having joint legal custody and with my having unlimited visiting privileges. He remarried. His wife had three children (two of them live with her and one with her ex-husband). The children get along as well as any large family. I am friendly with my ex-husband and his wife. We were able to plan our daughter's wedding together and be in photographs as family groups. I am invited to their family parties, although I rarely go. The in-laws and other relatives are very supportive of this arrangement.

We worked this all out, and the papers were drawn up accordingly. There was no opposition from anyone. My youngest daughter had some problems initially and wanted to live with me, but financially and to be with the rest of the family . . . this was not possible.

Legal joint custody is beginning to wear on another mother of two males, ages thirteen and twenty. The oldest, a sophomore at the University of Texas, had no terms set up for him. Both children are free to see their father whenever they wish, but

we always have to ask if the thirteen-year-old can go over to his father's home. Never has he [the father] asked him or his brother to come over for a visit or a meal. At first, I thought this was fine, but now I feel that I need some time away from teenagers and to be able to spend one weekend occasionally with my friends or go shopping, etc., without having to arrange for the thirteen-year-old to be taken in by one of our friends. His father does not take any initiative toward this, and I am getting a little tired of same. His reaction to this is "just call and ask."

Physical joint custody usually mandates that coparents live relatively close together. In many legal joint custody arrangements, however, great distances are involved:

My daughter lives with me, yet she sees her father every time it is possible for her to do so. Since the separation and divorce, we have lived from 1,200 to 3,000 miles apart. At seven years of age, she has flown alone five times to spend time with her dad.

[a mother whose daughter lives with the father] Since I am basically a private person, I do not suffer greatly from the arrangement [joint legal custody]. I do have periods of depression when I stop to realize all that I am missing from her life. But it has been five years, and we all adjust. It has not been too painful for me . . . for her I wonder. For him, I honestly do not care.

Flexibility versus Rigidity in Joint Custody Arrangements. There is tremendous variation in the child care schedules that joint custody families maintain. Some are extremely flexible, while others have everything nailed down to the minute. A thirty-eight-year-old father of a
five-year-old girl explained the go-with-the-flow approach that he
and his ex worked out over the years:

> After separation we naturally fell into a two months on, two
> months off routine. This time has varied from as short as one
> and a half months to just recently three and a half months,
> depending on work and vacation schedules.
> At times I've felt my ex-spouse did not consider my needs
> in scheduling, but mostly there has been a give and take. This
> process has evolved over three and a half years, from separation
> through our recent divorce to the present.

A mother with joint legal custody managed to get in a dig at her
ex for using flexible scheduling to his best advantage:

> There is no defined arrangement. The father calls and says he'd
> like to take the children fishing, and off they go. There are no
> defined weekends and never have been. It causes problems in
> that the children do not see their father enough. It is beneficial
> to the father, as it still allows him control over mother and chil-
> dren's schedules.

The mother goes on to describe in detail how things got this
way:

> When negotiating we had a third (female) party who was later
> to move into my household, and she assumed a parenting role
> with the children, which is a reason I never pushed for a set
> time for visitation. We discussed the visitation, and the father
> did not want to be "tied down" to a set pattern.
> The lady and I did not push for a set time either, as we
> wanted to have our alone time flexible. Well, now that my part-
> ner has moved out and is no longer even friends with me or the
> children, I am again exploring a set time for them, which would
> allow them to see their father and for me to have some alone
> time.

I have seen a family court counselor, who said he would contact my ex-husband in November. He has never done so because he says my case is not as serious as some and he is overworked. I am in the process of contacting the father. We live in the same town. I want to try to negotiate for one evening per week and one weekend per month to be arranged at the first of each month, looking at both of our schedules.

We are still playing power games with each other instead of looking at the best interests of the children, who are becoming distrustful of parenting figures after losing their father and now the lady who has lived here since the divorce.

We are considering making an ad for a new "housemate" but are being cautious!

Parent after parent in our study stressed flexibility. Though most families had a set structure so everyone knew what was going on and could plan ahead, the structure was not cast in bronze:

The agreement is basically that I, the mother, am available after school for supervision, doctor, sports appointments, and dinner—Monday night through Thursday night. We split up the weekend nights (i.e., Friday and Saturday). Sunday night they spend with me.

The plan is flexible and adaptable each week, according to meetings, working nights, and social plans. We talk on the phone to plan each week. If the kids want to split up on one or two occasions, that is usually okay. The plan has worked well for us. It is *very* flexible.

A key to this plan, of course, was positive communication between the parents. A forty-four-year-old father of an eight-year-old boy explained a similar situation:

Basically I have my son on Tuesdays and either Friday night and Saturday or Saturday night and Sunday. However, if either parent has something special to do or goes on vacation, the other takes care of the child willingly and happily.

Can such an idyllic arrangement last? Certainly, as a mother explains:

Only one child is still at home, one is married, and one is living
with his girlfriend. My fifteen-year-old lives with her father and
stepmother and stepsisters. She is at my apartment two to three
days a week. This works well. The days vary according to days
off, school schedule, activities with friends, and relatives.

We all communicate well regarding joint custody, and this
includes holidays, vacations, open house at school, family parties, and work schedules. We have never had a major problem
that was not worked out by good communication in seven
years.

When stepparents are added to the family configuration, the
ugly head of jealousy often rears up. An ex-spouse may refuse to
care for the children "while my ex goes off and fornicates in Colorado," and so forth. Other parents, however, see the trip to Colorado
as an opportunity to have more contact with the child and do not
play power games to try to forestall an ex-spouse's future happiness.

It is truly amazing to us how differently people will handle similar situations. The result, of course, is that some families run
smoothly after a divorce, and some are in shambles.

The divorce court often delineates schedules to the very second.
This is done to eliminate future hassles, because many ex-spouses
love to continue hating each other and do so by nitpicking over minute differences. A good number of joint custody families started
out in a lockstep, prearranged manner, and it evolved over time into
a more flexible and humane approach. A mother with twelve- and
fifteen-year-old children told us:

According to the divorce settlement, he gets the children every
other holiday and one month out of the summer. But I have
never said no to any additional time. He sends for the children
every opportunity he can and usually for at least two months
out of the summer. The arrangement works well, except that I
miss them very much.

Besides being helpful to the parents, a set schedule with good-
natured flexibility built into it seems to be best for the children also.
The children then have the security of knowing what is going to
happen to them ahead of time, without confining rigidity.

Adjustment of the Parents

When we compared joint custody parents statistically with sole custody parents, we found some interesting differences, as you will recall. Joint parents, on the average, experienced less burnout as parents, because having someone around to share the load was a big help. Parents with sole custody had acquired significantly more nervous habits than had joint custody parents (smoking, nail biting, and so on). And feelings of being overburdened by the children were less prevalent among parents with joint custody (as compared with sole custody parents). But when they were asked to come up with a simple rating for satisfaction with their particular custody situation as a whole, no statistically significant difference emerged between sole custody and joint custody parents. Both groups of parents were relatively happy.

The Ex-spouse Relationship. The divorced parent's relationship with an ex-spouse can be an important factor in his or her adjustment, for some degree of contact, whether direct or indirect, is inevitable as the two share responsibility for the children.

Some joint custody parents get along amazingly well; others, so-so; and others are continually at war. This is quite similar to the sole custody parents, though on the average joint custody parents interrelate more positively than sole custody parents do with their ex-spouses.

Let us look, first, at some joint couples who are relating well. A mother of fifteen- and twelve-year-old children told us:

> To adjust, I had to accept. It is over, and I just had to live with that knowledge. Someday I hope to remarry, but in the meantime, I let the kids know that I still love their father and will probably always care about him, but in a different way than one feels about a husband. I just take one day at a time and thank God for the good things we have.

A mother of three teenagers had thoughts complementing those of the previous mother:

> We respect each other and do not try to get the children to take sides. Hopefully, they will see that though we did love each

other at one time and had a close relationship, we could leave each other in an adult manner.

One mother of a four-year-old child who had been divorced one year reported that things were going well with her ex-spouse now but that the future may be different:

> We each stated that we would like to have her full-time, so it seemed that the obvious compromise would be to share half and half. We do have a very positive attitude toward each other, and we each realize that the child will benefit from contact with the other.
>
> It was decided in one friendly/sad conversation (most of our encounters are friendly/sad), with no outsiders involved. Our arrangement is very fair in that we both have the same job, the same income, the same house payments, etc., and share child-rearing expenses equally. The arrangement is flexible, so that if one parent has a ski weekend, the other keeps her longer and the schedule is adjusted.
>
> I anticipate problems if I remarry and quit work to have a child. I would want my daughter more often so she could be at home with me and the baby instead of at preschool for ten hours a day. I'm not sure her father would see the benefit to her from being in a home environment more (as he insisted that I go back to work when she was two months old, when I would rather have stayed home with her several months).
>
> I haven't brought this up for discussion, since the above situation may never come about.

Support Systems: Where to Go for Help. Divorced or not, all parents need a support system. The parents with joint custody of their children who participated in our study offered many suggestions and comments about parental adjustment.

One mother's advice was particularly poignant to us:

> Time alone will help the adjustment. Rely on a few good friends, and be open to their suggestions and love and accept their help. Read a lot of books on divorce. Jim Smoke's *Divorce Recovery* is the best.
>
> I have a strong religious conviction, but tend to think, what did I do to deserve this? still, after a year. Time alone seems to be the healer that we all need.

I desire to go out again, and maybe someday I will meet someone, but right now I feel that I have been wise in going slowly. My children are anxious for me to date and find someone to care for me again.

I am quite afraid, though, when I think of going out after twenty years with one person. I find that I want to laugh again and am seeking ways to do so.

"Read, read, read," a father with joint custody of his five-year-old son suggested. His list included women's magazines (because they deal with parenthood, while men's magazines tend to deal with sex, guns, and success), newspaper articles, lawyers' magazines, single-parent magazines, and the book *Saturday's Parents*. Besides reading, he said, joining a group is often helpful. He noted that it might take time to find one "you feel good with," so "try them all out."

One mother copes with the help of a good support group of friends she confides in, people who love her and whom she loves and trusts. She also has a group of friends who have personally experienced divorce and joint custody. This helps a newly divorced person to feel not so alone on the journey.

Another mother argued that a person must leave the past behind: "Once it has been determined that the marriage is over, accept the situation and start making a new life. Harboring bitterness, resentment, or pain won't change anything, and if not left behind can make it impossible to do anything with the rest of your life." She recommended Parents without Partners as an "extremely supportive and beneficial" group for aiding both males and females in the divorce process:

> They provide an opportunity to participate in activities both with and without children, to find new acquaintances of the same and opposite sex, and most importantly, because they have all been there, they understand. This organization provides the means of beginning a new and different life at whatever speed is comfortable.

Many joint custody parents suggested "really qualified" confidants and authorities, including ministers and counselors. Group counseling was also suggested as being helpful.

One mother recommended

> friendship networks, fulfilling hobbies and interests, and a
> moderately fast-paced social calendar when the kids are gone.
> Use time to keep self and home in order. I feel traditional ar-
> rangements burden the custodial parent and keep the noncus-
> todial parent from responsibilities.

Religion. Religion was a positive force in the lives of many joint custody parents. Several talked of God and prayer and Bible study.

Dr. Lew Moore, director of the counseling center at Harding
University in Searcy, Arkansas, studied how religious convictions
affected coping abilities in divorce among more than three hundred
divorced people. He concluded that religion is a positive force for
divorcing people who use their faith to gain the strength necessary
for working actively to survive the trauma.

According to Moore, those people who have a passive view of
religion—who assume they can sit on their hands while "God provides"—will generally have a more difficult time weathering the
crisis.

We want to conclude this section on religion by quoting one
mother's story at length. Joint custody often is portrayed as some
kind of panacea for the pain of divorce—that is, "the big dilemma of
divorce is what to do with the children, and joint custody should
smooth things out quickly," and so forth.

We have seen no easy divorces, however, in our experience as
clinicians and researchers. This mother with joint custody tells her
painful story well:

> I do not like to give advice. I can only state how it worked best
> for me—a troubled, emotionally unstable woman of forty-two
> seeking answers to a life that had become unacceptable.
>
> Because divorce was not a practice in my family, and cer-
> tainly not within my church (of which I was a compulsively ac-
> tive member), I struggled to find answers within my marriage
> (a good starting point, I believe).
>
> I was shocked into seeing divorce as something less than
> evil. I saw it as the only solution, no matter how undesirable,
> from the time I began to wish my husband dead.
>
> It was no passing thought, but a deep hope that someday
> he would die and solve the unacceptable choice. Yet, unbeliev-

able as it sounds, he did not know of the inner turmoil and distraction I was going through—such is the lack of understanding and caring between us.

We worked daily at our family business—we worked well together—yet all the time in those final months I was losing weight, was close to tears most of the time, and deeply afraid of what I might have to do.

I honestly believe, that even though I did not love him as people should, if he had approached me with tenderness and an open heart, we could have come to some settlement and would still be married. We did not touch each other. Our sex life was frigid and lifeless, an unendurable act to be endured, a wall that could have crumbled if we had just known how.

But this is how I finally approached the problem: number one. I did not discuss my heartache openly—although I alluded to it desperately in Women's Bible Studies, where we studied *love*, and I cried out, "Show me how!" I talked around my unhappiness to my book club, ladies whom I admired and appreciated as no other friends I have ever known.

I did not even discuss it with my best friend, yet she knew us well and knew our problems for all those twenty-plus years. She just accepted them as part of my life, as I did hers. (She has since divorced and is happily remarried—a situation I have been unjustly blamed for by both our ex-husbands!)

My solution for needing someone to talk to was the only one that works—prayer. The answers were not what I wanted, though, for I wanted, I begged, I wept bitterly for my marriage to last and be good. I could not stand the hollowness. I needed to be allowed to be affectionate and could not do it without encouragement.

To him, affection meant a quickie—not gentle touching and warm looks, not always followed by sex. To him sex was what little boys giggled through, and little girls pretended wasn't happening to them. He did not grow up in all those years—and I knew no better, except that I *felt* that life alone was better than life under such unreal circumstances.

What the prayer did was send me to find answers within myself, what I call my gut feeling. It has never failed me.

When I met and planned to marry my husband, I *knew* I did not love him. I chose to think it would come, or that real love only happened in books, since I'd been told that so many times. That is one time when I chose to override my gut feeling, and it proved out exactly as I should have known.

We *were* compatible, for he was quiet and easygoing, and I became strong in areas for which I had no ability. But what happened over the years is that he became less communicative as I became a bitch—however much a church-going bitch. He retreated further into his bottle and with his likeminded friends, and I retreated inward where there was not much to like.

So, after many years of this type of living, when I finally sought the answer (whether to leave and learn to live alone, or to stay and ask no more from life), it came in a direct way—an absolute rightness in my gut to *leave.*

Was I afraid? Strangely, no. The relief was so great, my assurance that I was finally doing the right thing—no matter how painful—carried me through difficult times with sureness. I was on a week's trip with my little boy when I knew where I was supposed to be. I honestly believe it was as much a spiritual decision as it was purely flesh.

I found a job, an apartment, told my sad little boy what I was going to do, and went back home to tell my husband and other children that in one week I was going to move two hundred miles away, and I did it with a new strength and calmness unknown before.

I honestly believe that this is where God wants me, and it is surely where I want to be, now that I can freely admit it. These past five years have been full of many conflicts. I've had deep periods of guilt and loneliness. I've felt out of it during the most important years of one child's life, yet I've not once regretted the divorce.

Dating. Going out with members of the other sex can be a source of both satisfaction and stress for joint custody parents. Just to go out in the first place for many is a big step—the gun-shy attitude is common. One veteran father reiterated some tried-and-true advice: "Don't judge a whole sex by a relationship with one person. And take time to think another relationship through."

These two bits of advice are difficult to heed, for the pain is great and the fear runs deep. Not many are willing to jump quickly onto another hot stove:

Overall, I'm very angry at the dishonest manner in which my exspouse has treated the children. He has not loved them but used them to serve his occasional needs.

No, I would never marry *him* again, but I would indeed like the benefits of a good marriage for both myself and my teenage children. But I'm also afraid I'd marry someone like him, and that frightens me.

He's very successful professionally but was married to career and not family, and that has been devastating to "our" children. As my children near adulthood, I'm starting to look forward to my new life *again*. I have not taken time for me, but I'm starting to.

The biggest advantage joint custody offers in the dating area is free time. Also, joint custody parents usually have fewer child support problems than do sole custody parents. So, money will be freed up a bit for leisure activities. Discretion is advised here, however. It does not make an ex-spouse ecstatic to get a call asking her to care for the children while her ex-husband flies off to Mazatlán with a girlfriend. Eventually it may work out this way, but a lot of divorce war wounds have to heal first.

One joint mother told us of how she jumped the gun on dating, and we infer that this added to divorce and custody issue tensions:

When we decided to divorce we both knew that we wanted the kids to feel loved and that they weren't responsible. We started working on the major problems. There were many major arguments—we tried to argue when the kids weren't present, but several times they were there. My ex sometimes tried to involve the kids in major arguments, which I didn't want. I felt that we should explain the decisions when we were more calm.

Most of the decisions we came up with were give-and-take decisions. I give on one thing, he'd give on others. It was a very painful, accusation-filled time. I think it was hard on all of us.

Most of the tension centered on the fact that I had started to date, which to me *now* was a mistake. We now, after several months, have a very good relationship.

Dating can often help heal the wounds, and it offers comfort for lonely and sad people. At the same time, it can be an enormous source of controversy for joint custody families, as it can be for divorced families with other custody arrangements.

The children can get incredibly angry about what is going on. Adolescents, concerned and confused about their own developing sexuality, often fill with rage over a parent's "indiscretions" (especially the mother's). Adolescents, like children of divorce of all ages, tend to hope that the parents will get back together. This blind hope can be held on to secretly for years. Signs of a mother's or father's sex life with an outsider can indicate to the youngster that there is no hope that the parents will reconcile. This can be very disturbing and can lead to volcanic outpourings: "So how many times did you ———— him last night, you ————?!" and other expletive-peppered interrogations are common.

All of this, of course, is no reason to foreclose the options on dating and relationships with attractive people. Adolescents have no right to run a parent's sex life. It is really none of their business. But at the same time, the parent who is aware of these possible complications can be more sensitive to the children's fears and concerns and can be more cautious.

Stresses: Distance and Money. These seem to be key stresses for joint custody parents, for they come up time and again in our clinical interviews with parents and in the questionnaires we received during the research project.

Distance is especially important for joint custody parents, because genuine coparenting or shared parenting almost necessitates living in close proximity, or providing lots of money for airfare.

One father with joint custody saw his time with his son drastically reduced by distance:

Originally time was to be split 50/50, and it worked well. Now my ex-spouse is remarried and has moved three hundred miles away. I rarely get to see my son. Hopefully, when school is out during the summer we can spend more time together. This arrangement works well for the ex-spouse, as she has him most of the time, and it is too costly to have him travel between us just for a weekend.

This situation happens often, sometimes because of remarriage, sometimes because an ex-spouse just wants to, as one said succinctly, "get the hell away from this mess."

Some divorcing couples protect each other at the time of disso-lution by agreeing in legal documents not to destroy joint custody by moving. Restricting one's freedom of movement like this is a somewhat drastic choice—but taking children away from a parent whom they love and who loves them is even more drastic.

Another solution is to have the spouse who moves away relin-quish joint custody and give sole custody to the ex-spouse staying put. A third solution is to have the mover guarantee to pay air trans-portation for the children's visits.

None of these solutions is without some cost, but an attempt to move away sparks great resistance in joint custody parents, and an expensive court battle can easily begin.

A father with joint legal custody of his three-year-old daughter told of the difficulties he faced in trying to continue to see his child grow up:

> With the distance involved (three hundred miles), visits are few and far between. Weather is a major factor. I must cross four major passes over the Rocky Mountains. I have the child for one-week periods when time and weather permit, approxi-mately once every two months, total time six weeks a year.

In many cases, parents will move out of town, and the children will resist the change. This is especially common in families with adolescents, who at least on the surface relate better to peers than to parents:

> At the time of the divorce, I had full custody and moved to a town unfamiliar to my son and me. (The custody arrangement was agreeable to my ex-husband.)
>
> My son disliked his and my living arrangement immensely—school, baby-sitters, school bus, large and new town. After sev-eral months of struggling, he chose to go back to his hometown and live with his father.
>
> I felt that it was the best for him, as he just could not adjust, and I was unable to cope with a very stressful situation. We have had this arrangement for several months now, and my son has done very well in his adjustment.
>
> I have our son every other weekend, part of his vacations, and holidays, which are agreed upon in advance. Father has cus-

tody the balance of the time. The father lives more than fifty miles away, which makes it difficult to pick up and return in a weekend. However, so far we've been able to work the visits out to our schedules.

A mother with joint custody noted how things worked out fine at first. "We wanted to share the responsibility equally and both be available to our child." But things soured as time passed:

The hang-ups are coming out more for me now, though. There are times when I would like to move back East, and yet I don't have the peace of mind to separate my daughter from me or from her father. I feel trapped and angry and blame myself for the divorce even more than is really fair on myself.

Money is a source of stress for many joint custody parents. When one parent is required to go a great distance to see the child or pay the child's airfare when the child comes to live with the parent, money can be a limiting factor in a parent-child relationship.

In a tight money situation where the problem is compounded by distance, joint custody becomes almost a mockery:

I have joint custody, but I live in Indiana, and they are in California. So, I get them six weeks in summer if I have $2,000 to go get them. I could have them Christmas and Thanksgiving a few days if I could afford it.

—the father of a three- and a nine-year-old

The following mother with joint custody of a three-year-old is in almost desperate financial circumstances and has entertained dark thoughts:

I have always felt guilty for being away from her so much when I'm at work. The hours between 5:00 and 8:00 P.M., and 6:00 and 7:00 A.M. are not the best times to be together, but when I work that's all we have. But now I have only half of that.

I sometimes entertain the fantasy of kidnapping her and moving somewhere and going on welfare, just so we could be together more.

Also, for the first time since college, finances are a big problem. I chose to buy a house after the separation because apartment living was awful after being a homeowner for six years.

But now almost three-quarters of my take-home pay goes for the mortgage payment, and I can't afford to eat out or buy things for myself or my daughter. That's a very difficult adjustment in life-style, since before, money was really no consideration.

And listen to the pinch this twenty-four-year-old father with three- and two-year-old children is in:

My ex was selling joint custody to me before I accepted the divorce. It was very hard for me to discuss this with her because I still loved her and I wanted the marriage to work. I was always close to my children from the second they were born.

The court ordered me to leave the house—but I couldn't keep myself from returning almost daily to see the kids and wife (who had a boyfriend).

Negotiating was simple, according to her—any way I wanted as long as she kept "physical joint custody" and kept getting my support checks.

My close family was a big help in supporting my custody effort. The divorce details—custody and payments—are not final yet. I have been making full support payments, yet caring for the kids half the time. In that respect it seems as if I'm being penalized for loving my own children and continuing to be a family man.

Joint custody, indeed, has many different meanings for many different people.

Advice on Parental Adjustment from Parents. Here is a collection of advice gained from our joint custody parents regarding personal adjustment:

I took a divorce adjustment seminar, which was worth tenfold the cost. It gave me positive reinforcement about myself, which helped me be a better parent, as well as get my act together. Don't be afraid to concentrate on yourself—you have some wounds to heal.

—a thirty-seven-year-old mother with joint custody of twelve- and eleven-year-old children

Be sure that divorce is the best answer for you before pursuing one. I spent eight years deciding (or questioning myself) as to what I really needed in life. Set yourself some goals and look ahead, not back. Try to rid yourself of the bitterness, as it consumes energy you can better use elsewhere.

—a mother with joint custody

Make sure you understand the difference between your needs and those of your children. Be honest with yourself concerning the issue of who is benefiting when a particular decision has been reached. If you can do that rationally, solutions won't be too difficult. The mechanics are not the problem. Understanding yourself is the barrier.

—a father with joint custody of a ten-year-old girl

1. Be sure that divorce is the only thing left to help your situation.
2. Go to a marriage counselor (sometimes more than one).
3. Have *no* self pity!
4. Attend counseling to be a one-parent family in the case of children.
5. Have a positive attitude toward your ex-spouse as an individual.

—a mother with joint custody

Seek professional help *before* you realize you need it. You will be more prepared when it hits, and you'll have an established relationship with a person who can help you through.

Make changes in life-style *only* that are necessary—there are enough changes beyond your control to deal with without you choosing to cause more disruption in your life.

In making that *final* decision to divorce, know *in your heart* that you've done all that you possibly can to save the marriage.

—a mother with joint custody

Time heals and there is a period of adjustment, so I would say, don't rush back into marriage for at least three years. Loneliness can become stressful, but meeting new friends and getting into some sport such as jogging (I did) will relax you and make you feel positive again.

—a father with joint custody

Remember the uncomfortableness and pressures and conflicts you experienced daily when you were married. Even though your life may be temporarily confused and scary or lonely, it will pass. At least you can relax and be at peace with yourself.

—a mother with joint custody of a four-year-old

I still love her dad. He loves and cares for us. And I know he will always be my friend as well as her dad. I would say: communicate—avoid a divorce if at all possible.

To me it is harder to return to a marriage after a "trial separation" than to stick it out and go for it. Positive attitudes always help. Knowing what you want will make your actions easier.

—a mother with joint custody

In ending a marriage I still had my job, which gives me positive strokes, and a healthy and loving relationship with my daughter. Friends and family were supportive. So, although a major part of my life changed, all the rest stayed the same. I did not disintegrate.

—a thirty-seven-year-old mother with joint custody of a ten-year-old

Whatever pain you are experiencing will pass. It's normal. Don't give in to it. Accept it and learn from it. Don't look for an easy way to reduce or eliminate it. Continue to follow your normal routine. Find something constructive to occupy your time. If necessary, counseling might help.

—a father with joint custody of a ten-year-old

Know that it will get better. That some rain must fall for the flowers to bloom. That though this seemed like the worst thing that could ever happen to me, it turned out to be the very best, as I sought to find myself and my capabilities, and in the process I found a new person (me) and a wonderful man to love.

—a thirty-five-year-old mother with joint custody of two girls, ages eleven and eight

It helps not to dwell on past mistakes. You also can't forget the past, nor should you try. Acknowledge to yourself the good and the bad, and then go on. Don't become a recluse. It's easy (in a small town) to shut yourself up because of "what people might say." Develop a social life and maintain old friendships and develop new ones. But remember that, although single, you are still a parent. If you feel you need help or counseling, *get it.*

> —*a father with joint custody of a six-year-old*

Don't feel you are stuck with the original arrangement! If you want to change custody, go ahead and change it. Nothing is forever.

> —*a mother with joint custody of a five-year-old*

Try to make sure both parents are involved. Discuss decisions with the children. We realized later that our children understood what was going on more than we realized. Try to understand what the other parent is feeling.

> —*a mother with joint custody of an eight- and a six-year-old*

Don't seek revenge. Don't deprecate the ex-spouse in front of the children. Talk about feelings openly with the children. Keep in mind that the children come first—and accept that as one rationale for divorce.

> —*a father with joint custody of a fifteen-year-old boy*

1. Feel and express all feelings.
2. Trust that new life will come.
3. Believe that you are forgiven.
4. Experience grief as normal and treat it as a friend, not an enemy.
5. Learn to enjoy yourself and others.
6. There is a purpose for your life.

> —*a mother with joint custody*

Everyone, I think, goes through several basic emotional problems. I was basically happy about the divorce, but I still had a period of loneliness, depression, and self-analyzing. Accept these things and realize that with time you get better. Also, realize that your children will have problems adjusting, too.

> —*a twenty-seven-year-old mother with joint custody of a nine- and a five-year-old*

In our study we found that a very positive statistical correlation existed between parental and child adjustment to the custody arrangement. It is important to "think of the kids first" as many divorced parents say, but if a parent does not meet his or her *own* needs, the children may suffer, also, as a result. There is a point of balance to be found between the needs of the children and the needs of the parents. If families can find this point, relative happiness will also be found.

Adjustment of the Children

We have found in our research that many divorced parents with joint custody are struggling to maintain or develop a strong bond with their children. In this struggle, joint custody parents are not much different from parents in two-parent families. Time for building bonds, however, may be more of a problem:

> I think the saying "Quality, not quantity" applies here. I probably enjoy my son to the fullest more now than when he was with me all the time. We have a more loving, concentrated relationship now than ever before.
>
> —*a mother with joint custody of a nine-year-old*

A father with joint custody described a lengthy process in which he gradually gained more and more time with his son:

> Well, at the time of separation, it was common procedure for the mother to get custody. I didn't want to lose contact with my child, so we agreed on an open relationship where I could set up certain days for seeing him.
>
> This continued until after her second divorce. Then I was more dominant and determined to see him more often. Even when I was out of town, I made special efforts to see him by flying home or by having my parents bring him to me.

Some Different Stories. The parents in our study told us so many fascinating stories. Below we quote a father at length. He is happy to say that after divorce and gaining joint custody, "I've never been this close to my son before." The man's story gives an excellent picture of how parent and child together adjust to the situation:

I'm on call at work three nights a week and try to use the other two for personal needs, entertainment, etc. I see my son on my days off, and he stays with me the whole forty-eight hours. I'm certain he would like to see me more, but there are not enough hours in the day. My ex-wife is neutral to the arrangement.

I insisted that my ex-wife allow me the time to get close to my son. We worked it out without much complication because she felt she needed time to herself.

We agreed that it would not be fair to Kenneth for me to pick him up on my night, on call, because to rush him back home would give him the feeling of being thrown away or cast off. Therefore, we had to agree on an alternating schedule for custody that coincides with my work schedule.

We kept everyone out of the decision making because a lot of problems stemmed from what I called "in-lawitis." Our divorce papers read that I will "take" Kenneth on my days off, instead of just being allowed to "visit." However, "legal custody" belongs to my wife. . . .

No two people or situations are the same. However, a child needs to know a parent during quiet moments; falling asleep together, eating, playing, walking, going to the zoo. I don't feel that this can be accomplished with simple visiting rights. Noon to 6:00 P.M. is not getting close to a child. In the same respect, neither is two or four days a week; however, it does allow more time for sharing. . . .

Conquer the guilt complex. If your marriage has gotten to the point where you can't make love to your partner and agreeing on almost anything is impossible, the child sees the stress each of you is under and he or she becomes the next target of your ill feelings. I felt very guilty about leaving my son. However, I'm positive that if I had remained married, my son was next in line for rejection, and he was not the cause of our divorce. . . .

A few of my friends only have visiting rights, allowing them Saturday and Sunday afternoon to see their kids. This is no way to get close to a child. Have them live with you when possible. I've never been this close to my son before.

I wish I had a nine-to-five-job so that when my son becomes of school age and gets home at 4:00 from school, we could spend a week at a time together.

We are accustomed to hearing much more criticism of lawyers and judges than praise, but in the following two stories a lawyer and a judge were important influences, encouraging parents to see that joint custody can be a great help to children adjusting to divorce:

> Our lawyer (we had just one) suggested joint custody. We had not thought about it before. I read everything I could find about joint or shared arrangements, and became more and more interested in its becoming an option for us. My husband did little reading, but listened to me when I talked about my findings.
>
> The one area of our relationship that is strong is our mutual responsibility for the children—my husband has played a very active, important, and loving part in the lives of our children since their births. He wanted to remain as much a part of their lives as possible, and I very much wanted him to, also.
>
> If there was any way to let the children and my husband remain as close as they had always been, I (and my husband) wanted it. There were no problems negotiating.

It is always somewhat saddening for us to see parents who both have invested heavily in their children and love them but have not been able to continue to love each other. Why does this happen?

A mother with joint custody who had a helpful judge tells her story below. Her main reason for wanting joint custody had to do with the children's adjustment to the divorce:

> I had recently read an article about a divorced couple obtaining joint custody—otherwise, I would not have known it was a possibility. My ex-husband was rather indifferent, and my lawyer didn't like it. He was afraid my ex would (in later years) use it against me as far as child support was concerned.
>
> My lawyer also thought the judge would not allow it. The judge, however, did not hesitate to grant us joint custody. My main reason for insisting was because I did not want our sons to *ever* feel that one of their parents had not wanted them.

One forty-year-old mother with joint custody of twelve- and eight-year-old children was as level-headed as any counselor or researcher we have ever run into when it comes to reasoning out custody issues and the children's best interests:

> I think each case has to be regarded individually. Different children have different needs—and these may vary with age. Other

factors to consider are: how much each parent wishes to be involved with his or her children; what their work situations are; whether they plan to remain in close geographical proximity to each other, etc.

Probably the best custodial arrangements are those that are flexible enough to cover changes in circumstances and in the children's needs as they grow older. If one or the other parent remarries, for instance, the children might want to become a more permanent part of the new household, or alternately, not to be.

Divorce is always a tough process to deal with, and as far as I'm concerned, trying to maintain one's relationship with one's children throughout and after the divorce is integral to keeping one's life going as positively as possible.

In order to do that it may be necessary to fight for the right to have the children there and to maintain responsibility for them—or on the other hand, to compromise so that your ex-spouse enjoys the same right. If one can keep arrangements as friendly as possible, the children benefit, and the split is easier to handle on all counts.

A mother with joint legal custody of three teenaged children wrote and told how hard it was for her to accept her fifteen-year-old daughter's wishes to live with the father:

I wanted a divorce from my husband, and as a result I am left living alone. When our fifteen-year-old girl wanted to live with her father, I was totally hurt as a mother, as a woman, but had to grit my teeth and try to understand her needs at the time. She always tells me she still loves me, and really since we're apart we are closer than ever. As I wrote Easter cards this year I cried.

"Keep communication open between kids, with him and with you," a thirty-five-year-old joint custody mother of five children, ages five to thirteen, advised. "Allow them to be responsible for their feelings and for sharing them with the appropriate source of concern themselves. . . . I feel I don't own my kids. Love them, but *they own themselves*."

A twenty-eight-year-old mother with joint legal custody of a four-year-old son truly enjoyed all the things she did with him:

skiing, horseback riding, walking, car rides late at night, cooking, seeing and being with animals. She did feel sad for her son. The ex-spouse lives so far away:

> It is both fortunate and unfortunate.... My son feels very strong and positive about his father and always will. I will never destroy that. He doesn't see his father often, which confuses him sometimes. But he talks to his father every Sunday night, and they send postcards back and forth at least once a week.
>
> My son does get male reinforcement from all his uncles, and his father realizes this and accepts it. He agrees our son can't have only my influence.

A mother wrote several pages on the trauma she experienced going through divorce, but according to her description, her four-year-old son's adjustment to joint custody appeared to be anything but traumatic for the boy. Many parents seem to do a good job of shielding their children from the pain they personally feel:

> Although James in the divorce decree is to live predominantly with me until age six, then go with his father, he lives with both of us (I guess equally).
>
> Jack picks James up from nursery school for me—he sees him every day. James usually spends almost every weekend with him, unless I have a special trip planned. It's a very free and flexible arrangement.
>
> Jack is a super dad, and James loves him. We let James go as he pleases. He has adapted beautifully. It hurts me to give him up so much, but Jack has a farm with cows, horses, chickens, a pond, and he flies an airplane. So with his girlfriend and her child, they have more activities for James than I.

"My ex-husband has become a *much better* father to our son. It's almost as if he had to lose our son before he could appreciate him," the twenty-seven-year-old mother of a two-year-old wrote. Her story, though unique, has this common element we see so very often: fathers fighting for sole custody or joint custody after divorce, though they ignored their children during marriage. Can these men turn over a new leaf and be good for their children?

Apparently, some can:

My ex has our son, Logan, on Tuesday and Thursday evenings. Logan spends the night with his father and then goes to the sitter in the morning, so I don't see him for a thirty-two-hour period. We both miss each other.

On Saturday evening, my ex picks Logan up from my house, and he returns Sunday about 11:00. Logan is with me the other four nights, Saturday afternoon, and Sunday afternoon. It means my ex and I see each other at least two times a week, which sometimes is okay, at other times uncomfortable. Logan was nineteen months old when this started, so he knows no other life-style.

The process of divorce and the negotiations over child custody created a very difficult situation for both of us, and there was considerable heated discussion and unpleasantness. It took about two months to settle the issue.

I felt Fred had no right to Logan, since he was a bad father before the divorce (spent no time with him, refused to help in his care or assume responsibility). Fred admitted he'd been at fault but wanted him now and would change. We bartered back and forth.

I began to feel sorry for Fred and felt that if he loved Logan half as much as I that I couldn't take Logan completely away from him. Fred also *threatened to fight a bitter battle in court* over Logan, and I didn't want to do that to any of us.

His other ammunition was that he would refuse to sign the quit-claim deed to my house which would allow me to take over the mortgage (plus a $15,000 debt) and not refinance the house at 13 percent interest. If I'd agree to joint legal custody, I could have sole physical custody, and he would agree to sign the quit-claim deed.

I kept trying to think of what is most fair to the child and what the long-term effects of the arrangement would be. Originally, I felt like my ex didn't want us when we were married, so he had no right to my son now.

I remembered him saying things like, "You're the one that wanted him, you take care of him," etc. But after I quit being so emotional, I realized it was important for him to know and feel loved by his natural father.

The divorced person has to realize that divorcing a spouse also is sort of like divorcing the family entity as it had existed. Therefore, things have to change. Selfishly, I wanted my son *all* the time. Be ready to sacrifice for the sake of your child.

My ex-husband and I have to see each other constantly, and I would just as soon not see him.

Sometimes my son is confused as to which house he is supposed to be going to: he doesn't always want to go with my ex-husband or have me leave. He'll take my hand and say, "Stay, Mommy," which makes me feel sad. I feel that I don't get to spend enough time with Logan, and there are occasions when I miss him terribly.

Words of Wisdom from Joint Custody Parents on the Adjustment of Children. Some two hundred parents who have experienced joint custody in all its many different forms are a powerful source of advice on child-rearing in such an arrangement. We have gleaned some of this wisdom from hundreds of pages of written testimony and hundreds of hours of interviews.

Some of the advice may work for the reader, and some may not.

Make sure the child understands that he or she is not the cause. Also, parents should take great care to let the child know that because they do not love each other, it does not mean they don't love the child. Parents should explain that the love for the spouse is very different from the love for a child.

> —*a thirty-two-year-old mother with joint custody of a two-year-old*

1. Get a good lawyer.
2. Sit down by yourself and really think of what is in the best interest of the children.
3. Believe very strongly in your position.
4. Don't compromise your children's lives away.
5. Make sure your children always know you love them.

> —*a father with joint custody of eleven- and nine-year-olds*

Love, love, love the children more than yourself.

> —*a fifty-three-year-old mother with twenty-five, twenty-four, and fourteen-year-old children*

It must be an agreeable and tension-free situation. Children, even small children, can pick up on hate and harsh feelings.

> —*a mother with joint custody of a four-year-old*

If at all possible, I would encourage parents to consider joint custody. I feel that the primary benefit to the children is that they do not feel that they have been abandoned by the non-custodial parent, nor do they seem to have the pressure of divided loyalties. Coparenting "forces" the parents to negotiate positively in order to provide the children with the security that is so important at this time.

—a thirty-four-year-old mother with joint custody of six-
and five-year-olds

If it's an amicable divorce, joint custody can work if you live close enough to make a regular exchange and if you trust the other to be as good a parent as you. I also think joint is probably better for the older child, who is at least at an age to understand what's going on and realize that it may seem odd to friends and teachers. The children must feel open to discuss any problems they have with it.

—a mother with joint custody of a ten-year-old

Try always to think of the children first. Everything affects them. Ask them what arrangements they would prefer, but don't force them to choose between their parents. *Never* use kids to punish the ex-spouse. It hurts everyone. *Never* bad-mouth the other parent. Remember that children need both parents, if not together, then separately, but as equally as possible. Joint custody will work only if both parents truly put the kids first. But it can work.

Don't be bound by traditional methods. Personally, I feel the child should have one residence and the parents should move back and forth. But that is not usually financially possible. Still, I think it is worth considering. It would be *best* for the children.

The good of the children should come first. All too often, parents use the children as pawns in a continuation of their battles between each other. I feel if you put the welfare of the child first, your chances of having a well-adjusted child are increased. Today's children are much more adept at sensing the motives of adults. The sex of the parent alone should not determine custody. Every family situation is different, and the final custody agreement should be discussed with the children if they are old enough.

1. Make sure you get time alone and with others.
2. Teach children to respect your alone space.
3. Don't make a custody decision in a hurry or because you feel forced or pressured.
4. Don't get in fights or hassles in front of the children.

> —*a mother with joint custody of twelve, eleven, ten-year-old children*

Explain your decision to your children as much as possible. Keep in mind that, in arranging custody, the parents *must* keep the best interests of the child in mind. Avoid continual jumping from one home to another so the child has enough time to adjust to each parent and that way of life.

> —*a mother with joint custody*

No matter what the parents want for themselves, they must put it aside and think what arrangement will be best all around for the children and what situation would change their lives the least in terms of spending time with both parents, friends, school, and familiar surroundings with no interruption in lifestyle.

I think it is very important to involve the children in what is going on, what decisions are being made, and why and what effects they will have on them. In my opinion, one of the worst mistakes to make is to forget that children are vitally involved and affected by what is going on between their parents. While there is little that can be done to change the circumstances, it certainly can ease the transition considerably if children know that they, and what they think, are important.

I would also advise that negotiations be conducted in as calm a manner as possible. If this is not possible, a meeting should be arranged outside the home without the children. Divorce is difficult enough for children without having to witness open hostility between their parents.

Sorrows

In summary, we asked the parents in our study to put everything together and tell us the good things and the bad things that have

come from living in a joint custody family. The list was long on both
the negative side and the positive.

A mother felt occasional sadness for her daughter, who did not
get to grow up "seeing positive male and female models under one
roof." Also, the mother felt confined to one community until the
daughter reaches age eighteen.

"I am filling out this questionnaire while cooking dinner for my
son and me," one father said, apologizing for his handwriting.
"Thank you for your research. [Signed,] The Two of Us." His only
complaint about joint custody of his five-year-old was "that I do not
have sole custody and my wife is not out of both of our lives."

Another father of one son could not really find anything bad to
speak of, except the fact that the divorce controversy dragged on for
twenty-two months. But all in all, "this begins a new chapter in our
lives that I hope will lead to a fuller life for all of us."

A mother of eight- and ten-year-olds told us:

> Fortunately, there has been very little sorrow involved in our
> custody situation. The sorrow that I have is for the fact that my
> children had to endure the pain associated with the breakup of
> their family and home.
>
> That pain and sorrow were present, there can be no doubt,
> but I feel that the way my ex-husband and I conducted our-
> selves during our divorce and custody arrangement has mini-
> mized the trauma as much as it is possible to do.

A mother with joint custody of a thirteen-year-old responded in
a similar vein:

> The only sorrow I have is, of course, that our seventeen-year
> marriage had to end. While both my ex-husband and I are hap-
> pier, better-adjusted people since the divorce, it is still sad to
> me that *any* marriage has to end in divorce.

How many times have we heard joint custody parents say this?
"I am forced to see my ex-wife each time I pick up or drop off the
kids. This can mean five times a week. It's hard to forget the pain
she has caused me with these frequent meetings."

Many parents couldn't think of any complaints:

We both not only recommend joint, we can't even imagine having it any other way. One very reassuring incident I wish to cite. During a conversation between some children regarding custody, our then eleven-year-old middle child announced, "No one has custody of me." We indeed never did discuss the question then, and she honestly did not know that the divorce even included that issue.

The images that many parents' stories created were often overwhelmingly sad: "I miss the closeness of having the boys around me, and I used to lie down with them at night until they fell asleep." The same father still has a good deal of anger toward his ex: "I still love my ex-wife but found that her insecurity and fondness for charging all over town were the downfall of our marriage. My main fault was *not* communicating!"

Calling a custody arrangement "joint custody" is no guarantee that a parent will feel he or she has enough contact with the children, nor will it ensure that situations like the following won't happen:

Missing vital steps in my daughter's development bothers me greatly. Not seeing her nearly enough to stay sane. Knowing that while father (me) works in his home six miles from his child (age four), grandmother is raising his daughter while mother works, and mother will not allow the child enough access to me.

"I cannot think of any 'sorrows' as such," one mother with joint custody of six- and five-year-old children wrote. "Although," she added, "I am concerned about how the children will be in the future. I believe we are making the best of a difficult situation; however, I'm sure there will always be questions until such time as they are adults and can share their observations and experiences with us."

The only problem that one joint custody mother could think of was that "occasionally, on holidays when I am with my folks and she is with her dad visiting his family," a bit of remorse comes through. "But we swap this out, and when we can we try to get our families to arrange things so she can be at both when we are having our family dinners. There isn't much of a problem with this." A joint father similarly feels "emptiness when she leaves to go live with her mom" and is apprehensive that the ex-spouse is not rearing the girl to his expectations.

Another father wishes that he had spent more time with his son in the past when he had the chance.

One father told us he made $50,000 a year and had a genuine 50/50 joint custody arrangement, but there are still considerable difficulties:

> Seeing the children spoiled by their mother's life-style and friends
>
> Logistical headaches
>
> Absence of a *whole* working family team and lack of control over the children's environment when with mother

One spouse often has a lot more money than the other after the divorce, and this can cause bad feelings: "The father takes them away many weekends, skiing and more vacations to Disney World, dude ranch, summer home, etc., and I can't afford all this, but we go camping, and the boys understand."

The word "custody" gives one father of nine- and seven-year-old boys a bad taste in his mouth: "Children aren't possessions to be controlled but joys to be equally shared all around."

And how many times did we read of these kinds of sentiments, not only from the joint custody parents but from all groups of parents?

> The feeling of separation we both experience on Monday mornings. Missing each other sometimes when something of common interest occurs. Occasional sentimental pain at the loss of the complete family unit.
>
> *—father of a nine-year-old boy*

and

> The children *still miss,* and I'm sure always will, the joys of a complete family. They love their father very much and were dismayed to learn of the separation.
>
> *—a mother of three*

and

The worst feeling is the absence of a "family feeling." I hope that will return some day. I miss them when they're with their father, but we can both see them whenever we want, and we do.

The sorrow is not so much with our custody situation—I feel good about that. The sorrow is that no matter how good the arrangement or how "friendly" the divorce, it still hurts the kids, and hurting them hurts me.

—a mother of two

Perhaps four out of five of these parents will be remarried at some time in the future. Remarriage will bring stepparents into the picture, and most likely stepbrothers and stepsisters. For those families already experiencing joint custody, the added challenge of step-relationships is often listed as a concern:

"My children don't always get along with their stepmother or stepsisters. I listen, feel guilty, and then try to explain that I used to yell and scream when they did not do the things I expected them to do."

And finally, some parents lamented the fact that joint custody children live, essentially, a double life:

"Knowing that, basically he must live two separate lives with separate environments, separate friends, separate everything." Many parents, however, see advantages to this type of arrangement for children, and we are reminded of a conversation we had with a child who was ecstatic about it: "I have four different sets of grandparents now. Do you know that's eight neat presents at Christmas?" Every cloud seems to have a silver lining somewhere.

And the Joys

Let us take one final look at the silver lining joint custody offers for many families. The benefits are not insignificant.

Leisure time came up time and time again. Parents discovered that life can be very interesting if they are not caring for children every second:

1. Having leisure time to myself for a social life while children are with father.
2. Spending more time with them on fun things when they are with me.
3. Less stress, less tiredness, less angry with them than if I had full custody.

—a mother of two

Another mother echoed these thoughts when she expressed surprise that she is involved in "no day-to-day drudgery." Fortunately, "the close relationship developed during the years can continue. The free time available can help you pursue new and exciting pursuits. Our time together is almost always special." She added that, "I get to let go of my children sooner than most mothers. It is probably very healthy."

A thirty-four-year-old mother with joint custody of a six- and a five-year-old compared her life with that of acquaintances and concluded that she was in pretty good shape:

I am able to have time as a parent and time as a single person. I do not have the pressures that so many women have who have full custody of their children. I appreciate my children now and thoroughly enjoy the time I can spend with them.

With time off from parenting, many parents feel renewed vigor to invest in parenthood during the reduced amount of time they had the children around:

A great deal of free time every now and then—privacy I've never known before. And then lots of good us-time.

—a mother with joint custody of a four-year-old

and

I have more free time than I ever did—I feel free again, yet I have family ties. I appreciate my children more.

—a mother with joint custody of an eight- and a seven-year-old

and

I feel I'm doing everything I can for my daughter under the circumstances. That feels really good.

—a mother with joint custody of a six-year-old

and

The greatest joy I derive from our custody situation is that our children appear to have not only adapted very well to our divorce and custody situation, but seem to have developed a healthy outlook about themselves and their parents. In fact, our daughter says she has it better than some of her friends because she has two sets of parents—her father and stepmother and my fiancé and me.

Many parents obviously liked what they were seeing in their children. One mother bubbled over with pride: "The sixteen-year-old is a delightful young lady, full of enthusiasm, and has worked things out for herself very well. She's compassionate and extremely knowledgeable in the dealings of human relationships."

A father of a nine-year-old boy spoke of the "wonderful love" he felt for his son. They share similar interests, and the private time the father shares with him is a special comfort.

Many parents were happy the relationship with the ex-spouse was working so well, for their own sake and that of the children.

A mother of a four-year-old wrote: "I am happy that my daughter can see her father. They have fun together. Just because he was a below-level husband doesn't mean he's the same kind of father. She loves him, and I intend to nurture that love throughout life."

Another mother felt "good knowing we worked out the best possible arrangement for the kids. I also feel good that my ex-husband has an equal share in parenting. And when I am with my kids it's *good* quality time."

A third mother put it extremely well:

It is good to know that my child is wanted by both parents and at the same time is shared so well. Unfortunately, some children are not wanted by either parent at a particular time.

We all have a great deal of affection and respect for each other as individuals. If you are doing what is best for everyone, perhaps the greatest joy is knowing that no child custody arrangement changes the love that you or your ex-spouse have for your children. It is knowing that my child is loved by me and by his father, regardless of where the child is living or who he is visiting, that gives me joy.

Also, it is seeing the child happy and doing well in what, at best, is a difficult situation: "The child loves both his parents equally."

Though many parents told of strained steprelationships, others saw some real benefits for the children and were eager to tell the kids as much:

As I tell my daughter, she has the best of both worlds. She can stay at home with me and be the "whole hog," or she can go to her father's and be a "piece of the pie" with her stepmother, stepbrother, and half-brother and sister.

—a forty-two-year-old mother of a seventeen-year-old

A number of parents told us how parenthood really begins for an ex-spouse after the divorce. For example, a forty-one-year-old mother of three adolescents was joyful over the "greater involvement of the father with the children. The girls will state that they didn't really know or have much to do with him until I moved out." A thirty-four-year-old mother with joint custody of eight- and seven-year-old children wrote it almost poetically: "I felt more like a single parent when I was married."

Many parents saw the differences between families as healthy for the kids. A thirty-seven-year-old mother of a ten-year-old told us, "Catherine has not had to make choices or take sides. She has lots of love and a variation in living arrangements—one house with two other kids, a zoolike atmosphere; the other quietly adult-dominated. She likes both."

A thirty-five-year-old woman with eleven- and eight-year-old daughters showed not a trace of jealousy as she wrote that "both parents have been able to provide lovely homes and new partners who share in the responsibilities of these children." A twenty-seven-year-old mother of children nine and five echoed the preceding words, saying, "The children have the benefits of both parents' ideas and opinions." Many people dislike diversity and different ideas and ways of looking at the world, but a number of joint custody parents saw this as a strength.

One Last Story

A long time ago, one of us, John DeFrain, was a kindergarten and first-grade teacher in a wonderful school. Besides living and growing with sixteen children each day in the school, he had to send home occasional evaluations—report cards, if you will. Writing a description of a five- or six-year-old child is a difficult, frustration-filled task. Young children are lively, exasperating, wonderful little people, and to write about them on an 8½-by-11-inch piece of paper does them an injustice. It is like describing a killer whale by dragging him out of Puget Sound, murdering him, pickling him, and hanging him on a wall in a dark and musty old museum.

Words just were not doing justice to Tom, age six, either. After rambling on for a couple pages, the young teacher found himself saying, with blushing face:

> I don't know how to describe Tom in school. He's fun to be around. He's sharp. And he's a pain in the neck sometimes.
>
> I'd like to stick him on this paper and simply say, "Here's Tom! Enjoy his company!"

The principal of the school always did say that the young, stumbling teacher's evaluations were "interesting"—whatever that means.

Likewise, writing about joint custody is dreadfully difficult. If you focus on one or two families, the reader gets a richer picture of what is going on—a better feel. But joint custody families are all unique, and to get an accurate picture of the families you need some statistics to compare them with sole custody and split custody families. And you need to listen to a lot of these families talk and read what they have to say.

In the end, the reader will have to do his or her own personal investigation of these families. Talk to them for yourself. Draw your own conclusions. On a parting note, we want to present to you one final parent, a very thoughtful young woman, age thirty-two. She is a lawyer by trade and has an eight-year-old son. She lives in Milwaukee, and she has many good things to say:

> My son's time is divided equally between us. He spends Monday and Tuesday nights with me, Wednesday and Thursday nights with his father, and weekends alternate. The schedule is subject

to alteration for holidays, out-of-town guests, vacations, emergencies, etc. My ex-husband and I confer at least twice a week.

The arrangement works well, for the most part. I do suspect that as he gets older the time periods will get longer.

We decided to separate two months before doing so. At that point it was a "trial." I was to move and wanted to take our son with me. After ten years of marriage, my ex-husband was having trouble coping with "losing" us. He raised the option of joint custody (we are both lawyers) and bought a book on the subject, which we both read. A close friend, whose father had died when she was four, encouraged the idea. She argued that any resulting instability would be compensated by our son's daily interaction with both of us and our families. I accepted it on a trial basis.

During this period, we were also seeing a counselor and in that setting aired our concerns and laid down the ground rules. This counselor later negotiated the divorce property settlement. An attorney I saw before the separation supplied additional literature, as did a judge who was sitting on the family court bench and was a good friend.

The only adverse reaction came from my family, who felt I was in effect abandoning my son. At the end of the first year they also were supportive.

The process is best described as cooperative. We both knew that if we could not preserve our underlying friendship and mutual respect, our son would suffer. I do not think joint custody could survive in a hostile atmosphere. Furthermore, neither of us is "unfit." Both of us work full-time. Either of us could support him without assistance. Our county was one of the first courts in the nation to award custody to a father without a finding of the mother to be unfit. I, quite frankly, was afraid (terrified) that I could lose custody by a toss of the coin!

As time went on, we discovered many things that made joint custody easier for all three of us. We used a nursery school at the time and explained the situation to his teachers. For kindergarten we chose a small private school. The principal, teacher, secretary, and bus driver all know our son's schedule. We both go to meetings and conferences.

I bought a house eleven blocks from his father. We can pick up the instruments, athletic equipment, etc., in five minutes. It is easy to "baby-sit" for each other.

We also stayed in the same church—that environment is stable for him. We are both active and comfortable there, in different areas.

We alert each other to behavior problems we're experiencing. He knows that he cannot lie to us—because we double-check.

We handle expenses in proportion to our respective incomes.

My advice: Read the literature and statistics on the various custody arrangements. Talk to professionals in the area; for example, court services. Talk to other divorced parents. If you see the other parent as "fit," caring, loving, work out the arrangement that preserves both parental relationships to the highest degree. Remember that a custody determination is never final. Divorce terminates a marriage, but the family continues. Try to preserve the friendship upon which the marriage began.

Once you have determined that a divorce is necessary, accept it as a *fact* and move forward. Otherwise, you will live with paralyzing guilt and be ambivalent about even minor decisions. Begin planning. Adopt goals. Budget money carefully. Realize that some friendships will end, and it is not a personal condemnation. I found a core group of friends who understood my pain and spent time with me. Seek them out. It is otherwise a very lonely time.

My son adores his father. I have seen him develop into a conscientious parent. He tried hard.

Freed from the conflict and unhappiness of a bad marriage, I'm free to love my child totally. I spend a great deal of time with him. He is a bright, happy child.

My career and family life have little conflict. I can work two evenings or two weekends a month, if necessary. Likewise, I have an active social life without feeling I'm neglecting my child. I schedule events when he is with his father, if at all possible.

I know someday joint custody will end when his schedule or desires dictate a single home. I hope he chooses to stay with me. Joint custody and ongoing interaction with his father are both good and bad. He's an old, good friend. But as the painful memories fade, we begin to question whether the marriage could have been continued. We have both remarried. I am resistant to his wife's influencing our joint decisions concerning our son. She is very conservative, my husband very liberal. Our son has several role models. If it (the difference between households) becomes stressful, in his best interests I will have to risk a judicial determination of custody.

Nonfamily members do not remember our schedule. My son is often left out of neighborhood activities because it is assumed that he is with his father.

My life isn't very well integrated. I have a life as a parent and a life as a nonparent. I often yearn for a child I don't have to share with my ex-husband, but I think a child who stayed when my son left would have an adverse affect on him.

In my situation, joint custody was the better alternative, preserving full parental relationships and rights. We must recognize that a custody determination is never final. If it ceases to serve the best interests of the child, it must be altered. That knowledge is a key incentive to the adjustments and sacrifices involved. No family is without conflict in the rearing of children. No relationship is totally secure. The divorced parent must be realistic and not assume that each and every problem his or her child encounters is the result of a broken marriage.

We hope that you have gained a sense of the richness and variety of these joint custody families. Some are joyful, some dreary; most alternate between peaks and valleys. The challenges they face never end and make their lives very interesting indeed.

7

Conclusion

W E can sum up the whole point of this book in one sentence: In a divorce situation, there are many different successful ways to arrange child custody. Rather than belabor the point by simply reiterating all we have reported to the reader in the preceding chapters, we would like to launch into a genuinely new discussion in this final chapter.

How to Decide What Is Best

The major problem remains: It is useful for a divorcing parent to know that maternal, paternal, split, and joint custody all can be successful approaches. But the question is still valid: "How do I, a divorcing parent, decide for myself and my family what is best?" In this final chapter we will outline what we believe to be a useful process to go through. An answer, or most likely a tentative answer, should surface.

The process involves thinking about and answering a series of difficult questions. It should take several hours. We encourage you to write down your thoughts—however tentative and imperfect and confused they may seem at this point. The confusion is good. Once it is out on the table, you can go back and clean up the problems and inconsistencies later.

For starters, make yourself sit down and begin finding answers to these questions:

Personal Background

What is happening to my life right now? Am I satisfied with how it is going? Personally and professionally? How did I get to this point?

(Be honest. Brutally honest. Take several pages if necessary to answer in writing.)

Why Is This Happening?

Who initiated the talk about divorce? What factors are contributing to the divorce? What is causing these marital problems? Does my spouse agree with my analysis? Does a counselor who has listened to *both* of us objectively agree with me? With my spouse? With neither?

Custody Issues

Have we talked about custody issues at length? Can we talk openly and in a friendly manner? Can we talk openly but in an unfriendly manner? Is it impossible to talk?

Have we talked with the children about what they want? Most likely they want us to stay together. How do we respond to this? Who do the children want to live with? Why? Is my spouse hearing the same thing or, very likely, something a little bit different? The kids are in a terrible bind. Can they afford to be totally honest with us?

If we do break up, what makes the most sense? Sole custody, split custody, or joint custody?

Will my ex-spouse or I move after the divorce? What plans have we made for this possibility? How will this affect the children?

Have I seen a lawyer? Has the lawyer made things better for me? Has the lawyer made things better for the family as a whole?

Have we sought out a professional mediator?

The Children

What is happening to the children right now? Are they being lost in the shuffle? Do we talk with them openly about the situation, or will our decisions hit them from out of the blue?

What's best for the children? Really. Can I separate this honestly from what's only best for me?

What will be the initial effects on the children if we break up? What about the long-term effects?

Do the children want us to reconcile our differences? Can we? If not, why?

Are the children disturbed by the situation now? How is it affecting their self-esteem? Schoolwork? Friendships?

If we choose joint custody, will the children eventually adapt to going back and forth?

How well do I communicate with the children? How well does my spouse communicate with them?

Do I feel guilty about the care I'm giving the children?

My Spouse

How do I feel about my spouse? How does he or she feel about me?

What type of attitude do I relate to the children about my spouse? How is the children's relationship with my spouse? How do I want it to be after the divorce? Do I feel that it is important for children to have a close relationship with both parents? Can we manage this in our family? Why? Why not?

Has my spouse ever indicated that he or she feels left out of the family? What has he or she done to contribute to this? What have I done? Do I feel left out occasionally?

Personal Well-being

How do I feel about myself now? Am I in good shape emotionally? Can I make important decisions rationally? Am I crying a lot, sleeping a lot, overeating, drinking too much? Do I yell at the kids a lot now? How often have I hit them recently?

How much alcohol or other drugs am I using? How is it affecting me? Can I really be honest with myself about this? Can I say these same things to a friend who has been through it or to a counselor without their telling me that I am lying to myself?

What part do my religious beliefs play in all this? Will the people in my church or synagogue be supportive?

Friends and Relatives

What about my extended family and friends? Have I explained the situation to them? What problems do they foresee? Will they be supportive of me? What do they think is best for the children? They can perhaps be more objective than I can, but will they be honest with me?

Roles in the Family

Before the split, approximately what percentage of the responsibility for child care (bathing, feeding, discipline) did I assume as compared with my spouse? _____ mother's percentage _____ father's percentage [must total 100 percent].

Before the split, who carried the responsibility for most major decisions concerning the family (coping with crises, making large purchases, planning vacations, and so forth)? How will this change after the split? Can I cope with the changes?

Before the split, approximately what percentage of the responsibility for "traditionally" female housework (cooking, cleaning, dishwashing, laundry) did I assume as compared with my spouse? How will this change after the split? Can I cope with the changes?

What percent of the "traditionally" male chores (lawn mowing, taking out garbage, home repairs) did I do before the split as compared with my spouse? How will this change after the split? Can I cope with the changes?

What percent of the family income did I earn before the split as compared with my spouse? _____ mother's percentage _____ father's percentage [must total 100 percent].

Approximately what percentage of the time do my children spend with me in comparison with the time they spend with my spouse? _____ mother's percentage _____ father's percentage [must total 100 percent]. After divorce, ideally, what would these percentages be? How does my spouse feel in regard to these percentages?

Finances

What is our financial picture like? Will two separate households crush us financially? The children will suffer from money problems, too. Can we devise an arrangement that minimizes their deprivation due to money?

What will I do for a job in the future? What realistic opportunities do I have? Have I consulted with employers or professionals in various fields to get a better picture of where I stand?

Love and Social Life

What will happen to my love and social life if I divorce? Will the custody arrangement affect my love and social life positively? Negatively?

If You Have a Lover Now. What does my lover feel about my getting a divorce? Does he or she honestly want it? Does it scare my lover?

Will he or she stand by me through the long months of transition? Does he or she genuinely like my children and like to be with them? Does he or she really view the children and me as a package deal?

I may have to continue interacting positively with my ex-spouse for the children's sake. Will my lover be jealous? Is he or she mature and experienced enough to deal with this situation for a long time?

If You Do Not Have a Lover Now. Do I want to date? Will I be able to?

What will the children think about my dating? How will they react to my having a sex life (if I choose to)? How jealous will my ex-spouse be? Will he or she try to sabotage my dating? Are we capable of meeting this issue head on and honestly?

Do I want to remarry sometime? How will the children respond? Would I cohabit before remarriage? How would the children react? How would my ex-spouse react?

Summing Up

All in all, am I physically, emotionally, and financially prepared to divorce?

All in all, am I physically, emotionally, and financially prepared for continuing the marriage?

If not, where will I seek help to better prepare myself?

When will I begin seeking help?

Reread your answers. It probably would be very valuable to go through them with an interested friend—maybe a single parent who has "been there"—or a trusted counselor.

Go back and compare your answers to those of the parents in the book who have experienced the custody options you are considering. Can you see yourself in them to some degree?

Do you have the courage to ask your spouse to go through the same questioning process and share his or her responses with you? Could you do this with a counselor present? The exploration of these important issues would be difficult for both of you, but looking at them together could be extremely helpful for you and the children in the long run.

What, Then, Have We Learned?

It is very hard to get the nerve to write a book. "Who am I to want to trumpet my silly ideas to the world?" the conscience seems to say. But once the writing starts to pour out, it is hard to stop the flood of thoughts and emotions.

A final question we have to ask is of ourselves, the writers. We have invested a good part of ten years looking at divorce and as researchers have been in a unique position to understand and synthesize countless impressions.

The question: "What have we learned that will be important in our lives?"

The answer: So many things that we really do not know where to begin.

We learned, for one thing, that people should not stay together in a marriage simply for the children's sake. But we also learned that divorce is dreadfully painful, and custody and visitation disputes can draw blood that flows for a long time. We learned, in short, that there is no easy way out in the world of marriage and divorce. *None.*

Our thinking on these issues has evolved over the years. Initially, we believed that couples should stay together at all costs. We were promarriage. Excessively promarriage.

But our thinking changed with experience. We saw some very grisly family situations: attempted murder and suicide, incest, chronic alcoholism and drug abuse, rampant loneliness in and out of marriage. We came to believe that divorce can be advantageous, often a lifesaver for abused women or spouses suffering from a partner's addiction to alcohol or other drugs.

Our current way of thinking is that both marriage *and* divorce are difficult. We urge people in troubled families to get as much help as they can—from friends, relatives, and professionals. We urge them to try very hard to change themselves for the better and to work with their partners to change the marriage for the better. As a last resort we counsel divorce. And we are quick to point out that divorce does not bring instant happiness. That just will not come. Divorce instead brings new problems: new problems in relating to the ex-spouse and new problems relating to other people—employers, new friends, relatives, lovers, children.

Perhaps human beings fool themselves by reaching for happiness, anyway. Life should be instead the search for manageable challenges.

The Future. And what will we, as authors, do in the years to come, now that we have finished a major task and are moving on to new challenges ourselves?

We will try as best as we can to enrich our marriages and to enjoy being with our children. We will try to preserve this family bond at all costs, for without our families we are lost. And, if or when crisis strikes in the future, as it has so many times in the past, we will reach out to those who love us and whom we love. They will give us comfort and support, and we will thank them for it.

The "Right Answer"

> The legal system seeks answers that are generalizable to all cases, while social scientists search for the "right answer." Sarason has argued that a search for the right answer is not the most fruitful one for addressing social problems. Rather, he cited the need to define a process and a set of parameters that can be used to generate best answers for social problems as they are viewed against a constantly changing background. Divorce is one of the social problems in which the "rules" change most quickly. Women entering the work force, fathers being entrusted with more child care, changing economic conditions, and a myriad of other shifting social variables make the right answer for child placement different from year to year, if not from day to day.
> —*Robert Felner and Stephanie Farber*[1]

Though we would agree with researcher Deborah Luepnitz that "joint custody at its best is better than sole custody at its best,"[2] such a statement can be correct and yet sublimely unhelpful to parents going through a divorce. The choices in life are rarely between two or three glowing alternatives. Rather, parents most often find themselves grappling with unpalatable alternatives and seeking to choose the least troublesome.

In short, joint custody at its best is not even an option for many families in divorce. It is just not in the cards. Many parents will have to remain content with an occasional visit with the children by the ex-spouse or a card or gift every so often sent from hundreds of miles away. The parent may not even be able to call this sole custody "at its best."

Though social scientists are constantly making comparisons of groups of people based on statistics or clinical impressions, individual people do not live in statistical boxes. They live in very real, unique families.

The key, then, is not to seek "the right answer" that seems to work for the most people in the world; rather, the key is to seek the "right answer" that seems to work for at least a short time in our very own little personal worlds and circles of love we struggle to build in our families. If we are lucky and skillful enough to reach even this modest goal, we should feel very proud and thankful, indeed.

Successful Single-Parent Families

It is clear, then, that the structure of a family is not the critical issue. Successful single-parent families are headed by fathers, by mothers, and in the case of joint custody by both parents. The outward design is not the key. What is most important goes deeper. The heart of the matter rests in what happens within that single-parent family.

Recent research led by Dr. Nick Stinnett indicates that successful families share six major qualities. The research team of more than forty professionals has done thirty separate studies involving 3,500 strong families. (For details, see the book *Secrets of Strong Families*, by Nick Stinnett and John DeFrain.)[3]

The researchers concluded that though successful or strong families are each unique and different, it can be argued that they do share a number of important strengths. The six strengths are:

1. Commitment to the family—a genuine bond
2. Appreciation and affection for each other—sincere, and frequently expressed verbally and nonverbally
3. Positive communication patterns—open and honest talk with emphasis on strengths rather than on weaknesses
4. Time together—quality time and in great quantities
5. Spiritual wellness—optimism, mental health, shared ethical or religious values, and a network of caring relatives and friends in the community
6. The ability to cope with stress and crisis—challenges to individuals are met head-on by the family together; crisis is seen not only as a troubled time, but also as an opportunity for growth and family unity

One does not have to study the researchers' list for very long to realize that single-parent families also have the ability to be very, very successful. The structure of the family does not dictate whether or not it is a strong family. The love and kindness and creativity each family member brings to meet the challenges of life are the keys to family strength, the keys to family success.

A strong single-parent family "is not a contradiction in terms," as one mother put it so well. A single-parent family can be a wonderful place in which to live and grow.

Shalom.

Appendix A:
Tables to Chapter 2

Table 1
LEGAL CUSTODY ARRANGEMENT AS DEFINED BY A COURT OF LAW

	Joint Legal Custody	Sole Custody	Split Custody
Number	152	534	40
Percent of total sample	21	73	6

Table 2
PHYSICAL CUSTODY ARRANGEMENT AS DETERMINED BY CALCULATING PERCENTAGES OF CHILD CARE[a]

	Joint Physical Custody	Sole Custody	Split Custody
Number	56	642	40
Percent of total sample	8	86	6

[a]Neither the father nor the mother has more than 60 percent nor less than 40 percent of the day-to-day child care responsibilities (measured by counting contact hours in a "typical" week).

Table 3
SEX OF PARENTS BY GROUP

	Joint Physical Custody	Sole Custody	Split Custody
Males			
Number	19	114	15
Percent of total sample of parents	3	15	2
Females			
Number	37	528	25
Percent of total sample of parents	5	72	3

Table 4
OCCUPATIONAL DISTRIBUTION BY SEX OF PARENT

Occupation	Mothers %	Fathers %
Homemaker	9	1
Professional	35	45
Proprietor	7	19
Clerical worker	36	5
Skilled worker	3	23
Semiskilled worker	5	6
Student	5	1

Appendix B:
Resources and Readings

Parent Support Groups

Most cities and large towns have support groups for single parents. These could include a local chapter of the nationwide group Parents without Partners or a grassroots group meeting in a church or synagogue, a home, or a social agency.

All groups are different, of course. Some tend to be educational in nature, bringing in speakers and sponsoring workshops. Others focus on social relationships and organize parties, dances, and outings. Some groups are a good blend of both approaches and offer balance to the parent sorely in need of both intellectual stimulation from other adults and some fun.

Picking a support group is like choosing anything else in the world: Shop around. Get ideas from friends, but do not assume that because your friend liked—or disliked—a particular group that you will react similarly.

And if all else fails, start your own support group. It can be formal or informal to suit your needs.

Counselors

A good counselor can help a person move more quickly and smoothly through a painful transition in life—and to learn from the crisis at the same time. Counseling usually has little to do with craziness, though we all feel at times that we are delicately balanced. More often, counseling focuses on reasoned analysis and skill building so that the client has the tools to manage life's difficulties.

Good counselors come from a variety of backgrounds; psychology, psychiatry, human development and family studies, social work, education, and theology are common backgrounds that counselors have. As important as academic training is the warmth and empathy necessary to make a client feel secure and understood.

Finding a good counselor is a process of shopping around, also. Many agencies offer counseling services; a Child Guidance Center, Family Service Association, Community Mental Health Center, or church- or synagogue-related social service all could be helpful. Private practitioners are also good possibilities.

Some counselors offer the first session free to see whether the chemistry exists between counselor and client. Fees can go as high as $50 to $70 a session or more. Sliding-fee scales based on financial need, especially in agencies, can set fees as low as $25 or $10 or $5 per session. We know one single mother who paid $1.47 per session for what she felt was excellent counseling at a local agency. Sometimes you get what you pay for, and many times you get a lot more. Do not automatically assume that cost and effectiveness of counseling perfectly match up.

Finally, if the counselor-client relationship just is not working out, make a clean, honest break, and try again with a new counselor.

Other Social Supports

Counselors and parent groups can bring emotional support, but a well-developed city or town will also have many other social services for single parents. Depending upon your income, these services might include financial support and counseling through a department of social services; food stamps; help finding and financing adequate housing through a housing authority; child care for low-income working parents or those going back to school; respite care for the children when a parent is in a pinch or feeling stressed; financial aid for college or a G.E.D. program; a home weatherization agency; and many other possibilities that creative agencies keep coming up with.

In fact, in a large city there will be so very many social support programs going on that no one person could ever know about them all. The person in need is urged, again, to do his or her homework and shop around. The blue pages of the telephone book are a good place to start. Five or ten phone calls should uncover a lot of possibilities.

And remember this rule of thumb: If there is a human need, a community can probably fill it. The needy person simply has to have the strength to keep looking for the right people to help. It takes courage to reach out for a helping hand.

Books

For Adult Readers

The list of books on marriage, divorce, and parenthood is almost endless. Among our favorites:

Jessie Bernard. 1956. *Remarriage: A Study of Marriage.* New York: Dryden Press.
A classic study by one of the nation's best researchers.

Paul Bohannan ed. 1970. *Divorce and After.* Garden City, N.Y.: Doubleday.
The excellent articles in this book are by a wide range of authors and will be helpful to the divorced person.

Diane Eisler. 1977. *Dissolution: No-Fault Divorce, Marriage, and the Future of Women.* New York: McGraw-Hill.
This systematic analysis of marriage and divorce laws can be appreciated by any person going through a divorce, although women may find it especially interesting.

Sonja Goldstein and Albert Solnit. 1984. *Divorce and Your Child: Practical Suggestions for Parents.* New Haven: Yale University Press.
A lawyer and a child psychiatrist discuss legal and practical issues surrounding divorce, child custody, visitation, and remarriage. Readable, and contains especially good explanations of how the courts work.

Morton Hunt and Bernice Hunt. 1977. *The Divorce Experience.* Hightstown, N.J.: McGraw-Hill.
A fine 1970s follow-up to their earlier study of the divorced, *The World of the Formerly Married*, published in the 1960s. Both authors are journalists, and their interviewing and writing skills are especially apparent. Morton Hunt has been described by one professor as "the best non-sociologist sociologist in America."

E.E. LeMasters and John DeFrain. 1983. *Parents in Contemporary America: A Sympathetic View.* Chicago: Dorsey Press.
A look at the many challenges of childrearing from the parent's perspective.

George Levinger and Oliver C. Moles eds. 1979. *Divorce and Separation: Context, Causes and Consequences.* New York: Basic Books.

An excellent book of readings; the topics are comprehensive, and the list of authorities with articles in this book is impressive.

David Mace and Vera Mace. 1977. *How to Have a Happy Marriage*. Nashville:
    Abingdon.
A step-by-step guide by two of the pioneers of the marriage enrichment movement.

Augustus Napier and Carl Whitaker. 1978. *The Family Crucible*. New York: Harper
    and Row.
An insider's view of family therapy follows one family through the painful process
    of healing and growth; perhaps the most readable introduction to family ther-
    apy available.

Isolina Ricci: 1980. *Mom's House, Dad's House: Making Shared Custody Work*. New
    York: Collier Books.
Ricci offers a readable solution for how parents can make two homes for their chil-
    dren after divorce. This refreshing and instructive book focuses on *reorganized*
    rather than broken homes.

Ruth Roosevelt and Jeanette Lofas. 1976. *Living in Step: A Remarriage Manual for
    Parents and Children*. New York: McGraw-Hill.
A nuts-and-bolts primer for stepfamilies.

Virginia Satir. 1972. *Peoplemaking*. Palo Alto, Calif.: Science and Behavior Books.
The enormously popular book on how families work and how they can learn to
    work better, by the renowned therapist and educator.

Nick Stinnett and John DeFrain. 1986. *Secrets of Strong Families*. Boston: Little,
    Brown and Co.
An exploration of the qualities that make families strong, based on research on three
    thousand families across the nation and around the world.

Abigail Trafford. 1982. *Crazy Time: Surviving Divorce*. New York: Harper and Row.
Trafford's book is a moving commonsense account of how to face the divorce process
    and build a new life. It is informative and honest, as well as comforting to read
    during the painful emotional journey of divorce.

Joan S. Wallerstein and Joan B. Kelley. 1980. *Surviving the Breakup: How Children
    and Parents Cope with Divorce*. New York: Basic Books.
Two clinicians with a great deal of experience explore the emotional difficulties that
    many families face.

Robert Weiss. 1975. *Marital Separation*. New York: Basic Books.
A sensitive book on the challenges people encounter by an eminent authority.

Lenore Weitzman. 1985. *The Divorce Revolution*. New York: The Free Press.
Weitzman, a Stanford University sociology professor, argues that no-fault divorce
    laws have had a startling and unforeseen result: "The systematic impoverish-
    ment of divorced women and their children." Studying the impact of no-fault
    divorce on 114 women and 114 men in California, she calculated that during

the first year after divorce the women experienced an average 73 percent decline in their standard of living, while the men enjoyed a 42 percent rise.

Persia Woolley. 1979. *The Custody Handbook.*
An excellent and easily read book by a professional writer. Full of nuts-and-bolts ideas for divorcing parents.

For Children and Parents

There are many good books for children. Here is a sample of our favorites:

Preschoolers (fiction)

Beth Goff. 1969. *Where is Daddy? The Story of a Divorce.* Boston: Beacon Press.
This book explores the confusing changes the preschooler must learn to face, and focuses on guilt and anxiety over abandonment.

Barbara Shook Hazen. 1978. *Two Homes to Live In: A Child's Eye View of Divorce.* New York: Human Sciences Press.
"Having divorced parents isn't so bad," a young girl finally concludes. "Lots of kids do. Besides, nobody divorced me." At first, though, it was not so easy to understand. A good book for preschoolers, early elementary children, and their parents. Noteworthy because the family is Asian-American.

Erica Jong. 1984. *Megan's Book of Divorce: A Kid's Book for Adults as Told to Erica Jong.* New York: The New American Library.
In this enjoyable book, an irrepressible four-year-old girl gives her own views on divorce. It is a book for all children who have two households and for all parents considering, or already involved in, a shared custody arrangement with their ex-spouse. In an effort to get her parents back together, Megan tells her daddy's friend Kate, "Daddy will never marry you, so just give up." She tells her mommy's friend Win, "Mommy will marry you if you don't watch out." This recent book is enlightening for both kids and adults.

Ianthe Thomas. 1976. *Eliza's Daddy.* New York: Harcourt Brace Jovanovich.
A young black girl is disturbed about her parents' divorce, her father's remarriage, and her new stepsister. When she meets the little girl, though, her jealousy fades, and they become good friends. Fine for preschool and early elementary children and their parents.

Preschoolers (nonfiction)

Earl A. Grollman. 1975. *Talking About Divorce: A Dialogue between Parent and Child.* Boston: Beacon Press.
A nice little book for parents and preschool- or early elementary-aged children to

read together. It will undoubtedly spark a good discussion and also includes a
parents' guide and sources for further help.

Janet Sinberg. 1978. *Divorce Is a Grown Up Problem*. New York: Avon Books.
A fine book for preschool- and early elementary-aged children dealing with the
common fears and guilt youngsters feel.

Elementary-aged Children (fiction)

Florence Adams. 1973. *Mushy Eggs*. New York: G.P. Putnam's Sons.
Two young (four- and seven-year-old) brothers, Sam and David, describe life in
their one-parent home. "Our mom works in the city on a computer. She is also
a good builder." "Our dad's house is in New Jersey. He doesn't live with us
because we are divorced. . . . Dad comes to see Sam and me every Sunday."
"Our babysitter, Fanny, loves us too." *Mushy Eggs* is a nice little book for the
early and middle elementary-aged child.

Rose Blue. 1972. *A Month of Sundays*. New York: Franklin Watts.
The story of ten-year-old Jeffrey, trying to deal with moving from his comfortable
suburban home after his parents' divorce to New York City, where he would
live with his mother and his father would visit only on Sundays. The author
uncovers Jeffrey's feelings and describes his development in a new and difficult
situation.

Judy Blume. 1972. *It's Not the End of the World*. Scarsdale, N.Y.: Bradbury Press.
A young girl's struggle to reunite her divorcing parents and to deal with the sadness
when she finds conciliation is out of the question. Recommended for middle,
late elementary, and older children and their parents.

Peggy Mann. 1973. *My Dad Lives in a Downtown Hotel*. Garden City, N.Y.:
Doubleday.
The story of a young boy's emotional reactions to his parents' breakup. A good book
to help children explore their fears, anger, guilt, and confusion. Especially appropriate for elementary-aged children and their parents.

Elementary-aged Children (nonfiction)

Terry Berger. 1977. *How Does It Feel When Your Parents Get Divorced?* New York:
Julian Messner.
The focus in this book is on the anger and confusion a youngster feels during and
after divorce. Good sections on divorced fathers, money problems, and the
"latchkey" child. An excellent book for early and middle elementary-aged children and their parents.

Richard A. Gardner. 1970. *The Boys' and Girls' Book about Divorce*. New York: Science
House.
The first book on divorce to be read by the children themselves; probably even

better if read along with parents. Especially appropriate for middle elementary years through junior high.

Adolescents (fiction)

Paula Danziger. 1982. *The Divorce Express.* New York: Delacorte Press.
Resentful of her parents' divorce, a fourteen-year-old girl tries to accommodate herself to their new lives and also finds a place for herself.

Norma Klein. 1974. *Taking Sides.* Toronto: Random House of Canada Ltd.
Twelve-year-old Nell knows other kids her age whose parents are divorced, but *they* all live with their mothers. She wonders what living with Dad will be like, even though she's always felt closer to her father. The adjustments Nell has to make range from sharing a room with her five-year-old brother, Hugo, and dealing with her father's serious heart condition. Sometimes she wishes for a more normal life, but all-in-all things seem to be working out pretty well.

Norma Klein's characters have the capacity to change and to love, and these are the qualities that make this a very special book for late elementary- or junior high–aged kids.

Stella Pevsner. 1975. *A Smart Kid Like You.* New York: Seabury Press.
A teenaged girl struggles to maintain allegiance to both of her divorced parents. A stepmother and two stepbrothers complicate matters. Excellent for junior and senior high students.

Doris Buchanan Smith. 1974. *Kick a Stone Home.* New York: Thomas Y. Crowell.
Boys, dating, school, agonizing self-consciousness, and a stepmother all combine to make adolescence a difficult time for a tomboy turning into a young woman. A fine book for junior and senior high youth.

Adolescents (nonfiction)

Eda LeShan. 1975. *What's Going to Happen to Me? When Parents Separate or Divorce.* New York: Four Winds Press.
LeShan speaks directly to readers with wit and wisdom. Especially good for junior and senior high children, though late elementary-aged children might find it helpful as well.

Arlene Richards and Irene Willis. 1976. *How to Get It Together When Your Parents are Coming Apart.* New York: David McKay.
A book for adolescents experiencing their parents' separation or divorce, by a psychologist in private practice and a junior- and senior-high school teacher. Full of insight and good illustrative stories teenagers will enjoy. The book will also help parents understand their children better.

Eric E. Rofes ed. 1981. *The Kids' Book of Divorce by, for, and about Kids.* Lexington, Mass.: The Lewis Publishing Co.

Twenty children, aged eleven to fourteen, discuss various aspects of divorce, including custody arrangements, parents' boyfriends and girlfriends, how they were first told about their parents' divorce, and how divorce has changed them.

Young Adults

Michael Jackson and Jessica Jackson (edited by their father, Bruce Jackson). 1981. *Your Father's Not Coming Home Anymore: Teenagers Tell How They Survive Divorce*. New York: Richard Marek, Publishers.

This is a book by a brother and sister, eighteen and sixteen, whose own parents are divorced. The authors interviewed thirty-eight young people between the ages of thirteen and twenty-one, asking them to discuss how they coped with their parents' divorce.

Peter Mayle. 1979. *Divorce Can Happen to the Nicest People*. New York: Macmillan.

Lively writing and excellent illustrations by Arthur Robbins. Perhaps the most honest and straightforward book on divorce for children from the middle elementary years on up through graduate school. This book explains, in an objective manner, how some parents can fall in love with another person.

Warner Troyer. 1979. *Divorced Kids*. New York: Harcourt Brace Jovanovich.

A journalist and divorced father of eight children reports the findings of his interviews with divorced children, mostly ages five to fifteen. He also includes interviews with young adults and adults in their thirties, forties, and fifties on their experience with divorce as a child. Fascinating reading for later adolescents, young adults, and parents.

Films

Lee Kimmons and Judith A. Gaston. 1986. "Single Parenting: A Filmography." *Family Relations: Journal of Applied Family and Child Studies* 35:205–11.

An invaluable description of a broad range of films, videotapes, and filmstrips that deal with the single-parent experience.

Notes

Chapter 1

1. Kahlil Gibran, *The Prophet* (New York: Alfred A. Knopf, 1978), 18–19.
2. The interview with Chief Justice Norman Krivosha was conducted in his chambers by graduate students of the Department of Human Development and the Family, University of Nebraska, Lincoln, in the spring of 1983.
3. John DeFrain, "Developing Educational Programs for Separated and Divorced Families" (Proceedings of the Sixtieth Annual Agricultural Outlook Conference, presented to Cooperative Extension family-life specialists, U.S. Department of Agriculture, Washington, D.C., winter 1984).
4. Maggie Hayes, Nick Stinnett, and John DeFrain, "Learning about Married from the Divorced," *Journal of Divorce* (October 1980).
5. Morton Hunt and Bernice Hunt, *The Divorce Experience* (New York: McGraw-Hill, 1977).
6. See the following: John DeFrain, "Sexism in Parenting Manuals," *The Family Coordinator: Journal of Education, Counseling, and Services* (National Council on Family Relations), July 1977; John DeFrain, "Androgynous Parents Outline Their Needs," *The Family Coordinator: Journal of Education, Counseling, and Services* (National Council on Family Relations), Apr. 1979; John DeFrain, Pamela Nelssen, Kendra Summers, "The Androgynous Parent as Societal Norm: Research Evidence" (Paper presented at the Groves Conference on Marriage and the Family, Washington, D.C., Apr. 1979); Rebecca Braymen and John DeFrain, "Sex-Role Attitudes and Behaviors of Children Reared by Androgynous Parents" (Paper presented at the Groves Conference on Marriage and the Family, Washington, D.C., Apr. 1979).

Chapter 2

1. Paul C. Glick, "Children of Divorced Parents in Demographic Perspective," *Journal of Social Issues* 35, no. 4 (1979).
2. L. Francke, "The Children of Divorce," *Newsweek*, Feb. 11, 1980, 58–63.
3. Arland Thornton and Deborah Freedman, "The Changing American Family" (Ann Arbor: University of Michigan, 1983).
4. Lynn Langway et al., "Rounding Up Delinquent Dads," *Newsweek*, Aug. 6, 1984, 76.

5. Sonja Goldstein and Albert J. Solnit, *Divorce and Your Child* (New Haven: Yale University Press, 1984), 1.
6. Robin L. Franklin and "B." Hibbs, "Child Custody in Transition," *Journal of Marital and Family Therapy* (July 1980):285–91.
7. A. Derdeyn, "Child Custody Contests in Historical Perspective," *American Journal of Psychiatry* 133(1976):1369–76.
8. J.W. Duncan, "Medical, Psychologic, and Legal Aspects of Child Custody Disputes," *Mayo Clinic Process* 53(1978):463–68.
9. Derdeyn, "Child Custody Contests."
10. Franklin and Hibbs, "Child Custody in Transition."
11. Chief Justice Norman Krivosha, interview by University of Nebraska, Lincoln, graduate students, spring 1983.
12. Norman Fenton, "What Courts Can Do to Develop Family Strengths," in *Family Strengths 3: Roots of Well-Being*, ed. Nick Stinnett, John DeFrain, Kay King, Patricia Knaub, and George Rowe (Lincoln: University of Nebraska Press, 1981), 270.
13. Colleen Cordes, "Family Mediation: Who's Helped, and How?" (published by the American Psychological Association) (December 1983):10–11.
14. Ibid., p. 10. Cordes reported a review of mediation studies done by Jessica Pearson, a sociologist at the Center for Policy Research in Denver for the American Bar Association's Special Committee on Alternative Dispute Resolution.
15. Cordes, "Family Mediation," 11.
16. Alan M. Levy, "The Meaning of the Child's Preference in Child Custody Determination," *Journal of Psychiatry and Law* (Summer 1980):221.
17. Robert D. Felner and Stephanie S. Farber, "Social Policy for Child Custody: A Multidisciplinary Framework," *American Journal of Orthopsychiatry* 50, no. 2 (April 1980):341–47.
18. E. Mavis Hetherington, "Divorce: A Child's Perspective," *American Psychologist* 34, no. 1 (1979):856.
19. Carol B. Stack, "Who Owns the Child? Divorce and Custody Decisions in Middle-Class Families," *Social Problems* 23(1976):505–15.
20. Joan Wallerstein, "Children Who Cope in Spite of Divorce," *Family Advocate* (1978):2–5.
21. Hetherington, "Divorce," 852.
22. S. Koslow, "Joint Custody: Is It the Answer?" *Town and Country* (October 1980):165.
23. J. Marks, "Crisis Intervention for Children: A Psychological Stitch in Time," *Town and Country* (October 1980):170.
24. F.I. Nye, "Child Adjustment in Broken and in Unhappy Unbroken Homes," *Marriage and Family Living* 19(1957):356–62.
25. D. Luepnitz, "Which Aspects of Divorce Affect Children?" *The Family Coordinator* 28(January 1979):79–85.
26. Helen Raschke and Vernon Raschke, "Family Conflict and Children's Self-Concepts: A Comparison of Intact and Single-Parent Families," *Journal of Marriage and the Family* (May 1979).
27. Nye, "Child Adjustment."

28. Judson Landis, "A Comparison of Children from Divorced and Non-Divorced Unhappy Marriages," *The Family Coordinator* 11(1962):61–65.

29. Hetherington, "Divorce," 851.

30. E.E. LeMasters and John DeFrain, *Parents in Contemporary Society*, 4th ed. (Homewood, Il.: Dorsey Press, 1983), 169–74.

31. U.S. Department of Commerce. "Population Characteristics," *Current Population Reports* 352(1980):3.

32. John DeFrain and Rod Eirick, "Coping as Divorced Single Parents: A Comparative Study of Fathers and Mothers," *Family Relations* 30(1981):265–74.

33. See Joseph Goldstein, Anna Freud, and Albert J. Solnit, *Beyond the Best Interests of the Child* (New York: The Free Press, 1973); Constance R. Ahrons, "Joint Custody Arrangements in the Postdivorce Family," *Journal of Divorce* 3, no. 3 (1980):189.

34. Persia Woolley, "Shared Custody: Demanded by Parents, Discouraged by Courts," *Family Advocate* 3, no. 2 (1978):6.

35. Bobette Adler Levy and Carole R. Chambers, "The Folly of Joint Custody: Children Are Not Negotiable; Battering Them in Divorce Actions is Bad Law and Even Worse Psychology," *Family Advocate* 3, no. 4 (1980):6.

36. Anita D. Fineberg, "Joint Custody of Infants: Breakthrough or Fad?" *Canadian Journal of Family Law* 2(1979):417–54.

37. Ahrons, "Joint Custody Arrangements."

38. Constance R. Ahrons, "The Continuing Coparental Relationship between Divorced Spouses," *American Journal of Orthopsychiatry* 51, no. 3, (July 1981):415–27.

39. Barbara Rothberg, "Joint Custody: Parental Problems and Satisfactions." *Family Process* 22, no. 1, (Mar. 1983):52.

40. J. Cox and L. Cease, "Joint Custody—What Does It Mean? How Does It Work? *Family Advocate* (1978):10–13.

41. Woolley, "Shared Custody."

42. Goldstein, Freud, and Solnit, *Beyond the Best Interests of the Child*.

43. Carol B. Stack, "Who Owns the Child?" 507.

44. Felner and Farber, "Social Policy for Child Custody," 346.

45. K. Kressel et al., "Professional Intervention in Divorce: A Summary of the Views of Lawyers, Psychotherapists and Clergy," *Journal of Divorce* 2(1978):119–55.

46. David J. Miller. *Family Law Quarterly* 13, no. 13 (Fall 1979).

47. Ibid., 361.

48. Kathy Jordan, "Parents' Perceptions of Their Children's Adjustment To Marital Separation" (Master's thesis, University of Nebraska, Lincoln, 1978); Kendra Schwab Summers, "Parents' and Children's Perceptions of the Effects of Marital Separation: A Longitudinal Study" (Master's thesis, University of Nebraska, Lincoln, 1979).

49. Patricia Welker, "What Children Feel about Their Parents' Marital Separation" (Master's thesis, University of Nebraska, Lincoln, 1978).

50. Lew Moore, "Religiosity and Coping with Divorce" (Ph.D. diss., University of Nebraska, Lincoln, 1979).

51. Lou Ann Patterson, "The Church and Divorce" (Master's thesis, University of Nebraska, Lincoln, 1979).
52. Linda Bader, John DeFrain, and Anne Parkhurst, "What Parents Feel When Their Child Divorces," *Family Perspective* (Spring 1982).
53. John DeFrain and Rod Eirick, "Coping as Divorced Single Parents," 265–74.
54. Those readers with a statistical bent will be interested to know that we used the Pearson Product-Moment Correlation, Chi Square, Duncan T, and Analysis of Variance to test the data. The hypotheses were tested for significance at the 0.05 level of confidence, while the 0.01 level of confidence was used to determine highly significant differences.

Chapter 3

1. L.L. Bumpass and R. Rindfuss, "Children's Experience of Marital Disruption" (Madison: Institute for Research on Poverty, University of Wisconsin, Madison, 1978).
2. Kendra Schwab Summers, "Parents' and Children's Perceptions of the Effects of Marital Separation: A Longitudinal Study" (Master's thesis, University of Nebraska, Lincoln, 1979).
3. Linda Bader, John DeFrain, and Anne Parkhurst, "What Parents Feel When Their Child Divorces," *Family Perspective* (Spring 1982).

Chapter 4

1. John DeFrain and Rod Eirick, "Coping as Divorced Single Parents: A Comparative Study of Fathers and Mothers," *Family Relations* 30(1981):265–74.
2. Ibid.

Chapter 6

1. John DeFrain, "Androgynous Parents Outline Their Needs," *The Family Coordinator: Journal of Education, Counseling, and Services* (April 1979).
2. Lew Moore, "Divorce: A Study of Coping Behaviors and the Interrelatedness with Religiosity, Loneliness, and Well-Being" (Ph.D. diss., University of Nebraska, Lincoln, 1979).

Chapter 7

1. See Seymour Sarason, "The Nature of Problem Solving in Social Action," *American Psychologist* 33 (1978):370–80; Robert D. Felner and Stephanie S. Far-

ber, "Social Policy for Child Custody: A Multidisciplinary Framework," *American Journal of Orthopsychiatry* 50, no. 2 (April 1980):346.

2. Deborah Anna Luepnitz, *Child Custody: A Study of Families after Divorce* (Lexington, Mass.: Lexington Books, 1982).

3. Nick Stinnett and John DeFrain, *Secrets of Strong Families* (Boston: Little, Brown and Co., 1986).

Index

About the Authors

JOHN DeFRAIN, Ph.D., is an associate professor of family studies in the Department of Human Development and the Family, University of Nebraska, Lincoln. He codirects a joint postgraduate training program in marriage and family therapy, and has done extensive consulting for courts and families on marriage, divorce, and custody issues. His other books include: *Coping with Sudden Infant Death* (written with Jacque Taylor and Linda Ernst, and published in 1982 by Lexington Books, Lexington, Massachusetts); *Parents in Contemporary America* (with E.E. LeMasters, and published in 1983 by Dorsey Press, Chicago); *Secrets of Strong Families* (with Nick Stinnett, and published in 1986 by Little, Brown and Co., Boston); and *Stillborn: The Invisible Death* (with Leona Martens, Jan Stork, and Warren Stork, and published in 1986 by Lexington Books). His research has been published in two dozen professional articles and reported in many newspapers and magazines, including: *Parents* magazine, Reader's Digest's *Families, Psychology Today, Good Housekeeping, Redbook, Ladies' Home Journal, Reader's Digest, USA Today,* McCall's *Working Mother,* and National PTA's *Today.* DeFrain received his doctorate from the University of Wisconsin, Madison. He and his wife Nikki have three daughters, Amie, Alyssa, and Erica.

JUDY FRICKE received her B.S. in elementary education and her M.S. in human development and the family from the University of Nebraska, Lincoln. She has taught in Alaska and Nebraska, and currently is teaching elementary-aged children in Lincoln. Judy is married to Don; they have three children, Julie, David, and Becky.

JULIE ELMEN is working on a Ph.D. in child and family studies at
the University of Wisconsin, Madison. She received her B.S. degree from Gustavus Adolphus College in St. Peter, Minnesota, and
her M.S. in human development and the family from the University
of Nebraska, Lincoln. She and her husband, Ken Gruys, have two
daughters, Kjerstin and Hanna.